ERIC SINGLER

Nudge Management

Applying Behavioral Science to boost well-being, engagement and performance at work

Translated from French by Ruth Simpson

Pearson

To my parents,
to Valérie, Thomas, Baptiste and Valentine,
to my brother Franck,
to my friends Alain, Gérard and Pascal,
to my colleagues at BVA and PRS IN VIVO
and to the brilliant Nudgers in the BVA Nudge Unit.

Layout: SPI

ISBN: 978-2-7440-6716-7

Contents

Nudging: A Very Short Guide

Some policies take the form of *mandates* and *bans*. For example, the criminal law forbids theft and assault. Other policies take the form of *economic incentives* (including disincentives), such as subsidies for renewable fuels, fees for engaging in certain activities, or taxes on gasoline and tobacco products. Still other policies take the form of *Nudges* – liberty-preserving approaches that steer people in particular directions, but that also allow them to go their own way. In recent years, both private and public institutions have shown mounting interest in the use of Nudges, because they generally cost little and have the potential to promote economic and other goals (including public health). Companies often use Nudges.

In daily life, a GPS device is an example of a Nudge. So is an "app" that tells people how many calories they ate during the previous day; so is a text message, informing customers that a bill is due or that a doctor's appointment is scheduled for the next day; so is an alarm clock; so is automatic enrollment in a pension plan; so are the default settings on computers and cell phones; so is a system for automatic payment of credit card bills and mortgages. In government, Nudges include graphic warnings for cigarettes; labels for energy efficiency or fuel economy; "nutrition facts" panels on food; the "Food Plate", which provides a simple guide for healthy eating (see choosemyplate.gov); default rules for public assistance programs (as in "direct certification" of the eligibility of poor children for free school meals); a website like data.gov or data.gov. uk, which makes a large number of data sets available to the public; and even the design of government websites, which list certain items first and in large fonts.

Nudges Maintain Freedom of Choice

It is important to see that the goal of many Nudges is to make life simpler, safer, or easier for people to navigate. Consider road signs, speed bumps, disclosure of health-related or finance-related information, educational campaigns, paperwork reduction, and public warnings. When officials or companies reduce or eliminate paperwork requirements, and when they promote simplicity and transparency, they are reducing people's burdens. Some products (such as cell phones and tablets) are intuitive and straightforward to use. Similarly, many Nudges are intended to ensure that people do not struggle when they seek to interact with government or the private sector, or otherwise to achieve their goals.

It is true that some Nudges are properly described as a form of "soft paternalism", because they steer people in a certain direction. But even when this is so, Nudges are specifically designed to preserve full freedom of choice. A GPS device steers people in a certain direction, but people are at liberty to select their own route instead. And it is important to emphasize that some kind of social environment (or "choice architecture"), influencing people's choices, is always in place. New Nudges typically replace preexisting ones; they do not introduce nudging where it did not exist before.

Transparency and Effectiveness

Any nudging should be transparent and open rather than hidden and covert. Indeed, transparency should be built into the basic practice. Suppose that a government or a private employer adopts a program that automatically enrolls people in a pension program, or suppose that a large institution (say, a chain of private stores, or those who run cafeterias in government buildings) decides to make healthy foods more visible and accessible. In either case, the relevant action should not be hidden in any way. Government decisions in particular should be subject to public scrutiny and review. A principal advantage of Nudges, as opposed to mandates and bans, is that they avoid coercion. Even so, they should never take the form of manipulation or trickery. The public should be able to review and scrutinize Nudges no less than government actions of any other kind.

All over the world, nations have become keenly interested in Nudges. To take two of many examples, the United Kingdom has a Behavioral Insights Team (sometimes called the "Nudge Unit"), and the United States has the Office of Evaluation Sciences. The growing interest in Nudges stems from the fact that they usually impose low (or no) costs, because they sometimes deliver prompt results (including significant economic savings), because they maintain freedom, and because they can be highly effective. In some cases, Nudges have a larger impact than more expensive and more coercive tools. For example, default rules, simplification, and uses of social norms have sometimes been found to have even larger impacts than significant economic incentives.

In the context of retirement planning, automatic enrollment has proved exceedingly effective in promoting and increasing savings. In the context of consumer behavior, disclosure requirements and default rules have protected consumers against serious economic harm, saving many millions of dollars. Simplification of financial aid forms can have the same beneficial effect in increasing college attendance as thousands of dollars in additional aid (per student). Informing people about their electricity use, and how it compares to that of their neighbors, can produce the same increases in conservation as a significant spike in the cost of electricity. If properly devised, disclosure of information can save both money and lives. Openness in government, disclosing both data and performance, can combat inefficiency and even corruption.

Testing

For all policies, including Nudges, it is exceedingly important to rely on evidence rather than intuitions, anecdotes, wishful thinking, or dogmas. The most effective Nudges tend to draw on the most valuable work in behavioral science (including behavioral economics), and hence reflect a realistic understanding of how people will respond to initiatives. But some policies, including some Nudges, seem promising in the abstract, but turn out to fail in practice. Empirical tests, including randomized controlled trials, are indispensable. Bad surprises certainly are possible, including unintended adverse consequences, and sensible policymakers in the private or public sector must try to anticipate such surprises in advance (and to fix them if they arise). Sometimes empirical tests reveal that the planned reform will indeed work – but that some variation on it, or some alternative, will work even better.

Experimentation, with careful controls, is a primary goal of the Nudge enterprise. Fortunately, many Nudge-type experiments can be run rapidly and at low cost, and in a fashion that allows for continuous measurement and improvement. The reason is that such experiments sometimes involve small changes to existing programs, and those changes can be incorporated into current initiatives with relatively little expense or effort. If, for example, officials currently send out a letter to encourage people to pay delinquent taxes, they might send out variations on the current letter and test whether the variations are more effective.

It is important to say, as Eric Singler does in this book, that Nudges can be used to create better workplaces, and so to enable people to make better decisions there. Employee well-being is important in itself. It is also important for productivity. This is an important area for both theory and practice.

Ten Important Nudges

Nudges span an exceedingly wide range, and their number and variety are constantly growing. Here is a catalogue of ten important Nudges – very possibly, the most important – along with a few explanatory comments.

(1) **default rules** (e.g., automatic enrollment in programs, including education, health, savings)

Comment: Default rules may well be the most effective Nudges. If people are automatically enrolled in retirement plans, their savings can increase significantly. Automatic enrollment in health care plans, or in programs designed to improve health, can have significant effects. Default rules of various sorts (say, double-sided printing) can promote environmental protection. Note that unless *active choosing* (also a Nudge) is involved, some kind of default rule is essentially inevitable, and hence it is a mistake to object to default rules as such. True, it might make sense to ask people to make an active choice, rather than relying on a default rule. But in many contexts, default rules are indispensable, because it is too burdensome and time-consuming to require people to choose.

(2) simplification (in part to promote take-up of existing programs)

Comment: In both rich and poor countries, complexity is a serious problem, in part because it causes confusion (and potentially violations of the law), in part because it can increase expense (potentially reducing economic growth), and in part because it deters participation in important programs. Many programs fail, or succeed less than they might, because of undue complexity. As a general rule, programs should be easily navigable, even intuitive. In many nations, simplification of forms and regulations should be a high priority. The effects of simplification are easy to underestimate. In many nations, the benefits of important programs (involving education, health, finance, poverty, and employment) are greatly reduced because of undue complexity.

(3) uses of social norms (emphasizing what most people do, e.g., "most people plan to vote" or "most people pay their taxes on time" or "nine out of ten hotel guests reuse their towels")

Comment: One of the most effective Nudges is to inform people that most others are engaged in certain behavior. Such information is often most powerful when it is as local and specific as possible ("the overwhelming majority of people in your community pay their taxes on time"). Use of social norms can reduce criminal behavior and also behavior that is harmful whether or not it is criminal (such as alcohol abuse, smoking, and discrimination). It is true that sometimes most or many people are engaging in undesirable behavior. In such cases, it can be helpful to highlight not what most people actually do, but instead what most people *think* people should do (as in, "90 percent of people in Ireland believe that people should pay their taxes on time").

(4) increases in ease and convenience (e.g., making low-cost options or healthy foods visible)

Comment: People often make the easy choice, and hence a good slogan is this: "make it easy". If the goal is to encourage certain behavior, reducing various barriers (including the time that it takes to understand what to do) is often helpful. Resistance to change is often a product not of disagreement or of skepticism, but of perceived difficulty – or of ambiguity. A supplemental point: If the easy choice is also fun, people are more likely to make it.

(5) disclosure (for example, the economic or environmental costs associated with energy use, or the full cost of certain credit cards – or large amounts of data, as in the cases of data.gov and the Open Government Partnership[1])

Comment: The American Supreme Court Justice Louis Brandeis said that "sunlight is the best of disinfectants", and disclosure can make both markets and governments much "cleaner". For consumers, disclosure policies can be highly effective, at least if the information is both comprehensible and accessible. Simplicity is exceedingly important. (More detailed and fuller disclosure might be made available online for those who are interested in it.) In some settings, disclosure can operate as a check on private or public inattention, negligence, incompetence, wrongdoing, and corruption. The Open Government Partnership, now involving sixty-four nations, reflects a worldwide effort to use openness as a tool for promoting substantive reform.

(6) warnings, graphic or otherwise (as for cigarettes)

Comment: If serious risks are involved, the best Nudge might be a private or public warning. Large fonts, bold letters, and bright colors can be effective in triggering people's attention. A central point is that attention is a scarce resource, and warnings are attentive to that fact. One virtue of warnings is that they can counteract the natural human tendency toward

---

1 opengovernmentpartnership.org.

unrealistic optimism and simultaneously increase the likelihood that people will pay attention to the long-term. There is a risk, however, that people will respond to warnings by discounting them ("I will be fine"), in which case it would make sense to experiment with more positive messages (providing, for example, some kind of reward for the preferred behavior, even if the reward is nonmonetary, as in apps that offer simple counts and congratulations). Research also shows that people are far less likely to discount a warning when it is accompanied by a description of the concrete steps that people can take to reduce the relevant risk ("you can do X and Y to lower your risk").

(7) precommitment strategies (by which people commit to a certain course of action)

Comment: Often people have certain goals (for example, to stop drinking or smoking, to engage in productive activity, or to save money), but their behavior falls short of those goals. If people precommit to engaging in certain action – such as a smoking cessation program – they are more likely to act in accordance with their goals. Notably, committing to a specific action at a *precise* future moment in time better motivates action and reduces procrastination.

(8) reminders (for example, by email or text message, as for overdue bills and coming obligations or appointments)

Comment: People tend to have a great deal on their minds, and when they do not engage in certain conduct (for example, paying bills, taking medicines, or making a doctor's appointment), the reason might be some combination of inertia, procrastination, competing obligations, and simple forgetfulness. A reminder can have a significant impact. For reminders, timing greatly matters; making sure that people can act immediately on the information is critical (especially in light of the occasional tendency to forgetfulness). A closely related approach is "prompted choice", by which people are not required to choose, but asked whether they want to choose (for example, clean energy or a new energy provider, a privacy setting on their computer, or to be organ donors).

(9) eliciting implementation intentions ("do you plan to vote?")

Comment: People are more likely to engage in activity if someone elicits their implementation intentions. With respect to health-related behavior, a simple question about future conduct ("do you plan to vaccinate your child?") can have significant consequences. Emphasizing people's identity can also be effective ("you are a voter, as your past practices suggest").

(10) informing people of the nature and consequences of their own past choices

Comment: Private and public institutions often have a great deal of information about people's own past choices – for example, their expenditures on health care or on their electric bills. The problem is that individuals, including workers, often lack that information. If people obtain it, their behavior can shift, often making markets work better (and saving a lot of money).

The Irish poet William Butler Yeats put it well: "Do not strike when the iron is hot, but make it hot by striking." For managers of all kinds – and indeed for all of us – that's an excellent Nudge.

Cass R. Sunstein

Robert Walmsley University Professor at Harvard Law School

Founder and Director of the Program on Behavioral Economics and Public Policy

Preface

Nudges: everyone is talking about them but no-one really knows what they are nor how they are used. At worst, they might be seen as the latest management fad. At best, someone might have read the excellent book by Eric Singler, *Nudge Marketing*, and will know that Nudges are ways to change behaviors while preserving freedom of choice by making subtle changes to the choice context.

Others may have a few well-established examples of Nudges. Such as the drop in energy consumption which is triggered by showing your neighbors' average energy use on your household bills. Or the massive increase in the number of organ donors that was achieved by switching from opt in to opt out on registration forms. Still, all the famous examples of Nudges are in the field of public action, which leaves people with the impression that nudging is only a tool for governments.

Eric Singler's new book, *Nudge Management*, is important because it masterfully dismantles these two preconceptions: that nudging isn't real, and that nudging is just for public policy.

In reality, nudging is the brainchild of the most recent advances and the most cutting-edge findings in behavioral science. This new discipline, represented by two Nobel Prize winners Daniel Kahneman and Richard Thaler, combines social psychology and experimental economics to better understand human behaviors as they really are, rather than as they should be. As a true connoisseur of this discipline and its main players, Eric Singler has the rare talent of being able to put this body of science into plain language, and shows that the Nudge concept is something very different from the unscientific anecdotes found in management books for the general public.

But the greatest merit of *Nudge Management* is certainly to show that the benefits of nudging venture far beyond the sphere of public policy. Because yes, Nudges can help you to be more effective in the workplace. Drawing on his vast experience as an entrepreneur himself, and as an advisor to leading companies, Eric Singler reveals how our decision making and behavior at work can be influenced by our bounded rationality. It also shows us the insufficiency, and sometimes even the perverse effects, of conventional incentives such as remuneration, which ignore the complexity of human motivation.

A word cloud featuring the most frequently mentioned words in the table of contents.

Nudge Management therefore identifies large- and small-scale interventions that have been proven to promote engagement and team spirit. It also addresses the criticism that Nudges are unethical because they are, by definition, manipulative. Unlike regulations or social conventions, Nudges always leave individuals or employees with the power to make their own choices. Moreover Nudges do actually work, and sometimes even work better, when people know they are in place. As reported by Cass Sunstein, who co-authored the book *Nudge* that started the movement with Richard Thaler, the best example of Nudge is the satellite navigation system we use in our cars, because it helps us reach our chosen destination by allowing us to make better decisions but without imposing them. More funda- mentally, Eric Singler's book helps increase performance and well- being at the same time. Clearly in today's world, companies can only be innovative, attractive and agile if they allow their employees to combine these two elements.

The book you are about to read is a valuable tool and will help you to be stronger and feel better in your place of work.

Pierre Chandon
Professor at INSEAD
L'Oréal Chaired Professor of Marketing, Innovation and Creativity
Director of the INSEAD-Sorbonne University Behavioural Lab

Introduction

The incentive revolution

"Nudge ... a lot."[1]

"Nudge ... a lot." That might sound like odd advice, but it's taken from an outstanding book entitled *Work Rules!* and given by one of the world's leading experts in human resources management, former Senior Vice President of People Operations at Google, Laszlo Bock.

He goes on to say: "Nudges are an incredibly powerful mechanism for improving teams and organizations."[2]

But what does he really mean by that? What's behind this powerful statement from a company that became the world's number one in 2016, while picking up the HR awards *Great Place to Work* and the *Best Diversity Employer*, as well as being voted the most desirable employer for undergraduates, and MBAs in several different countries?

The purpose of this book is to show how Nudge can be a management revolution and bring a real boost to employee engagement, well-being, and even business performance by explaining how to make high quality decisions and encourage winning behaviors.

As you'll see, Nudge is neither a miracle cure nor the latest fad that will soon give way to another. It is an approach based on the most recent findings in behavioral science, supported by a new key discipline: behavioral economics, and has been the subject of several Nobel Prizes in Economic Sciences[3] since the early 2000s. It has been put into practice by many different governments, international organizations and major pioneering corporations.

....

1 Laszlo Bock, *Work Rules!: Insights from Inside Google That Will Transform How You Live and Lead*, John Murray Publishers, 2015.
2 *Ibid.*
3 Daniel Kahneman in 2002, Thomas Schelling in 2005, Robert Shiller in 2013 and Richard Thaler in 2017.

Knowledge of behavioral science and the gentle encouragement of a Nudge can be a wonderful competitive asset for managers and companies. It can help them to make better decisions throughout the organization and focus on how to bring about useful behaviors. Sharing openly and communicating, stimulating employee and team cooperation, supporting innovation and facilitating internal transformations, the possibilities are endless.

Behavioral science, spearheaded by the Nudge approach, can create the structural conditions required for success by putting in place the physical and mental frameworks that encourage good decisions, incite people to adopt good behaviors within the company, and on the basis of these behaviors, bring more engagement and improved well-being.

The aim of this book is both simple and very ambitious: help companies to significantly boost their performance and generate well-being among their employees by drawing on the behavioral science revolution and its secret weapon: the Nudge.

It is mainly for business people and employees, especially leaders and managers, those who are striving to be pioneers in the most recent scientific teaching methods to boost their chances of success. It can be applied to any occupation, as long as it is involved with the overall running of the business. In addition to general management, people working in human resources, innovation and marketing, the employee experience, training and internal transformation are all concerned by the issues raised within its pages.

In addition to leaders and managers, employees who want to understand their work environment better, improve their everyday experiences, find greater meaning in their daily tasks and boost their individual and collective efficiency both for their own benefit and that of their company will find useful ideas from among the solutions I suggest.

Finally, management students may also be interested in the Nudge approach, if only to identify companies that are already involved in this revolution and could be a good fit for a future employment opportunity: both for their own well-being and for the chance to join a company that knows how to maximize its chances of success.

But let's start from the beginning, with behavioral science, and behavioral economics in particular.

A revolution in behavioral science...

Understanding why we act in one way or another on a given day or throughout our entire lives. Understanding what motivates us to behave or discourages us from behaving in a certain way. Understanding how other people's behavior influences our own, how elements in the world around us can influence our choices and how emotions or cognitive biases affect our decisions. That's what behavioral science aims to achieve.

Generally speaking, it's about drawing on rigorous scientific experiments to identify what really drives us to make the most fundamental decisions in all aspects of our life – the ones that have a lasting impact as well as the ones we make on a daily basis.

As its findings were gradually proven to be true, behavioral economics became "mainstream" to quote the famous consulting firm McKinsey[4]. Perceived in the early 1970s as marginal, the field of behavioral economics was gradually given more respect for its considerable contribution to the understanding of human behavior until finally it became a central focus. To date, no fewer than six Nobel Prize in Economic Sciences[5] holders have focused their work on this line of thought, including the 2017 winner, Professor Richard Thaler, who co-designed the Nudge approach with Cass Sunstein.

We'll see that discoveries made in this new field, which have benefited from more than forty years of research, fundamentally challenge how we understand human decision-making and behavior. The Economic Man from conventional decision-making theory – the famous *Homo economicus* – has been replaced by a being who looks much more like us, a sort of Homer Simpson in flesh and blood with

4   Dan Lovallo and Olivier Sibony, "The Case for Behavioral Strategy", *McKinsey Quarterly*, March 2010.
5   Daniel McFadden in 2000, Georges Akerlof in 2001, Daniel Kahneman in 2002, Thomas Schelling in 2005, Robert Shiller in 2013 and Richard Thaler in 2017.

impulses and emotions, and makes a series of never-ending mistakes, despite his good intentions.

We'll find that what we've learnt from this quest for a better understanding of human behavior is truly revolutionary.

No, humans are not rational beings as described long ago by Descartes and classical and neoclassical economists. No, we are not able to analyze the characteristics of each option involved in a choice in a cold and calculated manner to identify the one that maximizes its usefulness, in a demonstration of abject selfishness.

No, at work, people are not primarily motivated by a salary and material rewards, and yet this is precisely the basis of the motivation system that the vast majority of companies go on using every day.

No, making a good decision – individually or as a group – is not natural, and can actually be a huge challenge, not just because of the uncertainty of the environment and the effects of ongoing changes, but because of our own internal decision-making biases.

No, innovating or accepting change, let alone encouraging it, isn't self-evident for employees, because it doesn't fall in line with who we are deep down.

As we'll see when we take a look at recent findings in the field of behavioral economics, we are complex beings, and our behaviors are guided by many different factors. To quote Dan Ariely from Duke University in his enlightening book *Predictably Irrational*[6]: "we are really far less rational than standart economic theory assumes. Moreover, these irrational behaviors of ours are neither random nor senseless. There are systematic and since we repeat them again and again, predictable."

We will take an in-depth look into these irrational behaviors and why they occur, because by using this intimate understanding, we are going to put forward a new way of thinking about how companies are organized internally, with a view to achieving more team-based effectiveness and personal well-being by boosting employee engagement.

....
6   Dan Ariely, *Predictably Irrational: The Hidden Forces that Shape Our Decisions*, HarperCollins, 2008.

I'm a businessman. After a few years with Yoplait as a product manager in the marketing department, I founded my first company with my friend Alain Sivan in 1989. It was called IN VIVO, and now offers expertise for Fast Moving Consumer Goods businesses in the form of PRS IN VIVO, part of the market research and consulting firm BVA, of which I am the managing director.

Since we created IN VIVO, I have had the chance to go on developing the original concept of our business internationally, creating affiliates first in the main European countries, then in the United States and finally in Asia. For almost thirty years, I have been lucky enough to work with many of the world's biggest and best-performing companies, including Procter & Gamble, Nestlé, L'Oréal, Danone, Orange, Unilever, Mondelēz, Chanel, Coca-Cola, Mars, BMS, and many more. Over the years, I have watched how they work and operate, always driven by what I have been able to learn and understand.

As a businessman, I am interested in how companies perform. This book is extremely pragmatic and I hope it will be useful for both businesses and their employees.

I didn't write this book to share my beliefs and feelings about management, it is a work based on the most recent and proven scientific findings. What do we know about the basic ideas behind human behavior and how can we apply that knowledge to companies – using rigorous experiments that have been carried out for decades by the best researchers, and applied by the most cutting-edge companies – to enhance collective performance and improve individual well-being?

Because my enthusiasm as an entrepreneur has been spurred on by the world of academia and university research, I have always thought that studies and experiments of these kinds could help businesses and entrepreneurs to perform better. So I worked on and studied a great many academic publications; I also set up connections between the world of research and the business world by holding symposia to get feedback from businesses and researchers and by creating a prize for a thesis that was awarded to the best researchers. And I have always talked a lot with French and international researchers to improve my understanding of their results.

So this book is rooted in science. It draws on the most recent work carried out by behavioral scientists with a view to helping companies reach the holy grail of performance and well-being, individual and group effectiveness, and daily engagement.

Lastly, I see myself as both an entrepreneur and the builder of a "bridge to science". I wrote the book from this perspective, because it strives to take the realities and constraints of business life into account – any theoretically good solution might not be applicable to all companies – while putting forward innovative, tried-and-tested solutions that stem from research into behavioral science on the most strategic issues: how do we make the best decisions? How do we attract talent and build a great team? How do we innovate on a daily basis and stay ahead of the competition? How do we encourage cooperation among employees and break with convention?

We now know a lot about what motivates behavior in the workplace, about what encourages or hinders employee engagement, about what we need to do to succeed in terms of innovation, internal transformation and learning. But there is often a huge difference between academic theory and how practitioners use that knowledge. And that's the gap that this book will try to fill.

Nudge: the power of a boost

The Nudge – whose name is taken from the title of a seminal work[7] by professors Richard Thaler and Cass Sunstein – is an approach that aims to turn innovative insight from behavioral science into action.

When it was published in the United States in 2008, the authors made it possible to move from theory to practice, from the knowledge of what influenced behavior to how to use that knowledge for more effective purposes in public policy. Behavioral economics teaches us what drives human behavior. The Nudge idea is based on this knowledge, and encourages individuals to transform any harmful

....
7   Richard Thaler and Cass Sunstein, *Nudge: Improving Decisions about Health, Wealth and Happiness,* Penguin Books, revised and expanded edition, 2009.

behavior into behavior that is beneficial for themselves and for the community. The Nudge approach helps individuals to make better personal and professional decisions. It can be used to recommend effective actions, based on a new understanding of human behavior.

In concrete terms, behavioral economics researchers have drawn up a list of factors that influence behavior, cognitive biases and decision heuristics, all of which create – following specific analysis of a given situation – what is known as "choice architecture", that naturally encourages individuals to make better decisions and adopt desired behaviors.

And the Nudge approach has seen some spectacular results! A tiny detail intelligently added to the environment when a person is asked to make a choice can bring about a spectacular change in behavior, if that detail is able to activate an influence that behavioral science experiments have identified as important.

Just position a small sticker with a picture of a fly in the middle of a urinal at Schiphol Airport, and cleaning costs plummet, as travellers aim at the central target and splash back is dramatically reduced. When green footprint stickers appeared on the streets of Copenhagen, put in place by Professor Pelle Hansen and his team to show the path to the nearest trash receptacle, the volume of waste on the streets dropped by nearly 50% because the stickers reminded people of the right thing to do at the right time. Finally, a basic graph on an energy bill comparing a user's consumption to that of their neighbors in California potentially saved millions of dollars. There are now a great many examples of the incredible effect these tiny nudges can have.

From 2010, the governments of influential countries such as the United States and the United Kingdom began using the Nudge approach to tackle major public policy issues more effectively: encouraging people to take better care of their health, be eco-responsible, pay their taxes on time, take professional training courses, choose green energy solutions, etc.

But they aren't alone. Companies have also begun taking an interest.

From Nudge to Nudge marketing...

Enthusiasm from the business world has grown gradually, as the books by Sunstein and Thaler, as well as Dan Ariely's work, have been reporting worldwide success. Following on from this, the authors began receiving invitations to share their ideas at business conferences such as *The Marketing Research Event* – the biggest international meeting held in the United States each year for marketers from around the world – which hosted Richard Thaler in 2010, Daniel Kahneman in 2012 and Dan Ariely in 2015. Dan Ariely has also presented several TED talks, and notched up over a million views, the best one attracting over five million. He also created a Mooc[8] in 2013 to explain the ideas behind behavioral economics. With over 100,000 people registered, this initiative was another huge success.

I made my own attempt to contribute (a much more modest contribution than those made by the people I mentioned earlier) to sharing knowledge about behavioral economics and how it is used beyond public policy, in marketing, when I published *Nudge Marketing*[9]. The BVA Nudge Unit, that I created in 2013 with my friends Richard Bordenave and Étienne Bressoud, also helped boost awareness of these new approaches through various events.

The combined effect of these actions was soon felt. Proof of growing interest came in the form of Indra Nooyi – Global CEO of PepsiCo – who was quoted in the Harvard Business Review as saying: "We've taken lessons from Richard Thaler and Cass Sunstein's book *Nudge*."[10] The concept is growing in popularity within companies for the same reason that Nudge is gradually becoming more widespread in public policy: it can bring about impressive changes in behavior at a low cost! And just like governments, companies are also looking for greater effectiveness on smaller budgets. Businesses are discovering that in addition to communication and marketing, it is possible to encourage beneficial behavior from customers using a much more frugal approach. For

---

8   *A Beginner's Guide to Irrational Behavior*, Coursera.
9   *Nudge Marketing: Winning at Behavioral Change*, Pearson, 2015.
10 Adi Ignatius, "How Indra Nooyi Turned Design Thinking Into Strategy: An Interview with PepsiCo's CEO", *Harvard Business Review*, September 2015, hbr.org.

example, it can be used to make customers more loyal, try new products or services, find out about online services, ensure that patients comply with their treatments, use technical products correctly, make an application simple and easy, ensure that a point of sale experience is exciting or that a visit to a website leads to the desired action, etc.

The Nudge approach is developing quickly in private companies, where it is seen as a new and very effective addition to traditional tools, and a way to transform customer behavior into a win-win relationship that creates long-term value for business, for both parties. Of course this is just the beginning, but it's really starting to catch on. I know this from personal experience, because in my own business we worked for more than forty major companies last year using the Nudge approach, in many countries such as the United States, France, the United Kingdom, and Germany as well as Thailand, India and the Philippines.

Setting the course for Nudge management

As we developed quickly and on an international scale, however, one element became increasingly clear: the use of Nudge and lessons in behavioral economics had been mainly directed towards end users: private citizens, product consumers, customers buying a service or patients who were being followed up after a treatment. But they hadn't been used for promoting desirable behaviors within a company or an organization.

So why not use the behavioral science revolution and the Nudge approach within the company itself, for its own benefit and that of its employees?

That's what this book is designed to do.

My strong belief is that by gaining in-depth knowledge of the factors that influence behavioral economics – combined with the transformative power of the Nudge approach – companies can benefit their employees and achieve better overall performance. It is possible to think about your business with that understanding in mind to enable better decision-making, whether you're dealing with the CEO, team leaders, a project group or employees going about their daily tasks, as well as designing and implementing psychological and physical environments that encourage people to adopt beneficial collective behaviors.

While the first uses of Nudge have focused on transforming the behavior of "external" customers, there is no reason that it should only be applied in those cases. As Laszlo Bock pointed out, it is not only possible, but highly desirable, to build on the in-depth understanding of behaviors and motivational factors and apply this knowledge to companies to improve engagement, encourage employees to behave the way we want them to, and boost company competitiveness and employee well-being.

And it will bring about a revolution, because while some companies – Google, Facebook and even Tesla – have already understood and now rely on behavioral science to build a work environment that is conducive to performance and success, it is not the case for the vast majority. Of course most companies take the opposite approach, because they have remained under the influence, often unconsciously, of the long-dominant theory of a rational human being who is mainly motivated by the carrot and the stick. If employees are motivated to adopt the desired behavior because their salary, career or even presence in the company depend on it, then these levers must be activated to motivate them and generate the engagement that all entrepreneurs want from their employees.

But it is clear to see that this isn't effective, or at least that it could be a lot better, and that's why so many employees around the world now say that they are only barely committed to their work. In the Gallup global survey of 230,000 employees in 142 countries, only 13% of respondents say they felt engaged at work. At the same time, 63% of individuals say they are not engaged and, perhaps even worse, 24% say they feel actively uninvolved! Commenting on the results of this study, the renowned psychology professor Barry Schwartz states: "Work is more often a source of frustration than one of fulfillment for nearly 90 percent of the world's workers."[11] There is even talk of "bore-out": professional exhaustion brought about by the boredom that leads to demotivation.

....
11   Barry Schwartz, *Why We Work?* Simon & Schuster, New York, 2015.

All of this can and must change. There have been more and more scientific studies in recent years aimed at improving our understanding of individuals at work. This knowledge has expanded and is now available for anyone to access. But it's not only a question of knowledge. The challenge is how to apply this knowledge to everyday life within the workplace, to generate the behaviors we are striving to obtain.

It's a great opportunity, because we now have plenty of evidence to prove the strong link between well-being at work, employee engagement, and performance. The study carried out by the Great Place to Work Institute, in partnership with *Fortune*[12] magazine, shows that Best Place to Work companies perform twice as well on the stock market than others!

Improved performance is at your fingertips, it is possible to achieve both better results, AND increased well-being. And you can do it without investing millions. In the spirit of Nudge – keeping costs down – consider the company as a structure that needs to be shaped in order to incite employees to adopt more beneficial behavior, and promote good decisions as well as individual and collective effectiveness.

The Nudge approach is about taking a new look at how we manage, and is based on behavioral science. Its aim is not to mechanically motivate a rational human being who doesn't even exist in reality, but rather to incite, encourage and facilitate engagement and beneficial individual and collective behaviors by designing a relevant physical and psychological environment that takes into account the reality of human nature in all its complexity.

This book is separated into three parts, each of which corresponds to the three fundamental ideas on which Nudge management is based:

- *Understand*: The first part aims to share the fundamental knowledge required to apply the Nudge management principle with a two-fold goal: to share the lessons taught by behavioral science to understand what really influences human behavior; identify the consequences of these revolutionary discoveries

---

12 See greatplacetowork.com.sg/our-approach/what-are-the-benefits-great-workplaces.

through the four major challenges of corporate performance and how human beings really become engaged.

- *Build foundations:* The second part describes the two fundamental pillars of Nudge management that refer on the one hand to individual effectiveness and on the other hand to collective performance by designing a physical and psychological environment that creates the conditions for engagement and success.
- *Encourage beneficial collective behavior*: The third part lays out the specific conditions to encourage two main beneficial behaviors for 21st century companies: attracting talent that cooperates with one another and establishing the conditions for a naturally learning-focused and innovative company.

And now, let's see just how powerful Nudge management can be.

Part 1

Using behavioral science to solve business and societal challenges

Chapter 1

Behavioral science: from *Homo economicus* to *Homo psychologicus*

How do humans really think?

Let me start by asking you a series of simple questions about the sort of decisions we all make every day.

The first set of questions is about individual concerns, the ones you and I need to deal with each day of our lives.

Let's start with a particular profession, doctors: do you know what percentage of French doctors smoke? About 25%! About the same proportion of doctors smoke as there are smokers in the general population. Do you think that those doctors who smoke know that "smoking kills"? I know what you're thinking: "What a stupid question, of course they do!" And you would be right. So logically and on the basis of this knowledge, no doctor should smoke, because this behavior is a major risk to what we hold most dear: our precious existence. Voltaire said: "I know of nothing more laughable than a doctor who does not die of old age." And even today, the revered philosopher's words still ring true, two centuries after he wrote them. Doctors who smoke are fully aware of the consequences of their actions, but that's not enough to stop them from behaving against their basic interests. Keep that in mind and move on to the second question.

Do you know what percentage of the world's population is obese? According to the World Health Organization (WHO)[1] the figure was 13% in 2014 for adults aged 18 and over. In absolute terms, that's more than 600 million people. If you add merely overweight people to the mix, the WHO estimates the figure to be 1.9 billion! Not only are there

---

1   World Health Organization, *Obesity and overweight*, checklist No.311, October 2017, who.int.

a huge number of obese and overweight people, but their number has doubled since 1980.

Same question as before: Do you think that obese and overweight people know that their behavior puts their health at risk? Obesity is a major risk factor especially for cardiovascular diseases such as stroke but also for diabetes, musculoskeletal disorders such as osteoarthritis, and some cancers. Perhaps those who are obese or overweight aren't familiar with this level of medical detail but there is certainly a perception, however minimal, of it being a health hazard. I myself am overweight (yes indeed!), and my doctor (very nicely) and my wife (more firmly) remind me of it regularly. They make it very clear that there are serious potential consequences. In the same way that doctors know that "smoking kills", overweight or obese people are aware of the risks to themselves, but it doesn't matter enough. Again, the information alone doesn't have enough impact to make us change our behavior.

Let's move on to some more personal questions. And be honest! No one is watching, it's just between us.

The first question is for those of you who use a car: in the last month have you used your phone while driving? I have asked this question during conferences in many different countries – the United States, the United Kingdom, Singapore, China, and Germany – and response rates are usually around 50% (starting with myself, but as I write these lines I swear I'm going to stop). I then ask if the people concerned know that this behavior is very dangerous both for themselves and for the people sharing the road. The unanimous answer is yes! We all know that using telephones behind the wheel might kill us, or kill other people. And that's true. According to the French road safety department, more than one accident in ten in my native France is caused by someone using a phone whilst driving. In particular, typing a text message while driving multiplies the risk of having an accident by 23! In this respect, my typical conference audiences aren't representative of the population. In 2015, I worked with the road safety department in France to try to find out what we could do to stop young drivers from using their phones behind the wheel. The BVA Nudge Unit interviewed a number of young drivers to understand their behavior and to find out if they knew about its dangerous consequences: the answer was of course a resounding yes. So many of us, with *full knowledge and awareness*, behave in a way that we know is putting our lives, and the lives of others, at risk.

Here's another personal question. Do you do as much regular physical exercise as you would like, and as much as you need to do to stay healthy? I'll be honest again here, I don't. I'm a big fan of the Paris Saint-Germain soccer team, and I go to see them play at the stadium or I watch them on television, but that's about all the exercise I get. But I'm very active when watching the matches! What about you? If you are like 42% of French people[2], myself included, you don't do enough weekly physical exercise to keep you healthy. Are we aware that it isn't enough and that, again, the consequences of not exercising might be detrimental to our health? We certainly are! We know this because public health campaigns are another constant reminder of how important it is to get daily exercise. But again, we often intend to do the right thing, but don't manage to align our behavior with our remaining intentions – like most New Year's resolutions – and they are soon forgotten.

This doesn't just apply to a handful of individuals. The Centers for Disease Control and Prevention (CDC) have established that 40% of premature deaths in the United States – those that occur before the age of 80 – are due to individual decisions that have serious and preventable consequences. That's more than 900,000 people a year who smoke, drink too much, don't exercise enough, don't wear their seatbelt, stay in the sun for too long, or don't wear a helmet while riding a motorcycle, and then die too soon.

The personal decisions we make on a daily basis are therefore often far from rational: we know what should be done, we intend to behave in a way that benefits our bodies, but we don't manage it, even when the stakes are high.

If our individual behavior is often unreasonable, what about when these individual behaviors are pooled? Do they become rational when we look at the behavior of the species as a whole?

---

2   See the Insep survey by the French Ministry of Youth and Sports conducted in 2000 and published in Inserm, *Physical activity - Contexts and effects on health*, 2008.

Here again, I would like to share a fundamental question. It is no longer about the survival of an individual but of that of our planet, and therefore of our species. We're going to talk about global warming, and I'm going to ask you two simple questions.

First question: do you think the population is aware that our behavior is causing major disruption to the planet's ecosystems and that this behavior poses serious risks for the survival of this planet?

In its European barometer conducted for the European Commission, the TNS Sofres Institute writes[3]: "Climate change is still a key issue for Europeans. In all, 91% of them see climate change as a 'serious' problem, with 69% considering it 'very serious'. Nearly half of all Europeans (47%) think climate change is one of the most serious problems, and about one in six think it is THE most serious problem facing the world."

So we all know that the planet is in danger. But what about our behavior? In the same study, just over one in two (54%) – of those who consider climate change to be a 'very serious' risk – say they have taken personal actions to combat climate change. And in contrast, almost one in two people say they have done nothing, which goes against their own belief systems. Of course that's not the worst of it. Let's look at the reality of our behavior. For example, in various markets studied by Michal J. Carrington, Benjamin A. Neville and Gregory J. Whitwell[4], 30% to 50% of consumers say that they intend to buy eco-friendly products while the market share of these products is often less than 5% of total sales.

Referring to the most recent economic disaster the world has witnessed – the 2008-2009 financial crisis – President Obama said: "This recession was not caused by a normal reversal of the business cycle. It was caused by an outburst of irresponsibility and bad

---

3   *Special Eurobarometer 435: Climate change*, Wave EB83.34, TNS Opinion & Social, November 2015.
4   Michal J. Carrington, Benjamin A. Neville and Gregory J. Whitwell, "Why Ethical Consumers Do not Walk Their Talk: Towards a Framework for Understanding the Gap Between the Ethical Purchase Intentions and Actual Buying Behaviour of Ethically Minded Consumers", *Journal of Business Ethics*, vol. 97, No.1, November 2010.

decision-making that spread from Wall Street to Washington and to people on the street."[5]

Again, for the President of the United States, then in office and best placed to have an informed opinion, it is the nature of the decisions we make that caused the disaster.

This handful of examples, of which there are many more, bear witness to a very simple reality: contrary to what we have long believed, humans are not rational decision-makers. As a group, or individually, we often make bad decisions and adopt behaviors that go against our own interests, sometimes even when it comes to crucial issues, even matters of life and death.

So if we are not "utility maximizers" as neoclassical economists say, how do we make decisions? What really explains our seemingly irrational behavior? Behavioral economics tries to answer these questions. Let's take a look at this fascinating science to discover what's behind decision-making, before we return to the world of work and business.

Behavioral economics: unmasking the human

Rational human beings: an outmoded idea?

In conventional decision-making theory – which dominated 20th century thinking – humans are rational beings. A person makes decisions by analyzing the characteristics of each option in the choice which is made available, and selects the one which seems to be in his or her best interests.

The decision-maker, considered to be an economic agent, or *Homo economicus*, is a rigorous and logical calculator, driven only by his own interest, coherent in his choices and whose behavior is in line with his intentions. The strength of this theory is its ability to create a mathematical model. In making decisions, whether crucial

....
5   Quoted in Max H. Bazerman and Ann E. Tenbrunsel, *Blind Spots: Why We Fail to Do What's Right and What to Do about It*, Princeton University Press, 2010.

or trivial, individuals are supposed to identify each characteristic of a choice, evaluate its importance, analyze it and then mathematically aggregate the value obtained for each characteristic, obtaining an overall "usefulness" score. Decisions are made based on the option whose overall value is the greatest. And the actual behavior of the individual is in line with the intention that results from this calculation. Let's look at a specific case involving a car. First we select all available models (choice options); we then identify all the descriptive characteristics of a car (price, color, size, engine power, appearance, etc.); the importance of each of these characteristics is assessed (relative importance of the price, brand, etc.); all the characteristics of each model are evaluated (how is the Renault X positioned on each of the characteristics we have identified); and finally, a mathematical calculation is made for all the values, weighted by the importance of each factor, and each characteristic for each model (for the Renault: value of the brand + value of the price, and so on). The model that gets the highest score will be purchased.

The birth of behavioral economics

This vision was gradually challenged by some young economists and psychologists, starting in the early 1970s, using a very simple and very pragmatic method: conducting experiments during which participants are placed in situations where they need to make decisions. The economists and psychologists then set about trying to understand the logic behind those decisions by varying certain elements.

The path had been cleared by two pioneers who had already begun to question conventional decision-making theory, which seemed very far removed from the human reality: the Frenchman Maurice Allais and the American Herbert Simon. Both went on to receive the Nobel Prize in Economic Sciences (1978 for Simon and 1988 for Allais). For Allais, the assumptions that form the basis of this theory are invalid. This is the famous "Allais paradox" in which the researcher demonstrates that the independence axiom is very often violated by individuals when making decisions. If one of the fundamental axioms of conventional decision-making theory is invalid, then individual behavior is impossible to predict. The whole theory is undermined.

For the American Herbert Simon, the criticism is really about a human being's inability to process information in the manner described by proponents of the utility theory. We do have limits. And because of these limits, we can't proceed in the manner described by the theory when we make our decisions. The limits are cognitive: our brains are not able to analyze a series of options so rigorously. The limits also include information, because we don't have all the information about all the choices when we have to make a decision. Finally, they are also temporal in the sense that we simply don't have the time to go through all these actions for every decision we make. For example, when shopping in a grocery store, how much effort would it take to carry out an exhaustive analysis of all the characteristics involved in making a choice from the various brands available for each product that we would like to buy? And how long would it take? It wouldn't make any sense to do that, because the time we would use to make a high quality decision in comparison to a quick method would be time lost on doing something much more useful. Rather than proceeding in a perfectly rational manner through a comprehensive analysis, we stop at the first "satisfactory" choice. It may not be the best, but we weigh up the quality of the decision and the attention resources it requires with the time we have invested to achieve it. Simon's theory will be recognized as the theory of "limited rationality". We are not rational because we are quite simply incapable of being rational.

From the work of these pioneers, a whole generation of economists and psychologists leaped on this chink in the armor, based on a seminal article published in *Science* by a pair of psychologists who would later become famous – and Michael Lewis has just told a fascinating story about them in his latest book[6] – Daniel Kahneman and Amos Tversky. The first won a Nobel Prize in 2002 and the second would probably have received it if he hadn't passed away at such a young age in 1996. By conducting multiple experiments to gain

....
6   Michael Lewis, *The Undoing Project: A Friendship that Changed Our Minds*,
    W. W. Norton, 2016.

better insight into how decisions are made in real life, these young researchers gradually built a new vision that looks at previous knowledge in a completely new way. It was the birth of behavioral economics, which is based on a set of disciplines: economics, psychology, cognitive science and gradually neuroscience, all focused on the same issue: understanding how people make decisions.

Patiently, these brilliant researchers – mainly Richard Thaler, George Loewenstein, Paul Slovic, Robert Cialdini, Colin Camerer, Dan Ariely, Matthew Rabin, Max Bazerman, Drazen Prelec, Ernst Fehr – turned our understanding of how behavior is motivated completely on its head. At first perceived as "anomalies" in relation to the dominant standard theory, their discoveries actually constitute a new overall vision about how we make decisions. So if we aren't rational, how *do* we make decisions? What *does* motivate our behavior?

The real human: a social and emotional animal, the product of evolution and context

It all starts with survival: System 1, mental shortcuts and cognitive biases

The human brain is an organ that aims to maximize a person's chances of survival. In concrete terms, this means being "programmed" to take replenishment or reproduction opportunities when they present themselves in our environment and to identify and avoid potential risks.

Our brain is constantly, automatically and often unconsciously analyzing our surroundings in order to meet these specific objectives and more generally, to ensure our survival.

But we are not supercomputers that can constantly process everything in order to rigorously evaluate the situation in real time, and adapt our behavior to it by making the right decisions. We are simply incapable of that. When I'm looking at one thing I can't also be looking at something else. When I focus on a specific topic, reading a book for example, it's difficult for me to pay attention to something else, like watching TV or having a conversation. In a well-known experiment called "The Magical Number 7"[7], Harvard University Professor George Miller demonstrated how difficult it is to process multiple pieces of information at the same time. If you're in any doubt, why not try the exercise yourself? Participants in the experiment were asked to read information in the form of letters, words, and numbers, and then to reproduce that information from memory. On average, we don't seem to be able to recollect more than seven elements from a list of more than seven. There are limits to processing and memorizing information at a given time. And yet our environment is constantly sending out information of all different kinds for us to process. And analyzing this properly can be a matter of life or death.

So why, as a species, have we not only survived with such basic limits, but climbed to the top of the pyramid of the animal kingdom in an environment that could be considered highly competitive? While we have been on the Earth, many other species have, at least physically, been much better equipped than us to survive the world's dangers. If we consider that the planet was created three billion years ago and that humans in their present form (*Homo sapiens sapiens*) appeared just two hundred thousand years ago, our presence on Earth is very recent.

In terms of time, that's less than 0.0001% of the universe's existence. Nevertheless, over this short period, our species has expanded enough to colonize the entire planet and there are now more than 7 billion of us.

Our brain has been able to develop mechanisms to optimize our limited capacities, both on a personal and a collective level.

System 1 and System 2: two thinking speeds

In his major work *Thinking, Fast and Slow*[8] – the bible of behavioral economics – Nobel prizewinner Daniel Kahneman popularized the concept of a dual mode of decision-making in human beings, which he calls Systems 1 and 2.

....
7   George Miller, "The Magical Number 7, Plus or Minus 2: Some Limits on Our Capacity for Processing Information, *Psychological Review*, vol. 63, No.2, March 1956.
8   Daniel Kahneman, *Thinking, Fast and Slow*, Penguin, 2012 (revised edition).

System 1: quick decisions, occasional mistakes

System 1 is an automatic, unconscious, fast decision-making mode that is constantly solicited but requires almost no effort. System 1 works very transparently in all of us. It's like "autopilot" mode. It almost makes decisions for us in the sense that we do not need to assign resources to it. It enables us to constantly analyze our environment to identify potential opportunities or risks in order to draw instant conclusions and drive us forward in the right direction. To take a famous example by Kahneman, if I ask what's 2 + 2, the answer will be immediate. Finding the answer takes no effort. It comes to you almost instantly. It's a kind of miracle, except that we know how much effort we made at some point in our lives to learn the rules of addition and multiplication tables. But once the rules are acquired, the answer to the question is easy. System 1 results from both learning and from innate mechanisms. We learn to add, but recognizing an aggressive facial expression, which alerts us to a potential risk from an individual or an animal, is something we are able to do very early on in our development, and nobody needs to teach us about it. The huge advantage of System 1 is that we save our resources (our attention or energy), which allows us to perform a task automatically without thinking about it, and leaves us able to assign these saved resources to another action. Driving is a great example of this. When you learned to drive, you focused a great deal of effort on memorizing the various stages of each maneuver. But once they were memorized, you began to drive without thinking about the technique you used, which means that you can now carry on a conversation with your passengers. The attention savings you make through mental learning releases your brain so that it can focus on another task.

System 1 is a wonderful asset in our quest for survival as it allows us to improve how we manage our limited resources while helping us make the right decisions, most of the time. Why does it usually help us to make the right decisions in our everyday life? Because mainly, it looks back at our past experiences and learns from them. If any past experience has been positive or negative, we memorize it and its memory will be reactivated when we have to make a similar decision.

For example, if you enjoyed a particular restaurant, or had a great time on your last trip to Corsica (like I did), you can quickly decide to go back without getting into an exhaustive analysis of all the other places you could go. And the chances are good that you're making the right decision, because if you enjoyed a restaurant once, you will probably enjoy it again when you go back. So it's a great decision that doesn't take much effort. A very good return on investment!

System 1 also feeds on immediate impressions, sensations, perceived emotions at any given time, and, in general, any information that is easy to process – images rather than words, simple, rather than complex words, stereotypes, immediate associations – to enable quick and efficient decision-making using your cognitive resources. For example, System 1 will instantly interpret a beautiful visual of a piece of fruit on an item of packaging and make you think that the packaging contains a good product. That will prompt you to choose quickly from among the other options, without having to analyze the composition of each product in more detail, without attempting to evaluate the actual organoleptic qualities of the product in question.

System 1 is designed to make effortless decisions. And, again, it's fundamental to our survival because our resources are limited. System 1 allows us to make plenty of decisions and save our energy or attention. It automates most of the decisions we make in everyday life: what time we get up in the morning, when we take a shower, when we have breakfast, how we get to our usual destinations. We use System 1 when we go through the same motions, arriving at the office or buying the same brands and products when shopping. A study directed by Wendy Wood – now Provost Professor of Behavioral Science at the Sorbonne University-Insead center[9] – showed that 45% of the decisions we make are of this nature: habits which aren't really decisions because we spend no time thinking about them. And it doesn't only apply to micro-decisions. It also affects more important choices: we choose the same holiday destinations from one year to another, we go to the same restaurants, the friends we see are often the same for

---

9   David T. Neal, Wendy Wood et Jeffrey M. Quinn, "Habits: A Repeat Performance", *Association for Psychological Science*, vol. 15, No. 4, August 2006.

years, and so on. The researchers point out that "much of everyday action is characterized by habitual repetition."

We are creatures of habit. We use System 1 almost constantly for the vast majority of our decisions. For Daniel Kahneman, "most of what we think and do is rooted in our System 1."

But System 1 makes mistakes! And that's a key point. While it is generally a major asset to help us make a whole host of everyday decisions – several hundred each day – it does generate errors. The idea behind System 1 is to work quickly. It does not analyze the information available in detail, which would take time, but feeds on clues from the environment and quickly jumps to conclusions by telling us what decision to make. Let's take a look at a great example used by Daniel Kahneman to shed light on the bad decisions made by System 1. Try this simple exercise: a ball and a baseball bat cost $1.10 when they are purchased together. The bat costs $1 more than the ball. So how much does the ball cost? Quick, what's your answer? If the answer that springs to mind – thanks to your System 1 – is 10 cents, as was the case for me and the majority of students from the major American schools to whom the question was asked, you are wrong. Let's work it out step by step, starting with the two pieces of information:

- bat + ball = 1.10
- bat = ball +1
- therefore ball + (ball + 1) = 1.10
- therefore 2 balls + 1 = 1.10
- 2 balls = 1.10 - 1
- 1 ball = 0.10 / 2 = 0.05

Our System 1 has therefore given many of us a quick but incorrect answer (but well done if you got it right!). System 1 uses a fundamental mechanism called the mental shortcut. From clues perceived in the environment and past experiences, System 1 makes decisions based on simplified logic, which is needed to make decisions quickly. A little like keyboard shortcuts on computers, the brain has created a battery of mental shortcuts that are specific to each of us and based on our personal history, and we use them to make quick decisions. It is a tremendous asset in terms of efficiency, but carries the risk of error: clues might be misinterpreted, or a situation initially perceived as similar to a previous experience might be different, and this means we make bad decisions.

Stereotypes are one of those mental shortcuts, and we know that many stereotypes are wrong (are all blondes really stupid?). Others can be misleading: red is mostly perceived as a dangerous color because it is often used as such – often, but not always.

These shortcuts can lead to dead ends, and bad decisions. There is therefore a downside to the tremendous speed and economy of resources in System 1: the occurrence of errors.

But we have another system: System 2.

System 2: powerful, but soon exhausted

System 2 is a slow, deliberate, conscious decision-making process that requires thought and effort. How do you know when you are using System 2? Easy: you are making an effort. You weigh up the pros and the cons; you try to identify the main advantages and disadvantages of each option in the choice you have to make. This is of course the system you try to use for decisions you consider important: changing jobs, buying a house, making a significant purchase or taking out a loan, and so on. But it can also be used for everyday decisions. If I ask you to work out 25 x 37, your System 1 will have trouble responding instantly unless you're a math whizz, and you'll have to use your System 2 to get an answer. Except of course if your System 1 tells you to use the calculator on your cell phone!

System 2 therefore helps us to make more rational and well thought-out decisions, as we have paid more attention and spent more time finding the solution. I said "more rational", and not simply "rational". It's a fundamental difference because we will see later that, even in System 2 mode, we aren't immune to the errors of logic caused by cognitive biases.

System 2 also has a very powerful opposite number in everyday life. It is exhausted quickly because it uses a lot of energy and that makes us tired – psychologically, as well as physically. Psychologically, because we all know that it's very difficult to stay focused and attentive on a subject for more than an hour and a half. But also physically: experiments show that making decisions using System 2 consumes more energy than the automatic decisions generated by System 1. Our bodies simply don't allow us to make all our decisions using System 2. It would be impossible in our daily lives, given the time it takes to process information and it would be exhausting for our body, whose main goal is to survive. So these two decision-making systems run simultaneously: System 1 allows us to make lots of everyday decisions very quickly while saving up our resources, and System 2 helps us deal with more important decisions.

But when we consider how we weigh up our choices, we convince ourselves that we're rational decision makers. We believe that most of our decisions are made after careful thought, and we believe that other people do the same. We see ourselves as "System 2" beings. Why? Simply because – as I explained when I defined System 1 – we're not aware of what we're doing. Whenever we make a decision in System 1 mode, we don't know what the brain is doing because it all happens at a very early stage of perception. We act without knowing that the action has been prepared by our brain. That's why the answer to the math problem 2 + 2 leaps to mind without a conscious triggering of the mechanics that led to this correct answer. On the other hand, we know when we are using System 2 because it requires conscious reflection and careful deliberation. Daniel Kahneman concludes: "When we think about ourselves, we identify with System 2, the conscious, the reasoning and the thinking, the choice, and the decision to think and what to do. Although System 2 thinks it's at the heart of the action, the real hero is actually automatic System 1."

And this misguided belief in the reality of System 1's role has huge consequences.

A fundamental mistake: "System 2" actions to convince "System 1" beings

This perception that we are "System 2" beings, thinking beings, is fundamental to the way we convince others, whether in our personal or professional lives. We use an argument to inform and convince people we believe are "System 2" beings when most of our decisions and behaviors are driven by System 1. But why is that a problem? Because the same reasoning can't be used successfully for both systems. As I explained above, System 1 feeds on past experiences and memories, clues that are easily processed within the immediate surroundings; impressions and emotions; images, simple words and combinations of immediate ideas. All the elements in the environment – including the behavior of people around us or places and how they are organized – can have a tremendous impact on our behavior. By contrast, System 2 is influenced by facts, figures, reasoning and information, to which System 1 resists because it does not have time to process elements of this nature.

This difference is one of the main reasons why efforts to convince individuals to behave in a way that is beneficial to them simply don't work, despite the conclusive information that is presented. We will come back later to this fundamental point which can be used to explain many failures, and business transformations in particular.

But while our internal decision-making system is the key to understanding our behavior, its energy comes from the environment in which we evolve. And that environment is also occupied by other people.

The social human

Other people are important to us. Because humans are incredibly social creatures! And that means many of the decisions we make and the behaviors we adopt are directly influenced by what others think, do and say.

For a lot of researchers, especially in evolutionary psychology, social connectivity is even one of the major characteristics that explains our success as a species on Earth. Our ability to form communities, first in very small units and gradually in larger and larger groups, has enabled the human species to overcome the main challenges of its survival and reproduction. Groups are better at defending themselves against predators of all kinds, and are often much more powerful than individuals. They are better at hunting animals or organizing the farming of products to feed themselves. But in general, our social skills give us the ability to think together, to design more and more sophisticated societies. The social dimension of human beings is fundamental, because this is where we draw our strength.

Matthew Lieberman, professor of psychology, psychiatry and life and behavioral science at the University of California points out that "While we tend to think it is our capacity for abstract reasoning that is responsible for *Homo sapiens* dominating the planet, there is increasing evidence that our dominance as a species may be attributable to our ability to think socially."[10] Drawing on this fundamental idea, David Brooks in his book on the human social behavior writes: "In truth, what distinguishes us from other animals is the phenomenal social skills that allow us to teach, learn, sympathize, express emotions, create cultures and institutions, build the complex mental scaffolding of civilization."[11]

And this social capacity in humans, this ability to form groups, forge bonds including friendship, which is extremely rare in the animal kingdom, to think of others and their interests, to feel part of a community and act in the interests of that community, and not just in our own interests, is deeply rooted within the inner workings of our brains. It's not a choice; our brain leads us intrinsically towards these social connections. Neuroscientists call it "social cognition by default." This concept has been demonstrated through experiments using brain imaging techniques. Neuroscientists have observed the way our brain works – especially the areas that are activated – during tasks we need to perform. But what about when an individual under observation is not asked to perform a task? Or when the person is asked to rest and do nothing? Does the brain remain motionless? Certainly not. Scientists have noticed that it is always active: these areas of activity are called the default network. And this is where things get really interesting: this default network is exactly the same as another network identified by neuroscientists, one that supports social

----

10 Matthew Lieberman, *Social: Why Our Brains Are Wired to Connect*, Crown, 2013.
11 David Brooks, *The Social Animal: The Hidden Sources of Love, Character and Achievement*, Random House, 2011.

cognition, thinking about others and our relationships with others. It's almost as if, when we don't have any specific tasks to perform, we return to a default thought setting, which makes us think about other people. Professor Matthew Lieberman writes: "The default network directs us to think about people's minds – their thoughts, feelings and goals. It promotes understanding and empathy, cooperation and consideration."[12] We are therefore "built" to think about others and be connected to them.

So it's not surprising that behavioral science experiments have shown that what other people do and think, and how we interact with them, influences our own behavior and decisions. This flies in the face of the ideas in conventional decision-making theory that our decisions seek to maximize our own selfish interest independently of others. Other people are actually the key to our decisions.

Research into behavioral science has highlighted the mechanisms that influence our relationships with others and identified the most important:

- Fairness
- Reciprocity
- Social standards
- Social proof
- Peer pressure
- Figures of authority
- Love

Fairness

Fairness is essential. If we do not feel fairly treated by others, it has a strong impact on our attitudes and decisions, and can even go so far as to work against our own interests. On the other hand, we are also capable of highly altruistic behaviors that can drive us so far as to give our lives for another person.

Experiments carried out in game theory have shown that in the context of our relationships with others, including with people we

....
12 *Ibid.*

have never met and have little chance of seeing ever again, we make decisions taking this essential element of fairness into account. Let's now look at how fairness is demonstrated in experiments by one of the world's specialists on the matter, Professor Ernst Fehr from the University of Zurich.[13] His experiments are simple: they involve two participants, and one is given a sum of money. The first participant must share the money with the second participant however he or she wishes. In the "dictator's game", the one where the first player decides on how the money should be shared without the second one being able to refuse the offer, you would expect the "dictator" to keep it all and give the other person nothing. If they had 10 euros, it would be 10 for the first participant and nothing for the second. It's in the first participant's own material interest. And this is the behavior of a rational decision-maker, maximizing utility, in accordance with the conventional theory of *Homo economicus*. But in reality it doesn't apply. The "dictator" usually offers between 10 and 25% of the sum. While what is offered cannot be refused by the other participant, and there is no fear of reprisals against someone you don't know and will never meet again, people don't actually keep it all and give nothing to the other person. The "dictator" tries to make an offer that goes against his or her own financial interests, but one that he or she perceives as fair. "Other people" are important, even when we don't realize it, and this impacts our behaviors and decisions. Everything seems to suggest that acting fairly is a reward in itself that boosts our ego. We want to have a good self-image, and that involves the image we project to others when we behave in a certain way.

Another more balanced version of the game also shows the importance of perceived fairness, this time by the second participant who receives the offer. In this version, this second participant can refuse the offer: the transaction is then abandoned and none of the participants gets anything. Again, regardless of the amount offered – as long as it is greater than 0 – a rational individual should accept it,

---

13 Ernst Fehr and Klaus M. Schmidt, "The Economics of Fairness, Reciprocity and Altruism: Experimental Evidence and New Theories", in Serge-Christophe Kolm and Jean Mercier Ythier (dir.), *Handbook of the Economics of Giving: Altruism and Reciprocity*, vol. 1, Elsevier, 2006.

having gone into the game with nothing. If an offer is made that costs nothing, the logical decision is to accept. This is the logical decision, but it is not the decision made by most humans: if the offer is less than 20%, then most participants refuse. It is preferable not to receive 20% rather than accept an offer we perceive as unfair, and in doing so, cause the person making the unfair offer to lose out as well. Again, the value of the consideration and respect we believe we should be shown is greater than the amount of money on offer.

Reciprocity

The other aspect of fairness is reciprocity. We tend to treat other people in the same way as how we think they are treating us. "Kindness breeds kindness", yes, but the opposite is also true. In a search for balance, we adapt our behaviors to the behaviors of those around us. The perception of a negative behavior – or simply indifference – generally leads us to adopt the same type of negative behavior. Positive behavior will, on the contrary, generate positive behavior.

Reciprocity dictates that when we receive a gift, we feel that we have to do the same in equivalent circumstances: return an invitation to someone who has invited us for dinner, do a favor for someone who has done the same for us. According to the works of sociologist Alvin Gouldner, no human society is immune to these rules of reciprocity, which generate a sense of obligation. And for paleoanthropologist Richard Leakey, "We are human because our ancestors learned to pool skills and food as part of a network of mutual obligations."[14]

Numerous experiments highlight the tangible effect of reciprocity. One of them was led by Professor Dennis Regan of Cornell University. Participants were told that the study was about artistic judgment. The participants were invited to look at a collection of artworks accompanied by an individual, who happened to be an experimenter behaving in a specific way. In one scenario, the guide left the room a few moments to return with two bottles of Coca-Cola saying to the participant: "I asked if I could get a Coke, and I was told I could, so I

....
14   Richard Leakey and Roger Lewin, *Origins*, Penguin Random House, 1991.

took one for you." In the second scenario, the person returned empty-handed. The purpose of the two scenarios was to set up a potential opportunity for reciprocity in the first case, with a control situation in the second case. At the end of the visit, when all the artworks had been evaluated, the chaperone asked the participants if they would be willing to buy lottery tickets at 25 cents each, which would give them – depending on the number of tickets sold – a bonus of $50. In the scenario in which the coach had offered participants a Coca-Cola, the number of tickets purchased was double compared to the other scenario. Reciprocity therefore led the participant to modify his behavior to settle a "social debt". Extending his experiment, Dennis Regan was also able to demonstrate that, even among participants who found the coach unfriendly, the offer of a Coca-Cola generated the same disproportional lottery ticket purchases. We feel compelled to enter into this mechanism of reciprocity, regardless of the feelings we may have for those who will benefit from it.

Social relations are much more important to us than we might imagine. We are very strongly affected by the positive or negative behaviors of other people. This has also been demonstrated by Professor Matthew Lieberman. Prof. Lieberman has conducted some fascinating studies in this field, comparing brain activity in victims of physical or social pain. Intuitively, we're drawn to think that physical pain is more intense and specific than social pain. But from the brain's point of view it's actually the same. The brain processes "social" pain, for example being rejected by someone, in the same way as physical pain. The brain has no pecking order: the same neural mechanisms are activated.

This is because the need to connect with others is so strong and important to us that any negative event is very traumatic. We need others to survive and to feel good. This need for a connection to others manifests itself in our desire to belong to a community.

Sense of belonging and social standards

Our species needs to feel part of a group, whether it's a family, a group of friends, neighbors, coworkers or a wider community. It is both reassuring and rewarding to belong to a group of individuals whose company we enjoy and for whom we are equally important, because we share a certain number of values or common interests.

But belonging to a group often means that we need to follow a set of rules and values. Sometimes those values are explicit, like a company's guidelines or the laws of a country, but they can also very often be implicit. These are the rules that a group must follow for everyone involved to live peacefully together. If you wish to belong to a group, you will have to comply with the standards that the group upholds, or you will be rejected from it. These standards are all the elements that individuals in the same community uphold, whether that community is a formal construct (a business, a family, a sports team or an association, etc.) or perhaps less clearly defined. These social norms have a strong influence on how community members behave, but also affect those who would like to join that community. They encourage people to adopt certain specific behaviors, ranging from dress codes to language and the way people talk, to the emblematic figures and the way the community goes about its business generally.

Social proofs

But beyond the norms within a community, the behavior of others also has an impact on us through what one of the world's leading influence specialists – Professor Robert Cialdini of the University of Arizona – calls "social proofs". His idea is that "One of the ways to determine what is good is to find out what other people think is right."[15]

Just like me, you have probably surprised yourself while wandering around a new city and having to decide between two restaurants, you went for the busiest. Because a mental shortcut implemented by your System 1 told you that the high number of customers is one proof of a superior quality restaurant. Or, to choose a hotel for your forthcoming trip, you've taken TripAdvisor reviews into account. Here again, we judge that other people's perception is undoubtedly a good

....
15   Robert Cialdini, *Influence and Persuasion*, Harvard Business Review Press, 2017.

way to anticipate our own perception. And that's the effect of social proofs. This mechanism is even more effective when two significant conditions are satisfied:

- On the one hand, when we don't have a confident opinion about a choice we need to make, we tend to think that if a large number of people behave in a certain way, it is probably the best thing to do;
- On the other hand, we feel a sense of similarity towards those whose behavior we observe. The more similar to ourselves we think the people are, the more willing we are to behave the same way.

In fact, when we don't have a specific preference for a choice we need to make, and when other individuals who appear to be similar to us have behaved in a certain way, that behavior naturally seems like the best thing to do, and the one that will maximize our chances of making a good decision.

We will see later how this social proof mechanism can be a powerful influencing factor when attempting to change behaviors. But influences from other people are also more directly affected by our decisions when we are dealing with a group of people who express a unanimous opinion, or all behave the exact same way.

Peer pressure

Studies of how other people influence the decisions we make can be quite amusing. This certainly applies for the seminal experiment led by Solomon Asch that I advise you to watch on YouTube[16]. In it, a group of people is invited to comment on a simple question with an obvious answer. The experiment supposedly focuses on the perception of length, using different lines drawn on a sheet of paper. Participants are presented with an image showing one line on the left side and, on the right side, three lines of different sizes, numbered 1, 2 and 3. They have to look at the lines on the right and say which is the same size as the one on the left. The answer is obvious, because the lines are of very different sizes: it is therefore very easy to identify the correct answer.

....
16 youtube.com/watch?v=sno1TpCLj6A

However, with the exception of one person, the group of participants is made up of actors playing a role. Having repeatedly given the correct answer, the actors then unanimously give the wrong answer. How will this unanimous group behavior influence the decisions of the only "normal" person? Well, it's simple, rather than going against other members of the group by giving what he believes to be the right answer, the individual conforms and yields to the answer given by the others. The pressure from the group – through the unanimous formulation of an answer, even though it is perceived as incorrect by our participant – is enough to make him doubt himself, and give the same incorrect answer. We have a tendency to conform to the response or behavior of a group to which we belong. And that goes a long way to explaining our sometimes very irrational behavior. For example a "normal" person can behave extremely badly when he or she is in a group of excited fans during a soccer game: from singing very aggressive songs to insulting their team's opponent or the referee, and even getting into violent clashes with supporters of other teams. But without going to these extremes, our behavior is largely influenced by the behavior of others, to the point where we make decisions that go against our intentions.

Other people count, but not everyone has the same importance. Some words or behaviors are followed more easily than others, because of the specific perception we have of the individual in question.

The messenger

When someone you love, whom you particularly respect or consider to be an expert in a particular area or who has a specific function, says or does something, then that person's actions and words will have more of an impact on your own behavior than another person's actions or words. This is called the weight of the messenger: all messages are not received in the same way; it depends on who is sending them. The most famous messenger impact experiment on receiver's behavior is one that Professor Stanley Milgram[17] conducted in 1963: the participants

---

17   Stanley Milgram, "Behavioral Study of Obedience", *Journal of Abnormal and Social Psychology*, vol. 67, No. 4, 1963.

in this study working under the direction of a supposed researcher, behave in a gradually more inhumane way, sending electric shocks to students who give incorrect answers to a set of questions. Fortunately the electric shocks are not real, and the students are actors. But the participants responsible for sending these fake electric shocks don't know they aren't real. And, under the influence of the researcher, the figure of authority, they follow instructions even if it means torturing the person, and in spite of being able to hear the pleas of the "victims". Two-thirds of the participants even agree to apply the maximum current of 450 volts. An observer of this experiment explained: "I observed a mature and initially poised businessman enter the laboratory smiling and confident. Within 20 minutes he was reduced to a twitching, stuttering wreck, who was rapidly approaching a point of nervous collapse. He constantly pulled on his earlobe, and twisted his hands. At one point he pushed his fist into his forehead and muttered: 'Oh God, let's stop it.' And yet he continued to respond to every word of the experimenter, and obeyed to the end."[18] Submission to figures of authority can cause people to behave very differently from how they would like to behave themselves. And figures of authority are everywhere: from the family doctor to a police officer on foot patrol, from a civil servant giving instructions to an expert being interviewed on the television or, of course, as we will see later, a manager in the workplace.

But figures of authority aren't the only ones who influence our behavior: the feelings we have for the messenger can also have a significant impact. For example, if someone who is friendly gives you a piece of advice, we are more inclined to follow that advice than if the person is unfriendly.

The same message is perceived differently depending on who conveys it, which generates a behavioral response that is also different.

The power of other people

Our decisions and behaviors are therefore not the direct, mechanical translation of our own intentions, but stem from the attitudes and

---

18 *Ibid.*

behavior of other people. In fact, our decisions are the result of our interactions with our environment: other people and the situations we are in when we make those decisions.

The emotional human

The reason for emotions, or emotional reasoning

The wonderful research by Hanna and Antonio Damasio, reported in the international bestseller *Descartes' Error*[19], brings the key role of emotions in human decision processes up to date. The unfortunate Phineas Gage, a foreman at a railway company, suffered a terrible accident on September 13, 1848. While fitting an explosive inside a rock to clear a path so that a railway could be built, the explosive was detonated and sent the iron bar he was holding into his skull, and out the other side. Amazingly, he survived, but his left frontal lobe was irreversibly damaged. Studies by Antonio and Hanna Damasio fifty years later on the preserved skull of Phineas Gage showed that the parts destroyed by the accident mainly affected his emotions, especially social emotions. And the consequences of this damage on Gage's life were very severe. Although his cognitive and reasoning abilities were not damaged, he no longer experienced any emotion, which made his behavior anti-social. Despite many new career opportunities, his behavior and reactions toward other people left him a failure. His personal life was affected in the same way. He died twelve years after his accident, having seen his personality and behavior transformed by the loss of his emotional capacities. Damasio states that "emotions and feelings aren't a luxury, they're our way of communicating our mental states to other people. But they're also a guide for us to make decisions."[20]

In order to make decisions in a social context, we must be able to experience emotions. There can be no reason without emotion. One of the world's leading experts on emotions, and director of the Emotional Brain Institute at New York University, Professor Joseph

....
19 Antonio Damasio, *Descartes' Error: Emotion and the Human Brain*, Vintage, 2006.
20 *Ibid.*

LeDoux believes that: "Minds without emotions are not really minds at all."[21]

The laws of emotion under the microscope

Some experts, such as psychologist and international emotion specialist Nico Frijda, have tried to define a set of rules that govern our emotions. In his book, which is aptly named *The Laws of Emotion*[22], he suggests a series of laws.

First, emotion is the outcome of specific situations. It is caused by the occurrence of an event that has meaning for the individual who experiences it. Emotion is therefore not a characteristic of the event itself, but lies in the meaning that the individual gives to the event. So the same event, which may be usual for one individual and surprising for another, does not generate the same emotional intensity. We react strongly to change and what is new to us, and we don't react strongly to events we are used to experiencing. Not only must the trigger have meaning for the individual, but the event must be important enough to generate an emotion. What matters isn't the reality of the event and its characteristics, but how it is perceived and interpreted by the individual. It's how we react to what we deem to be real, even if it is not, like emotional scenes in a movie that pertain to a situation that could be possible, or could be perceived as being real. On the other hand, positive or negative situations generate different levels of emotion. For negative events, the reaction is usually much stronger than for positive events, to which we easily become accustomed. In addition, negative experiences tend to generate more lasting emotions over time than positive experiences. When we feel intense emotions, they can prevent us from considering alternative viewpoints and other people's opinions. We appear to be locked into the need to defend our point of view, or driven to do something specific. Lastly, we can only

....

21 Joseph LeDoux, *The Emotional Brain: The Mysterious Underpinnings of Emotional Life*, Simon and Schuster, 1998.
22 Nico H. Frijda, *The Laws of Emotion*, Lawrence Erlbaum, 2007.

modify the emotions we feel by changing how we interpret the events that have occurred.

Emotions are a rich source of opportunities for analysis and thought, and countless experts have debated them.

Conventional theory about emotions states that they are a result of our evolution as a species. Emotions have contributed to our survival by generating immediate responses to potential opportunities or threats we perceive in our environment. Emotions are useful, because they are warning signs that trigger very quick instant reactions – mental short circuits that make us respond to our perception of a situation. The fear that drives us to flee from a source of possible danger is an excellent counselor. If we see emotions as universal, each one – anger, joy, surprise, etc. – is linked to a circuit in our brain that generates specific changes and reactions. Human beings, whatever their age, race, culture, all feel the same kinds of emotions. They derive from our primitive brain, the same brain that causes physiological and behavioral reactions. This vision is widespread and dominant among philosophers such as Plato, Hippocrates and Aristotle, as well as Descartes, Freud, Darwin and contemporary researchers like Steven Pinker and Paul Ekman.

Other researchers including Lisa Feldman Barrett – professor of psychology and director of the Interdisciplinary Affective Science Laboratory at Northeastern University, have conducted many experiments proving that emotions are actually much less universal and more acquired and constructed than traditional theory would have us believe. This line of thinking suggests that emotions are crafted by each of us as a result of our culture and our specific individual history: "They emerge as a combination of the physical properties of your body, a flexible brain that wires itself to whatever environment it develops in, and your culture and upbringing, which provide that environment."[23]

----

23   Lisa Feldman Barrett, *How Emotions Are Made: The Secret Life of the Brain*, MacMillan, 2017.

Emotions: a huge impact on our behavior

Are emotions universal and deeply rooted in our brain as a result of evolution or are they of our own making, a result of our education and specific environment and an adaptable brain? These two theories cannot both be true, and the study of the foundations and mechanisms of emotions and how they are controlled is still the focus of lively debate among experts. But alongside these theories, there is a consensus among researchers: when we feel emotions, they have a huge impact on our behavior. Emotions are a response to our environment. Something happens to provoke an emotional reaction that will itself trigger physiological and psychological changes. Depending on the nature of the emotion and how intense it is, specific behavioral reactions will occur. The higher the emotional intensity, the greater the influence on the decisions made and the resulting behaviors. For neuroscientist Joseph LeDoux, "once emotions occur they become powerful motivators of future behaviors. They chart the course of moment-to-moment action as well as set the sails toward long-term achievements."[24] The same is true for one of the major experts in behavioral economics, Professor George Loewenstein of Carnegie-Mellon University, who, in a famous research article[25], uses the term "out of control" to characterize the consequences of experiencing very strong emotions. When they occur, we are highly prone to losing control in order to satisfy the need that underlies the perceived emotion.

There are indeed a great many studies that show how the emotions we feel or expect to feel impact our behavior. In a very provocative and fun experiment[26], Dan Ariely and George Loewestein (again) showed that a high state of sexual arousal among students participating in a study made them report much riskier or more deviant sexual practices than when the same students were in a neutral emotional state. The

---

24 Joseph LeDoux, *The Emotional Brain, op. cit.*
25 George Loewenstein, "Out of Control: Visceral Influences on Behavior", *Organizational Behavior and Human Decision Processes*, vol. 65, No.3, March 1996.
26 Dan Ariely and George Loewenstein, "The Heat of the Moment: The Effect of Sexual Arousal on Sexual Decision Making", *Journal of Behavioral Decision Making*, vol. 19, No.2, April 2006.

same individuals, faced with the same decisions, gave very different answers when their emotional state changed.

But the impact of much more subtle emotions can also be significant. For example, the mere perception of sadness changes our behavior. This was demonstrated by another research project[27], during which three groups of participants were invited to watch different types of films, one of which brought about sadness as it dealt with the death of a child. After this first stage of the experiment, the individuals had to suggest a price for a pen they had been given at the beginning of the session. The participants who had watched a neutral film gave a very different price to those in the "sadness" group. The temporary sadness experienced by the members of this group impacted a decision that had nothing to do with the sadness, and was totally unconscious.

The stress emotion, which is very common in the workplace, also has a huge influence on our behavior. Studies[28] show that in a situation of excessive stress, it's not only the quality of our decisions that is affected, but also our behavior. We become less social and demonstrate a higher level of irritability, while our capacity for imagination and creativity lessens.[29] We show a greater preference to familiar approaches as well as a reduced ability to follow our own path and resist unethical decisions[30].

Not only do emotions change our behavior, but the mere anticipation of emotions can also have the same effect. So if we anticipate that we might experience painful regret based on a decision, then we look for more information to limit the risk of being disappointed. But

27 Jennifer Lerner, Deborah Small and George Loewenstein, "Heart Strings and Purse Strings: Carroyer Effects of Emotions on Economic Decisions", *Psychological Science*, vol. 15, No.5, May 2004.

28 Mara Mather and Nichole R. Lighthall, "Both Risk and Reward are Processed Differently in Decisions Made Under Stress", *Current Directions in Psychological Science*, vol. 21, No.2, February 2012.

29 Lars Schwabe, Martin Tegenthoff, Oliver Höffken and Oliver T. Wolf, "Simultaneous Glucocorticoid and Noradrenergic Activity Disrupts the Neural Basis of Goal-Directed Action in the Human Brain", *Journal of Neuroscience*, vol. 32, No.30, July 2012.

30 Jooa Julie Lee, Francesca Gino, Ellie Shuo Jin *et al.*, "Hormones and Ethics: Understanding the Biological Basis of Unethical Conduct", *Journal of Experimental Psychology: General*, vol. 144, No.5, October 2015.

beyond the consequences that emotions provoke on an individual scale, a major characteristic of emotion is its impressive ability to spread.

Contagious emotions

Many studies have highlighted something very surprising: the way emotions can spread throughout a group of people, just like a virus.

In an experiment conducted by a team of Princeton researchers[31], during which participants listened to eloquent speeches by politicians while their brain activity was monitored using a CT scan, individual reactions were parallel and identical, as if they were synchronized. The emotional reactions, especially during certain parts of the speeches, were the same from one participant to another: the people appeared to be feeling emotions in unison.

Based on these initial results, another study conducted in Israel by the Weizmann Institute of Science sought to better understand the phenomenon by asking participants to watch the movie *The Good, the Bad and the Ugly* (proof that scientists are capable of choosing fun stimuli) while researchers recorded brain activity. Once again, participants' brains seemed to be synchronized, with some periods generating such similar readings that it was difficult to distinguish one individual from another. Researchers have tried to identify these results and then analyze their characteristics: clearly the times when all the brains were in unison were during emotional scenes: a twist in the plot, an explosion or shots. In these cases, participants' brains reacted in a similar way. The reaction is the result of a particular area, the amygdala, being activated. It sends a kind of warning signal to the brain so that it can react immediately to a potential danger.

Tali Sharot, professor of Cognitive Neuroscience and Director of the Affective Brain Lab at University College London, describes the results of this experiment in her fascinating book *The Influential*

---

31   Ralf Schmälzle, Frank E. Häcker, Christopher J. Honey *et al.*, "Engage Listeners: Shared Neural Processing of Powerful Political Speeches", *Social Cognition and Affective Neuroscience*, vol. 10, No.8, August 2015.

Mind: "Emotion promotes brain synchronization by automatically allocating everyone's attention in the same direction and by generating a similar psychological state, which prompts people to act and view the world in a similar way."[32]

But there is something even more surprising in this idea of contagion, which is revealed in other studies cited by Tali Sharot. Another experiment[33], again conducted by a team of Princeton researchers, shows that after a while, the synchronization occurs not only in the brain of the person sending out the emotional message and the brains of those who receive it, but also when people expect to feel that emotion, a sort of predictable empathy. For Tali Sharot and emotion experts, this phenomenon is due to an "evolutionary" advantage. Connections and emotional diffusion improve people's understanding of a message and the impact it can have on them. Emotional contagion is not only to do with words. Evidence of that can be seen in a study on mothers and their babies. The experiment involved analyzing the mothers' strengths and weaknesses when faced either with an audience of angry judges or an empty room. The goal was to create stress in the first group of mothers to evaluate the possible reactions of the babies when they came back together again. Were the babies affected by their mothers' stress when they had not faced the scene in question? The answer is yes: the physiological state of the babies matched that of the mothers. Heart rates accelerated when the stressed mothers returned, whereas they didn't speed up with the other moms.

And that's not all. Not only did the babies' physiology change, but their behavior also changed: the babies with the stressed moms avoided the researchers' gaze, while the babies of the other moms were more inclined to play with them.

....

32 Tali Sharot, *The Influential Mind: What the Brain Reveals About Our Power to Change Others*, Little Brown, 2017.

33 Greg J. Stephens, Lauren J. Silbert and Uri Hasson, "Speaker-Listener Neural Coupling Underlies Successful Communication", *Proceedings of the National Academy of Sciences*, vol. 107, No.32, August 2010.

Of course this doesn't only apply to children. Another – ethically controversial – study carried out by Facebook[34], showed the impact of positive or negative posts received on news feeds on the subsequent behavior of Facebook members. Those who received more negative posts started to post more specific negative messages on their wall, while those who received positive posts did the opposite. And this behavioral contagion doesn't only affect how we communicate. Another study[35] quoted by Tali Sharot demonstrates that students who were initially contaminated by a bad mood expressed by a fake participant in their group, were then less successful than a control group in the tasks they had to perform. Not only was one person's emotion transmitted to the other people in that group, but once the bad mood dominated the group, the work and potential for success of that group were also affected.

In the end, all the studies conducted show that humans are fundamentally emotional creatures: emotions dictate our decisions and influence our System 1; they are highly contagious and cause behavioral changes. And we'll see later how all of this has a huge impact on the workplace.

Real humans are far from being as rational as popular conventional theory would have us believe, we are in fact highly social and emotional beings. We are also influenced by cognitive biases, which have a huge effect on how we decide, and we'll now see just how powerful they can be during our experiences at work.

34 Adam D. I. Kramer, Jamie E. Guillory and Jeffrey T. Hancock, "Experimental Evidence of Massive-Scale Emotional Contagion through Social Networks", *Proceedings of the National Academy of Sciences*, vol. 111, No.24, June 2014.
35 Sigal G. Barsade, "The Ripple Effect: Emotional Contagion and Its Influence on Group Behavior", *Administrative Science Quarterly*, vol. 47, No.4, December 2002.

Chapter 2

The four challenges of behavioral science in the workplace: cognitive biases in action

One of the most important discoveries in behavioral science was underlined by Dan Ariely (see previous chapter): the existence of systematic *cognitive biases* that influence our behavior and decisions.

So what does this term really mean? Human thought mechanisms produce errors in logic or in how they perceive the reality of a situation and lead us to make systematic errors or behave in a way that prevents us from achieving our objectives.

We'll see how cognitive biases have been identified during many different scientific experiments carried out by the world's best behavioral science researchers. Of course, science is constantly changing and what is true today will soon evolve as new research and discoveries emerge. Nonetheless, I'd like to show you the most recent and most reliable findings about what influences our decisions and drives our behavior on a daily basis. Most importantly, we'll see how cognitive biases, which creep up on us all the time, can be a major challenge in business. We'll approach the issue by looking at four main themes:

- The decision challenge
- The winning behavior challenge
- The personal effectiveness challenge
- The engagement challenge

The decision challenge

Decisions within companies – whether they are strategic or operational, made by directors or employees depending on their skills – are supposed to be based on a rigorous analysis of any given situation. These decisions are made by people who have been trained, are experts in their field and can draw from a wealth of information. In order to achieve the business objectives, these decisions must enable effective strategies and action plans to be put into place. The quality of decision-making is therefore a fundamental factor in a company's performance.

But we'll soon see that this is much more of a challenge than you might think. As well as the mistakes that can hinder System 1, all the decisions we make can be affected by cognitive biases to which nobody is immune, from the CEO of the company through to all of the firm's employees.

It's not only difficult to make decisions every day within a company because of the uncertain environment, developments in technology, constraints of all kinds or suspected reactions from current and future competitors, it's also difficult because of the way we make decisions internally. Even with the right information, the most talented teams and individuals end up playing tricks on themselves.

Let's start by looking at the main cognitive biases and identifying how each one's influence can lead to bad decisions or inappropriate behavior within a company.

There are more than a hundred cognitive biases. Some are minor and only occur in very specific contexts; others are still under review and experts don't agree on them; while some biases simply don't apply to the specific workplace context. I have selected the five biases that I see as major challenges to good decision-making in companies.

The overconfidence bias or: it's easier to be the best

"If you had a magic wand, what bias would you eliminate?" When this amusing question was put to Daniel Kahneman by a journalist from *The Guardian*[1] during an interview about cognitive biases, the answer given by the Nobel Prize winner in Economic Sciences was: "Overconfidence"!

---

1 David Shariatmadari, "Daniel Kahneman: "What Would I Eliminate If I Had A Magic Wand? Overconfidence", *The Guardian*, 18 July 2005, theguardian.com.

But what's really so dangerous about overconfidence?

Simple: we overestimate our performance, our knowledge, and our abilities compared to those of others, as well as the relevance and accuracy of our judgments. And this fact has been proven by a whole host of scientific experiments. Generally speaking, all of us think we're better than we really are!

In a famous study[2] on young car drivers in the United States in 1981, during which they were asked if they rated themselves better than average drivers, 93% said yes! This mathematical impossibility is proof of the overconfidence bias.

On a lighter note, 84% of French respondents said they were better lovers than average. I can't prove them wrong, but again, it's a mathematical impossibility!

The broad-reaching overconfidence bias not only impacts how we judge our skills, it can also be perceived in other areas:

- We tend to be overly optimistic about how successful we think we'll be.
- We overestimate our ability to control the situations in which we find ourselves.
- We overestimate the accuracy of our judgments.
- We overestimate our ability to complete actions or projects within a specific timeline.

In a way, this bias is very useful because it can spark action. For example, it can motivate aspiring entrepreneurs to start developing their idea rather than just talking about it. Overestimating your abilities and chances of success helps you accept risks that you wouldn't take if you had analyzed the situation more objectively and more rigorously. The overconfidence bias can be a good thing, because it encourages potential entrepreneurs to try out new ideas. But it's also why – as well as the inherent difficulty in starting a business – 50% of new companies[3] fail after five years.

....

2   Ola Svenson, "Are We All Less Risky and More Skillful than our Fellow Drivers?" *Acta Psychologica*, vol. 47, No.2, February 1981.

3   France Entrepreneurs.

More broadly speaking, the overconfidence bias is extremely dangerous in decision-making within companies and it brings several types of risks, whether in strategic decisions by directors or members of the management team, or day-to-day decisions.

It can all start with directors feeling overly confident about the stability of their company. This optimism may lead to their being less vigilant about their technological and competitive environment, and solutions to adapt to it being implemented too late.

The overconfidence bias creates a feeling that a situation is under control, whatever it may be. We think we are in the driver's seat, but a rational analysis of the context would suggest otherwise. The vision we have of our own influence is skewed.

But the overconfidence bias is not just about influence. It seeps into all our decisions and actions, every day of our lives. It can incite excessive optimism in the managers of an important internal trans-formation plan, when in actual fact McKinsey has proven that 70% fail. What's important about the overconfidence bias is that it's not enough to have run tests and acquired the right information. Overconfidence still wields its power. It plays out unconsciously and independently of these elements, and affects the quality of our decisions.

One of its most consistent negative influences is related to what is known as the "planning fallacy"; setting out an overly optimistic timeline as a project is planned. We very often, and very wrongly, think that our initial deadlines are achievable. Why? Not because of events beyond our control that disrupted and slowed the project's progress, but because we optimistically think those events won't happen. In fact our initial planning is designed without taking the reality of a situation into account. This is of course also true when assigning budgets. Optimism leads to underestimation, so costs end up being higher than expected.

This bias is universal, but it particularly affects people who consider themselves experts in a field. They don't just think they are better than the average people in their area of expertise (which could be a fair analysis) but much more surprisingly, they think they are better than *other experts* in their field. For example, in a survey of 300 professional investors[4], 74% rated themselves as better than average compared to other investors. The more we consider ourselves experts, the more often we fall victim to this overconfidence bias by thinking we are better than others. Expertise does not bring humility, but dangerous arrogance.

In today's business world, and in an environment that has become highly complex over the last few decades, everyone is now an expert in his or her field. As developments accelerate, especially in technology, there are now managers for digital marketing, social networks, data sciences or key account merchandising. We are all expected to be experts in a specific area of competence. So we can all potentially be influenced by this overconfidence bias. And remember, this bias is unconscious, which means that you are very likely to think you won't be affected by it. Other people are affected, but certainly not you! In general, the more convinced you are that you're not a victim of that bias, the more you should wonder how it might be influencing your decisions. Look back at some of the recent mistakes you have made, and evaluate how the bias might have had an impact. And that's where wisdom begins to take root.

Kahneman believes that overconfidence is the most dangerous bias we face, because it reduces our vigilance in the face of danger, while giving us the illusion that we can cope with it easily. And Kahneman gives one last piece of advice to professionals and experts: "Overconfident professionals sincerely believe they have expertise, act as experts and look like experts. You will have to struggle to remind yourself that they may be in the grip of an illusion."[5]

The confirmation bias or: the objectivity illusion

The confirmation bias is another of the most dangerous threats to making good quality professional decisions.

....
4   James Montier, *Global Equity Strategy: Behaving Badly*, Dresdner Kleinwort Wasserstein, 2 February 2006.
5   Daniel Kahneman, "Don't Blink! The Hazards of Confidence", *The New York Times*, 19 October 2011, nytimes.com/2011/10/23/magazine/dont-blink-the-hazards-of-confidence.html.

It is defined as an unconscious tendency to select, interpret and memorize information in a way that confirms our initial opinion on a subject.

When trying to make a good decision, it is important to try to collect information about the advantages and disadvantages of each option as objectively as possible. Only by collecting the most exhaustive data and rigorously analyzing them can we identify the best course of action.

The challenge of the confirmation bias is that despite such an objective process, the way we select, process and store information is far from neutral. And we're not even aware of it!

It all starts with how we look for information. When we really want to be rigorous and make the very best decision, we need to collect information from a variety of sources and retain no pre-conceived ideas. But right from the start, a study conducted by Amazon in 2012[6] during the United States presidential elections proves that this isn't the case. The study's researcher analyzed the link between the type of books purchased by those wishing to learn more about Obama and the political preference of the purchasers, and came to a very simple conclusion. Individuals who started out being in favor of the President bought books that showed him in a positive light. On the other hand, people who were against Obama chose more critical books. While the readers' initial objective was to learn more about the presidential candidate, they spontaneously selected the books that matched their original opinion.

In our search for information, we unconsciously value the information that is aligned with our beliefs, and this has a very clear outcome: we are certain that the facts – stemming from this "objective" and "rigorous" research – confirm our initial point of view. We think we have been meticulous, but the confirmation bias has tricked us by reinforcing our initial predisposition. We are even more convinced by the opinion we started with, because we're sure that we have analyzed all the facts and that those facts have demonstrated that our original intuition was accurate.

....
6   thenetworkthinkers.com/2012/10/2012-political-book-network.html

But the influence of this bias does not stop with how we collect information, it continues with how we interpret it. Again, we don't analyze data objectively, but in a way that is strongly guided by our initial opinions, as demonstrated during a particularly striking study by researchers at Stanford University[7] in the USA. It involves the death penalty and how it affects criminal behavior within the population. Two groups of participants – one in favor of the death penalty and the other against it – were invited to read identical texts relating to the consequences of an abolitionist or conservative policy in certain American states. After reading these texts, each group of people maintained their initial opinion: the ones who were favorable emphasized the futility of the arguments presented in the text to prove their point, while the individuals against the death penalty did the exact opposite. Reading the same text, containing identical information and arguments, led the members of each group to opposite conclusions. We therefore interpret the same facts differently, depending on our initial beliefs. Here again, this interpretation bias is dangerous because individuals are even more convinced that they are right, and think they have analyzed the facts that are objectively presented to them. I don't believe what I believe because of an initial predisposition, but because the facts have proven that I am right. This is where the confirmation bias can lead.

It also plays out on a third level, when we are memorizing information we have analyzed. Yet again, the process is not neutral and our memory is selective: we remember the information that reinforces our initial opinion and information that goes against it in different ways. And, of course, we memorize information that confirms our initial opinion more effectively, and therefore when we think about the same subject again later, that's the information we find easiest to remember. This bias of selective memorization in favor of information and arguments that fit our initial position also reinforces them.

....

7   Charles G. Lord, Lee Ross and Mark R. Lepper, "Biased Assimilation and Attitude Polarization: The Effects of Prior Theories on Subsequently Considered Evidence", *Journal of Personality and Social Psychology*, vol. 37, No.11, 1979.

The confirmation bias is therefore a huge threat to any sort of effective professional decision-making. Whether in terms of strategic decisions made by directors or more everyday choices, it is a potential source of error because it creates a tremendous barrier to accepting solutions from other people. Once again, it leads us to think that we are right not by mere conviction, but as a result of a painstaking and objective analysis of the situation.

Think about the danger of combining the two first biases: over-confidence leads to overestimating our situation and abilities, while the confirmation bias unconsciously selects facts and arguments that reinforce our initial convictions. It's a deadly trap.

The mental availability bias or: how the last one who speaks is right

The bias of mental availability shows how elements we remember most easily have a strong impact on how we make our decisions. If I'm thinking about whether to eat a wonderful Italian ice cream, and the event I can recall most easily is a delicious taste experience rather than my doctor telling me to keep an eye on my waistline and giving me healthy-eating advice, the chances are that I'll give in to temptation and let myself have a well-deserved treat. The elements we recall most easily – regardless of their relative importance to any part of the decision – are those that will carry the most weight.

An amusing study[8] highlighted the power of this once again unconscious mechanism. The question put to participants was simple: are there more words in the English language that start with an R or whose third letter is an R? The majority of participants chose the first answer. But is it correct? No. So why did people get it wrong? Because it is easier to remember English words that begin with an R than it is to find words that have the letter R in third position!

Our System 1 has built this shortcut of mental availability to cope with our inability to process a lot of information all at the same time.

....

8   psychologytoday.com/us/blog/creatures-habit/200909/mental-habits-taking-the-shortcut-part-3

When we make a decision, we can't possibly consider every possible outcome. We can't think of all the advantages and disadvantages of each option. The elements that we have in our minds when we make a decision are therefore those that will play a fundamental role in what we eventually decide to do. And of course the danger lies in the fact that what we can easily recall in our minds when we make a decision may not be the most important element in that decision: it is simply the most accessible. It may be the final point that a colleague has just talked about, or the end of the conversation with the team.

Certain arguments stick more easily in the mind, so the quality of decision-making is put at risk. In fact, another bias may intervene and reinforce the effect of the first: it's easy to recall the information so we think the information must be correct. The effect is two-fold: the memorized element benefits from a quantitative advantage relative to other elements, but also a qualitative advantage because it is perceived as being better than the competing arguments. If a plane has just crashed somewhere in the world, this very rare event is likely to be covered by the media. So people think about the risk of air travel during the weeks after the accident. And this idea will lead to an overestimation of how likely another accident may be. The ability to easily recall the event results in a misjudgment that may lead us, for example, to choose to drive rather than fly. That's what happened in the months following the September 11 attacks in the United States. Many people preferred to travel by car rather than by plane and this actually resulted in a huge spike in the number of road accidents and deaths compared with statistics from the previous year.

And remember that the confirmation bias makes us memorize the arguments that support our initial position more effectively. We therefore believe that we are making a sensible decision based on a rigorous analysis of the advantages and disadvantages of each option, when what we are actually doing is having our initial opinion confirmed by the confirmation bias and our mental availability.

And the more mundane the decisions, the more we slide under the influence of these biases because we don't want to waste time, we want to work quickly and trigger our System 1 using mental shortcuts. But minor decisions are of no less importance, because those are often the ones that bring about genuine business performance.

Fighting the bias of mental availability is therefore essential if we are to avoid its negative influence.

The possession bias or: how ownership can be blinding

The possession bias is valuing something that you own, simply because you own it. Once again, Daniel Kahneman, along with Jack Knetsch and Richard Thaler, identified this bias through a very simple experiment[9] using an everyday object, a coffee mug. The same mug – depending on whether or not it belongs to the participants in the survey – is evaluated in a very different way. When owners of a mug are asked if they'd like to sell theirs, the price they set is an average of twice the price that potential buyers offer. It's the same object, but possession changes how we perceive it.

Many different experiments have since confirmed that possessing an object changes its owner's perception of its value. And even the idea of potentially possessing a coveted object also significantly modifies its value. A study led by Dan Ariely, James Heyman and Yesim Orhun[10] showed that auction participants who lead the bid for most of its duration tend to outbid aggressively when a higher bid is made. The mere idea of a future possession is enough to trigger this possession bias.

Owning an object creates an emotional attachment that reinforces its value, and when we imagine how it feels to own an object, we already start feeling that emotion.

Think how dangerous the influence of this bias might be in business acquisition processes. Discussions and audits usually take several months. As they negotiate, potential buyers who feel well positioned

9   Daniel Kahneman, Jack L. Knetsch and Richard H. Thaler, "Anomalies: The Endowment Effect, Loss Aversion, and Status Quo Bias", *The Journal of Economic Perspectives*, vol. 5, No.1, winter 1991.

10   James E. Heyman, Yesim Orhun and Dan Ariely, "Auction Fever: The Effect of Opponents and Quasi-Endowment on Product Valuations", *Journal of Interactive Marketing*, vol. 18, No.4, autumn 2004.

against their competitors may tend to overestimate the value of the target company. Ultimately, the risk of overbidding can lead to paying more than the company is worth and may be very damaging for the future growth of the business.

The possession bias is accentuated when we have worked hard to obtain the object. It's what Dan Ariely calls "the Ikea effect".[11] This is illustrated in a fun experiment that involves asking participants to create origami sculptures from sheets of paper. At the end of the process, the creators of these "works" evaluate them much more favorably than when they are judged by individuals who were not involved in making them. It is as if self-directed efforts add value – whether the value is aesthetic or financial – to the end product. So it would be particularly difficult for someone in charge of a specific project in a company to give up on it, even if there is mounting evidence that it probably won't be successful. The efforts made affect the impartiality of the judgment.

The possession bias is not restricted to objects. It also happens with regards to something very familiar and intangible: our ideas. We tend to overvalue the usefulness of our ideas. By the simple fact that they come from inside our own heads, we think that they are better than ideas presented by other people. We do not see our ideas objectively, but perceive them with a positive filter that enhances their value. In discussions within project groups, this distorted perception can be very dangerous, because each person in the group tends to defend their own ideas, not because of their actual benefit, but simply because that person "owns" the ideas. This risk is even greater when it comes to business leaders, or team or project managers: as victims of the possession bias's negative influence, they may try to impose their own idea on the other members of the group, and those members will be reluctant to go against an idea put forward by their superior.

....
11　Michael I. Norton, Daniel Mochon and Dan Ariely, "The 'Ikea Effect': When Labor Leads to Love", *Journal of Consumer Psychology*, vol. 22, No.3, July 2012.

The present bias or: why it's hard to take long-term benefits into account

Having the ability to consider a company's long-term prospects, and making the right investment decisions for future success are vital for business leaders. Not only thinking about the present, but being able to take a step back and think about tomorrow is the key to lasting success. But as we'll see with the present bias, humans find this highly unnatural.

One of the greatest researchers in behavioral economics, Professor George Loewenstein of Carnegie-Mellon University, conducted a wonderful experiment that shows in a very simple way how this fundamental bias affects the human mind. The experiment is about choosing a movie from a selection of 40 options that include "easy" and "demanding" films. The researchers based the selection on a rather unusual criterion: the perceived ease or difficulty experienced by the viewer, when watching the movie. For example, the "easy" movies (which Loewenstein calls "vice") include *The Specialist*, with Sharon Stone and Sylvester Stallone in the leading roles. The "demanding" films (those that Loewenstein calls "virtue") include *Schindler's List*. Of course, study participants don't know if a movie is considered to be a vice or a virtue. They simply have to choose what they would like to watch for the next three days, but a different set of instructions is given to each group of participants:

- Members of the first group had to choose a movie for the next three days on the very first day.
- Participants in the second group had to choose a movie the day before they watched it. So on the first day they chose a movie for the second day, etc.

You might think that these rules wouldn't change a rational individual's film choice, because the list of movies is identical and the instructions are pretty similar, but as you have probably understood by now, the choices were very different. Let's take a look at how different they were, and why.

- For participants from both groups, the choice for the first day was the same: a "vice" film.

- But for the following days, the choices differed: for the first group, the films chosen for days 2 and 3 were "virtuous" films; whereas the second group chose "vice" films.

In fact, when we make a decision for that same day, "vice" wins. But when we decide for later, we are prepared to make an effort to watch a more "virtuous" film. This attitude doesn't just apply to movie choices. Countless experiments by researchers in behavioral economics have demonstrated its persistence, and it has been called the "present bias". When, like me, you can't resist a delicious ice cream or a burger, even though you know that it's probably not the ideal choice for your health, you are being influenced by the present bias. When you make good resolutions at the beginning of the year and you have a hard time adopting them, you are also under the influence of this very devious and powerful bias. It wields its power so that effort is delayed until later, and today's rewards are perceived as very attractive. I decide to watch a "vice" film for tonight (the reward) and leave the "virtuous" movies (the effort) for tomorrow and the day after tomorrow. But when the day comes, the reward is attractive again – the "vice" film – and we put off the effort we need to make to watch the "virtuous" film until tomorrow.

Evolutionary psychology again provides an explanation for this type of behavior. While it may seem irrational in today's world, it would have been much less surprising to our ancestors who had to fight for survival day after day in an extremely hostile world. Being focused on an immediate benefit, and not on its potentially dangerous long-term effects, made more sense, because the long term was a very theoretical concept. So our brains encourage us to go for short-term profit rather than a more beneficial long-term reward.

Be that as it may, in today's world it's a very dangerous bias and it affects both our personal and collective decisions. Personal: remember the example of the irrational behavior of the smoking doctors I used in the introduction, or the bad eating habits many of us have? Collective: think about our behavior towards the planet; are we not victims of the present bias by being too focused on our short-term interest and by putting off the efforts we need to make to protect our environment?

The present bias is also a deadly trap in the business world: decisions are made by overestimating the company's short-term interest rather than its long-term prospects. Major investments – even though amortization spreads the cost over several years – can be deferred to show a higher year-end result. A company can even turn its back on a breakthrough technological innovation out of fear for the disruption it may bring in the short term and the immediate effort that will have to be made in learning how it works. Internal transformation plans may also be put off when short-term hardships are considered, and long-term benefits may be deemed more hypothetical. In his famous book *Leading Change*[12], John Kotter emphasizes the risk of failure in bringing about internal transformations due to a lack of focus on long-term benefits, compared to the high visibility of the short-term effort that everyone will have to make. We will take a look at this very important topic later in an attempt to understand how to bring it under control using behavioral science.

But serious strategic issues are not the only ones that can affect decision-making. Everyday decisions are not immune to the harmful influence of the present bias. If you are a manager, think about the time you don't spend with your staff, just chatting with them for a few minutes every day, because you are dealing with an onslaught of daily emergencies. It is true that we need to make an effort to invest in this time, and your short-term effectiveness may be reduced, but as we'll see below, it can have a huge impact on your ability to create a dedicated team. In our day-to-day work as salaried employees, don't we often put off tasks that we know are important and whose potentially positive effects will only be felt far off in the future?

Thinking about the short term is often a lot easier. We deal with emergencies rather than what's fundamentally essential. Until one day we realize that we haven't thought about the long term, and considerable damage has been done.

The challenge of decision-making in companies – and it is a big challenge in itself – is not only about making choices in an uncertain situation, but also about how we work internally. The negative

....
12 John Kotter, *Leading Change*, Harvard Business Review Press, 1996.

influence of cognitive biases makes analyzing the costs and benefits of each option very tricky, because we need not only to consider a complex environment, but also be aware of how we collect and interpret the available information. It's a bit like using a decision-making computer – our brain. It is certainly very powerful, but plagued with viruses and biases that can distort the analyses we perform.

The good news is that with the help of behavioral science we know about these viruses, and as we will see later, this knowledge is the first essential step to protecting ourselves against their potentially negative effects.

But our biases do not only influence our decisions. They can also steer us away from behaviors that benefit the company.

The winning behavior challenge

Companies have never had to face as many challenges as they do today. Competition is now completely global, and your most threatening competitor may be right next door or on the other side of the world. Your business model, which has allowed your company to develop and perform brilliantly for years, might become obsolete in just a few months with the unforeseeable creation of the next Uber, Airbnb or Amazon. Customers are better informed and fickle, and they are armed with increasingly powerful sources of information and ways to communicate. Social networks act as powerful echo chambers and can create an overnight success or break a company with negative buzz in a matter of days.

In this new world, each company must face the specific challenges inherent to its own history and environment: its sector, positioning and internal organization, its customers, current competitors, and so on. But in addition to these particular elements, with which all companies seek to cope by defining a relevant strategy and carrying it out effectively, the key success factors are strikingly similar.

Whatever its market, an ability to innovate, reinvent its offers and products, and tailor them to new possibilities in a constantly evolving technological world, being able to constantly transform a company with new features and new knowledge, developing intelligence and learning to anticipate future advances have all now become absolutely essential for any business that wants to avoid rapid obsolescence. And take the opportunities for growth that this changing world presents. And of course being able to innovate, transform, and learn isn't something you can pick up from a rulebook! A company is not an abstract entity, but a collection of individuals who contribute to its success or failure when dealing with these huge challenges. Those individuals facilitate or hinder the developments the business wants to achieve by behaving in certain ways.

Here again, behavioral science teaches us that nothing goes without saying: some of these desired behaviors are unnatural and present a challenge in themselves. We'll now find out about the winning behavior challenge, through the most firmly established biases in human nature:

- Aversion to loss and risk;
- The status quo bias.

Aversion to loss (and risk) or: how to protect yourself against the unknown

As its name suggests, an aversion to loss or risk means having a tendency to reject a choice that includes the risk of a loss, rather than trying our luck for an equivalent gain. We are structurally very resistant to risk-taking and hate to suffer a loss even more strongly than we love to experience a gain. And this has a huge impact on how we behave each day.

Kahneman and Tversky first demonstrated the phenomenon in the 1980s[13], through very simple experiments. One of them involved offering participants the chance to play a heads or tails game to win or lose an identical amount. On average, individuals refused to participate if the amount they could win or lose was the same when the probability was the same (50%). This bias exists because the negative

....
13 Daniel Kahneman and Amos Tversky, "Choices, Values, and Frames", *American Psychologist*, vol. 39, No.4, January 1984.

feelings we have when we lose are stronger than the positives feelings we experience when we win. The mere opportunity to win a sum of money is not enough to make us accept a 50/50 chance that we will lose the same amount. From a mathematical point of view, it's not rational – we should see the same ratio in people's decisions to play or not to play – but from a human point of view, it is perfectly logical.

We are affected more deeply by a loss than we are satisfied by an equivalent gain. As a result, we tend to refuse a risk when there isn't a significantly greater probability of success than the probability of loss. In quantitative terms, Kahneman and Tversky estimated this ratio at 2.5. In order to accept a loss of 100, there must be a potential gain of 250.

This aversion to risk and loss can be interpreted in light of teachings from evolutionary psychology. When our ancestors were living in the savannah, losing something when they had almost nothing could mean a high risk of dying, while having more merely increased their existing chances of survival. Loss aversion is therefore a primary survival mechanism, and it still affects us today.

This structural risk aversion in humans is a major obstacle to one of the most important winning behaviors that companies look for: the ability to innovate. This means that generally speaking, individuals at work are not spurred on by a desire to innovate, and that's down to the risk-taking we associate with anything new. To encourage innovation, we'd need to design a system that counteracts one of the most powerful default human behaviors.

This risk aversion doesn't just apply to the actions we take or don't take. It also applies to how we treat ourselves. We don't like to risk seeing our image take a knock in other people's eyes.

In the professional world, our image is important and plays a key role in the advancement of our careers. We therefore seek to preserve it by avoiding the many different and risky behaviors in everyday professional life. For example, asking colleagues at a meeting for a better explanation so that we can understand a point we haven't quite grasped means taking the risk of being perceived as stupid or ignorant. By criticizing a project or idea put forward by a coworker – or worse, a supervisor – we run the risk of appearing negative, even though the objective may simply be to improve the project or idea by asking legitimate questions. Admitting errors in front of your peers to move the company forward by trying to set up processes to avoid the occurrence of the same error means taking on the risk of appearing incompetent. Accepting responsibility for managing an innovative project means running the risk of failure, with possible negative consequences on your career prospects, the list goes on.

Risk aversion therefore often encourages us to behave in a way that goes against desired behavior, and this has serious potential consequences: the sum of individual behaviors that are hostile to risk creates a company that ambles along, but is not able to evolve in a world that requires evolution, and runs the risk of disappearing. And risk aversion is aggravated by another very powerful bias: a preference for the status quo.

The status quo bias or: the draw of familiarity

The status quo bias is our preference for existing situations, regardless of the objective benefits of these situations in comparison to possible alternatives. When faced with a decision where one of the options is to stick with the current situation instead of exploring various other possibilities that might involve a change, the status quo is more attractive, regardless of the specific advantages and disadvantages of the other choices. We tend to opt for the absence of change, not because the current situation is better, but because it is the current situation.

Many different experiments in very different fields have highlighted both the existence and the power of this phenomenon. In a study by Raymond Hartman and Chi-Keung Woo on consumers of an electricity provider[14], participants were interviewed to determine which offer they preferred from a choice of six different levels of price and service reliability. Two consumer groups were created, each with different plans, one of which was representative of their current provider. In

---

14   Raymond S. Hartman, Michael J. Doane and Chi-Keung Woo, "Consumer Rationality and the Status Quo", *The Quarterly Journal of Economics*, vol. 106, No.1, February 1991.

each group, most participants chose that option. Presenting an option as the current solution was enough to change their preference. So the specific characteristics of each price-service reliability combination aren't what wield the most power, but which one is the current plan.

Dan Ariely summarizes the key outcome of the status quo bias: "People generally avoid changes, even if they are minor and even when another path is clearly better."

There are a number of factors that bring about this bias, and boost its influence. Firstly risk aversion, because the current situation is seen as a starting point to which you may not be able to return if you make a different choice. Options that bring about change are inherently risky because they are unknown. In contrast, the current situation has the advantage of being familiar, and is therefore reassuring.

We prefer the status quo because it has an emotional advantage and is linked to a feeling of coherence with our previous decisions, a feeling we don't get when we make a different choice. The current situation recalls a choice we made at some time in the past: changing that might be seen as going back on a good decision we have already made. Unless there is a major turnaround in a situation, not changing can psychologically reassure decision-makers that their choices have been the right ones.

Change also has a cognitive cost. It involves looking at new options, understanding the advantages and disadvantages of each, and ultimately making an effort, in contrast to the ease of just keeping things as they are. And because we've been living with it until now, it seems to be a fairly acceptable state of affairs. The effort required to make a change has an immediate psychological cost, for a potentially far more remote benefit. And you already know that because of the present bias, we don't like making an effort in the present to acquire benefits in the future.

Finally, the status quo bias has a major advantage to do with the attraction we feel for the familiar: and that's what researchers call the mere exposure effect. Many experiments have shown that familiarity breeds not contempt, but preference. The more we are exposed to certain things – objects, people, places – the more we develop a preference for them. One of the first researchers to have demonstrated this effect is the psychologist Robert Zajonc, and he did this using some very striking experiments. He exposes participants to various stimuli, for example meaningless words such as "iktitaf" that he presents as being of Turkish origin, or Chinese symbols, and asks them for their preferences with regard to these different elements. Note that the individuals were exposed differently to the stimuli: some people were subjected to certain stimuli much more frequently than others. The consequences of this more frequent exposure were very clear: the number of times participants are exposed to a stimulus reinforces their preference for it. Participants always prefer the unfamiliar words they have seen more often, or the Chinese ideograms they saw more frequently. And, of course, like all cognitive biases, this influence is unconscious. When asked why they prefer this or that ideogram, they justify their choice using various theories but aren't able to say that it's because they have seen them more frequently. So we tend to like the status quo because it has the emotional advantage of familiarity.

Here again, evolutionary psychology provides an explanation for our preference for the status quo. Changing a situation by choosing a new option means venturing into the unknown and possibly running a risk, whereas the current situation appears, by nature, to be less dangerous because it is familiar.

The brain spontaneously leads us to see change as something potentially dangerous and, as a result, to avoid seeking it out. When it is imposed on us our first reaction is to resist or struggle more directly to maintain our current situation.

If changes are required in business it means bringing in behaviors that oppose the status quo. Whether these are individual changes affecting employees about how their tasks are defined, what their work environment is, which colleagues they interact with, the appointment of a new manager, or even collective changes related to an overall restructuring process, an employees' natural reaction is to oppose them. Change is unnatural, and many business transformation plans fail: the power of the status quo bias has been underestimated, and we tend to think that a rational explanation about the need for change, and the new structure, should be enough to convince employees that the intended transformation is positive. If it is to succeed, a transformation plan must start by tackling the very strong resistance that is expected when the change is brought to the table, and then a suitable strategy must be devised, as we will see below. Change is possible, but it is a large-scale challenge even, to paraphrase Ariely, when it is minor or clearly positive.

The combination of risk aversion and the status quo bias makes is hard to establish the behaviors required for the success of any business: innovation, transformation and evolution. Only by being acutely aware of this, then by designing tailored psychological environments and specific action plans can we successfully tackle the deadly challenge.

The personal effectiveness challenge

Making a good decision is difficult. Adopting and promoting good behavior is also a challenge, but we will now see that being effective at work – as an individual – isn't straightforward either. Again, behavioral science has identified structural limitations that reduce our productivity, regardless of our engagement or good intentions.

We are not computers: we simply can't process a massive amount of data simultaneously without it compromising our efficiency, and our cognitive abilities decline as we use up our resources, which also leads to a drop in job performance.

Limited and dwindling attention spans

The first fundamental point has to do with our limited ability. Despite the power of our brains, our ability to pay attention and process information is limited. As we started to see with the magic number 7 experiment, our cognitive resources are quickly exhausted. And if we seek to increase our productivity by working on several tasks at the same time, the opposite happens: we become less effective.

Many experiments have shown that simply performing two tasks at the same time is enough to greatly reduce our productivity. A team of researchers from Vanderbilt University[15] tested the differences in how long participants took according to whether they had to perform the same two tasks at the same time or perform one after the other. The results were very clear: 30% more time was needed to perform two tasks simultaneously rather than one after the other. But above all, the errors in how the tasks were performed were doubled for the "multitaskers" compared to those doing one at a time. Trying to be more effective isn't easy, because we quickly come head to head with our physiological limits.

And don't forget about the overconfidence bias: we tend to overestimate our abilities, so we think we can do more than we really can without it having a negative impact on the quality of our work.

Not only are our abilities limited, but our ability to pay attention is very fragile and if we start to lose focus when doing a task, it has a huge effect on how effective we are. As I'm writing this, my phone has just pinged: I've won a bid on eBay! That's great news for me, but bad news for my book-writing progress. A study by Microsoft's Eric Horvitz and Shamsi Iqbal from the University of Illinois[16] showed that when we're interrupted by a notification on a computer we're working on, it takes us fifteen minutes to get back to our previous level of concentration.

In another experiment, researchers at the University of Washington[17] demonstrated that not only do interruptions to a main task result in a loss of time spent regaining our initial focus and efficiency, but also that the interruption actually increases the likelihood of making

15 Paul E. Dux, Jason Ivanoff, Christopher L. Asplund *et al.*, "Isolation of a Central Bottleneck of Information Processing With Time-Resolved FMRI", *Neuron*, vol. 52, No.6, December 2006.

16 Eric Horvitz and Shamsi T. Iqbal, "Disruption and Recovery of Computing Tasks: Field Study, Analysis, and Directions", *Proceedings of the 2007 Conference on Human Factors in Computing Systems*, San José, California, 28 April-3 May 2007.

17 Erik M. Altmann, Gregory J. Trafton and David Z. Hambrick, "Momentary Interruptions Can Derail the Train of Thought", *Journal of Experimental Psychology: General*, vol. 143, No.1, February 2014.

subsequent errors. And it's no small difference: the number of errors are doubled and sometimes even tripled!

Unfortunately, given the above information, our working environments are causing us to become less, rather than more efficient. Our working day is packed full of tasks. Many employees often wear several different hats or are responsible for several different projects. So it's tempting to work on several different tasks. But we do run the risk of being less efficient.

Interruptions are part of our daily experiences with all the tools we have, starting with the simplest: instant messages and smartphone apps with their irresistible visual notifications and beeps. In the study by Eric Horvitz and Shamsi Iqbal that I mentioned above, researchers found that participants were interrupted in their main task by an average of 4.28 e-mail alerts and 3.21 other alerts per hour. Of course this applies to just one study, but it no doubt rings true for many employees. Interruptions are commonplace, and as we've seen, efficiency is the price we pay. How can we find the strength to resist temptation and not read the text message that has just come in, or take a quick look at the Facebook comment that has just popped up in the corner of the screen? How can we put off replying to an e-mail marked "Urgent" or answering a call that might be important?

Willpower gradually wears away

Again, behavioral science has unfortunately shown that we have a hard time resisting temptation and that our willpower lessens as we use it throughout the day.

Roy Baumeister, Ellen Bratslavsky, Mark Muraven and Dianne Tice ran a study[18] that was both pioneering and amusing, and shows how our willpower weakens as it is used up. The people involved in the experiment were sent into a room with a buffet offering cookies

18 Roy F. Baumeister, Ellen Bratslavsky, Mark Muraven *et al.*, "Ego Depletion: Is the Active Self a Limited Resource?" *Journal of Personality and Social Psychology*, vol. 74, No.5, May 1998.

and bowls of radishes. Some participants were invited to try the cookies, while others had to eat the radishes and resist the temptation to taste the cookies, which looked very appetizing. After that, all the participants had to work on a complex geometric puzzle for thirty minutes, but could give up if they found it too difficult. Participants who had been lucky enough to eat the cookies – and who had not used up their willpower resisting temptation – gave up after an average of nineteen minutes. On the other hand, the unfortunate individuals who had only eaten the radishes, and had already drained their resources, stopped after eight minutes. The previous exercise when they'd had to resist the temptation of the cookies had used up some of their resources and meant that they were less able to make an effort in the following exercise. Willpower is like a muscle that tires if doesn't have time to recover.

As we've just seen, we're constantly coping with tiny jabs of temptation, which become more and more difficult to resist, and our efficiency takes a huge tumble when we give in to them.

Our dwindling willpower isn't just a result of resisting temptation from the many different forms of distraction around us. It also happens whenever we practice self-control to avoid a kneejerk reaction that we rationally deem inappropriate. Whenever System 2 intervenes to stop a spontaneous behavior generated by System 1, we draw on our limited self-control resources, which gradually ebb away.

For instance, the control we have over our social interactions. When you force yourself to smile at a coworker you do not like or when you show diplomacy during a challenging meeting to calmly listen to each other's arguments – and face hostility from some of your colleagues – you consume your self-control resources. Managing our limited willpower resources by using them on important issues rather than frittering them away on minor tasks is the key to enhancing personal effectiveness.

But as well as leaving us with very little willpower, general tiredness can creep up and impede our efficiency at work, and have an impact on the decisions we make. And that's known as decision fatigue.

Decision fatigue impairs efficiency at work

A study by researchers from Ben Gurion and Columbia Universities[19] has shed light on decision fatigue by studying the quality of judicial decisions depending on how tired judges are when making their rulings. The experiment involved more than a thousand court decisions, and researchers analyzed the decisions according to whether they were made at the beginning of a session when the judges were rested, or at the end of the sessions. The results are both staggering and worrying. When the judges were rested – in the early morning, after the mid-morning or early afternoon break – prisoners who applied for parole had a 65% chance of receiving it. When they were seen at the end of the session, the percentage was almost 0, with no difference in the types of cases! And for each session, there was a gradual decline in the number of prisoners being granted parole. When the judges were more tired, they had less energy to really look into each case, so were more likely to go with the easiest decision: the status quo, and leave the prisoners behind bars.

And the effects of decision fatigue don't just apply to a handful of business sectors or specific decisions. It's a widespread phenomenon.

In another study carried out in hospitals[20], researchers from Pennsylvania and North Carolina universities looked into the influence of decision fatigue on a very important public health issue: how often medical staff wash their hands before coming into contact with patients, to avoid the spread of hospital-acquired diseases. The study involved 35 hospitals, and more than 4,000 people in charge of providing care throughout a working day were observed. And again, the results are very clear. An 8-point drop in the compliance rate of hand washing was observed between the first hour of the working day and the last, which is a 20% reduction in compliance. As the day goes

---

19 Shai Danziger, Jonathan Levav and Liora Avnaim-Pesso, "Extraneous Factors in Judicial Decisions", *PNAS*, vol. 108, No.17, April 2011.

20 Hengchen Dai, Katherine L. Milkman, David A. Hofmann *et al.*, "The Impact of Time at Work and Time Off From Work on Rule Compliance: The Case of Hand Hygiene in Health Care", *Journal of Applied Psychology*, vol. 100, No.3, 2015.

on and fatigue increases, more hand washing routines were ignored, despite the medical staff being aware of how important they were.

Another large-scale experiment[21], because it was conducted over a period of several years, also highlights the mechanics of decision fatigue. Decisions and behavior decline in quality as the day goes on, because our cognitive functions begin to weaken. The analysis involved more than 2,200 UK civil servants, who were asked to perform a series of tests to assess their cognitive abilities: short-term memory, vocabulary, verbal fluency, and logical reasoning. The researchers compared the scores obtained for individuals who worked more than 55 hours per week with those achieved by employees on a 40-hour working week. The results show a decline in cognitive performance, and reasoning in particular, for those who worked the longest hours.

Decision fatigue, which manifests itself as a gradual decline in decision quality, and reduced energy due to intense work, drives us to use more simplistic reasoning, to go for less complex solutions, to succumb more easily to distraction and various forms of temptation away from our main task, and behave in a more basic manner. Once again, we are neither robots nor computers, but human beings, and our limited capacities can be exhausted. When we act as though that were untrue – pushing the machine to its limits to try to make it more efficient – we end up with the opposite result: less efficiency, poor decisions, and inappropriate behavior!

Procrastination skews our priorities

But our effectiveness isn't only reduced when our cognitive abilities are compromised. Even when they are still at their peak and we are not suffering the effects of fatigue, we are influenced and debilitated by a powerful bias every day: procrastination.

We often tend to voluntarily postpone finishing a task – or making a decision – even when we know that it would be best if we got on with

---

21 Marianna Virtanen, Archana Singh-Manoux, Jane E. Ferrie *et al.*, "Long Working Hours and Cognitive Function: The Whitehall II Study", *American Journal of Epidemiology*, vol. 169, No.5, March 2009.

it right away. And we know we're doing it! Many studies show that we are more than ready to admit to procrastinating. When questioned on this subject[22] 95% of college students in the United States say that they are prone to procrastination, and 75% consider themselves as "procrastinators". From a non-specific sample of employees[23], more than 25% of those interviewed considered that they had a personality prone to procrastination. But we know that behavior is doubly harmful: first, those victims of procrastination recognize the negative impact on their effectiveness and they also suffer from it psychologically. So it's a dangerous trap, because it happens in spite of our intentions, and results in less efficiency and weaker performance. In a study by Caroline D'Abate and Erik Eddy[24], the cost of procrastination to a company was analyzed and estimated to be about $9,000 per employee per year.

As the phenomenon is significant and universal, many studies have set out to gain a better understanding of why it happens. One of the world's leading specialists – Professor Piers Steel from the University of Calgary – did a meta-analysis[25] on all the research that exists on the subject to find out what really happens. Fundamentally, procrastination is part of a bias that we have already encountered, the present bias. We tend to focus on actions that provide short-term rewards and postpone those that will require effort.

The first reason for procrastination is the type of tasks we have to perform. The more a task is perceived as uncomfortable in comparison with other tasks, especially because it requires effort, the more we tend to postpone it. And this applies even more if the benefits associated with carrying out this task are remote or unclear. Meanwhile,

....

22 Albert Ellis and William J. Knaus, *Overcoming Procrastination: Or How to Think and Act Rationally in Spite of Life's Inevitable Hassles*, New American Library, 1977.

23 Joseph R. Ferrari, Juan Francisco Díaz-Morales, Jean O'Callaghan *et al.*, "Frequent Behavioral Delay Tendencies by Adults: International Prevalence Rates of Chronic Procrastination", *Journal of Cross-Cultural Psychology*, vol. 38, No.4, July 2007.

24 Caroline P. D'Abate and Erik R. Eddy, "Engaging in Personal Business on the Job: Extending the Presenteeism Construct", *Human Resource Development Quarterly*, vol. 18, No.3, autumn 2007.

25 Piers Steel, "The Nature of Procrastination: A Meta-Analytic and Theoretical Review of Quintessential Self-Regulatory Failure", *Psychological Bulletin*, vol. 133, No.1, 2007.

the more enjoyable the other tasks are perceived as being – even if they are less important – the more we tend to favor them over fundamental but less tempting tasks. As well as the effort required to perform the task, the more it is perceived as being dull or uninteresting, the more we tend to procrastinate.

Task deadlines also play a role in procrastination. The closer they come, the less we procrastinate. And then we're motivated to avoid potential negative consequences if we don't finish the task.

Lastly, the more distractions there are, the more we procrastinate. The more temptation we have to deal with, the more we give in to it by pushing back a task we need to use our willpower to perform. We see the distraction – an e-mail, a phone call, a colleague coming into our office – as a sort of alibi, a way to justify our postponing the important but boring or complex task.

Procrastination and the present bias are part of the human experience, and in our current corporate context there is an endless list of tasks to complete in an environment packed with potential distractions. Procrastination is a serious challenge, given the decline in effectiveness that it provokes.

The engagement challenge: the limits of the carrot and the stick

Default disengagement

The three previous challenges – decision-making, winning behavior and personal effectiveness – relate to specific times during which our work performance may suffer under the negative influence of a bias, a decision method, or structural limit that is simply part of our human condition.

The challenge of engagement is doubly different: on the one hand it is all-encompassing and on the other hand it stems from how we perceive our external environment.

It is all-encompassing in that its consequences can continually influence our behavior and affect, to a varying degree, everything we do. Engaged employees will always seek to do their best – at all times – in the tasks entrusted to them. One of the specific outcomes of engagement is that they will even go beyond the call of duty when they believe the action could be beneficial. Conversely, disengaged employees at best simply perform their tasks in return for their salary, and at worst do their very least or regularly criticize their own company on a daily basis. Whatever the case, the consequences of engagement apply across the board, and affect how we behave each day.

The second characteristic of the engagement challenge is that it isn't innate – like the previous challenges – but actually emanates mainly from the perceived perception of the work environment and signs that are sent explicitly or implicitly to employees. And here, environment is used in the broadest sense of the word: how other people in the company behave – members of the board, your direct supervisor, your coworkers – the characteristics of the physical environment – your office, the meeting rooms and the shared spaces – your business itself starting with its sector, positioning and image, the products or services it sells, its customers; and of course the specific characteristics of your occupation and how it is defined, possible career changes, what training is available, and so on. We'll soon see that in a company and its environment, employees consider all these factors as signs, and they have positive or negative impacts on engagement.

But before going into detail about what behavioral science can teach us about professional engagement, let's try to understand why engagement is such a big challenge.

First of all, it's because the default situation is employee disengagement. As we saw in the introduction with the Gallup study, the vast majority of the world's employees don't feel engaged in their daily work.

Engagement: a game-changer for competitiveness

Employee engagement is a challenge because it is a key factor in competitiveness and as such, a critical issue for the company. If the engagement-performance relationship had never been established, we could legitimately think that from the strict point of view of company management, employee disengagement isn't a strategic problem and shouldn't be given priority over all the other challenges that companies face.

But this simply isn't true: the link between the performance of a business and the engagement of its employees has been widely proven, through both global analyses and experiments on individual behavior.

The link between engagement and performance

This key lesson is nothing new! As far back as in 1998, in an important book on the subject, *The Human Equation*[26], Professor Jeffrey Pfeffer of Stanford University presented a summary of the studies that show how results, employee motivation, and managerial practices are affected according to whether the company views individual development as a priority. And the results are striking: in an analysis of more than 3,400 companies across all major industries, Professor Mark Huselid[27] from Rutgers University came up with the following figures for human-focused companies: +$27,044 in sales per employee; +$18,641 in business value per employee and +$3,814 in profit per employee.

Since this analysis, many different projects have confirmed the strong link between engagement and a company's economic performance.

In fact Gallup regularly produces a fascinating meta-analysis on this topic. The latest publication[28] from 2016 counted a total of 339 studies on 230 organizations in 73 countries, employing over 1,800,000 people. It generated the following results:

....

26 Jeffrey Pfeffer, *The Human Equation: Building Profits by Putting People First*, Harvard Business School Press, 1998.
27 Mark A. Huselid, "The Impact of Human Resource Management Practices on Turnover, Productivity, and Corporate Financial Performance", *Academy of Management Journal*, vol. 38, No.3, 1995.
28 Gallup Q[12®], *The Relationship Between Engagement at Work and Organizational Outcomes*, April 2016.

- The business units that ranked in the top half of the table for employee engagement are twice as likely to succeed as those in the bottom half.
- Companies in the top 25 have better scores than the companies in the last quartile on all performance indicators: +10% on customer ratings, +21% on profit, +24% on sales revenue for large companies and +59% for small businesses.

And these results don't stop at financial scores and the customer experience. Accidents at work are less frequent, absenteeism is lower (-41%) and quality defects are reduced (-40%). Jim Harter, Scientific Director at Gallup Research, states: "Engaged employees are more attentive and vigilant. They look out for the needs of their coworkers and the overall enterprise because they personally 'own' the result of their work and that of the organization."[29]

The authors conclude: "The relationship between engagement and performance at the business/work unit level is substantial and highly generalizable across organizations."[30]

Using a different methodology, the Great Place to Work Institute reaches the same overall conclusions. Companies where employees feel happy also enjoy a significant advantage over other companies. An analysis carried out from 1997 to 2010[31] highlights an average annual stock market return rate of 11.6% for the 100 companies ranked "Best Places to Work" compared to an average of 4.6% for the Russel 3000 index and 3.83% for the S&P 500. If we combine these results over the period, results from the Best Places to Work companies are four times higher than the average of those obtained by the other companies on the main stock market indexes.

....

29 Quoted in John Baldoni, "Employee Engagement Does More than Boost Productivity", *Harvard Business Review*, July 4, 2013, hbr.org.

30 Gallup Q12®, "The Relationship Between Engagement at Work and Organizational Outcomes", *art. quote.*

31 gptwcontent.nonprofitsoapbox.com/our-approach/what-are-the-benefits-great-workplaces

The impact of individual engagement

The results of all meta-analyses point to employee engagement being the key to performance. And that's hardly surprising, given what behavioral science researchers have learned about individual behavior.

A study by Dan Ariely, Dražen Prelec and Emir Kamenica[32] – a fun and informative initiative as is often the case when Ariely is involved – highlighted the link between the meaning people give to their work and the performance they achieve. Researchers asked participants to make characters (known as "bionicles") out of Lego. Two groups of participants were formed, and given different instructions:

- In the first group, participants were asked to build one character in return for a fee of $2. They were informed that this character would then be dismantled. When they had finished their first character, participants were offered a lower amount to make a new one ($1.89), and so on until the participants decided to stop making them.
- In the second group, the participants were offered the same amounts to go on making the characters, until they decided to stop. The only difference was that the experiment leader dismantled the character in front of the participant as soon as it was finished. So all of the participants knew that their character would be dismantled, but only the members of the second group saw it with their own eyes.

The researchers wanted to find out if a different set of rules had an impact on the participants' performance in terms of how many characters they made, and how much money they earned. And if it did, to what extent? While they were receiving the same payment, did seeing the character being dismantled affect how the participants behaved? It certainly did! In the first group, the participants built 11 bionicles and earned just over 14 dollars. In the second group, the participants only built 7 bionicles. While the financial incentive remained the same, the members of this group decided to give up earlier, simply because they could see their characters being taken apart. And as a result,

....
32 Dan Ariely, Emir Kamenica and Dražen Prelec, "Man's search for meaning: The case of Legos", *Journal of Economic Behavior & Organization*, No.67, 2008.

they earned less. Ariely calls this condition "Sisyphus", recalling the legend in which the gods condemned Sisyphus to roll a rock up a hill before letting it roll down again and again. A meaningless task.

The researchers underlined that even the participants in the second group who had said they particularly enjoyed making Lego characters gave up after 7. Even though they enjoyed the task, its lack of meaning meant that those participants gave up sooner than the others. And the meaning wasn't life-changing, it was actually fairly mundane. But that's what makes it so interesting: even for minor tasks, the absence of meaning led to weaker performance. Yet the compensation – which is supposed to be the key to motivation – remained the same.

The surprising relationship between remuneration and performance

Bonus and performance

Continuing his research on the impact of pay on performance, Ariely ran two other studies that focused more specifically on the bonuses obtained when specific objectives are achieved.

The first experiment[33] deals with how bonuses affect performance. The basic belief behind the variable bonus systems for individual performance is that rewards enhance individual motivation, effort, and ultimately, the chances of achieving the original objective. The researchers wanted to evaluate this assumption by varying bonus amounts in order to measure any differences in performance. The study was conducted in India to test a very high level of bonus (given the low pay level in rural Rajasthan). Participants were asked to perform a series of six different tasks: some involving memory, others involving creativity, and others calling upon motor and functional skills. Depending on the level of performance achieved on each task, participants were eligible for a bonus. But the absolute value of the bonus was different – from low (4 rupees) to medium (40 rupees) to

....
33   Dan Ariely, Uri Gneezy, George Loewenstein *et al.* "Large Stakes and Big Mistakes",
     The Review of Economic Studies, vol. 76, No.2, April 2009.

very high (400 rupees) – so that its impact could be evaluated. The "very high" level was equivalent to the cost of living for one month, which meant that participants achieving a "very good" evaluation for each task they performed could obtain a sum equivalent to six months' living expenses.

The main results were as follows:

- There were no significant differences observed in the performance achieved according to whether the participants could obtain a "low" or "average" bonus. Multiplying the available bonus level by 10 (from 4 to 40) did not lead to any improvement in performance.
- Even more surprisingly, the level of performance achieved with the maximum bonus of 400 rupees was actually weaker in comparison with the "low" or "average" bonuses. The stress generated in participants who could receive a very high bonus actually resulted in a weaker performance compared with those who were offered a lower bonus.
- Finally, no difference was observed in the types of tasks performed.

The researchers wanted to go further, to assess whether the results obtained were specific to this population, who were unaccustomed to incentive systems. They also wanted to measure the impact – on the same individual – of a higher or lower incentive and the possible difference depending on whether the tasks to be performed were more intellectual or more physical.

So they ran a second study in the United States. Participants were all given the opportunity to earn a low, medium or high bonus, depending on the level of performance they achieved. But they were divided into two groups. In the second group, the bonuses were ten times higher than in the first group.

The results of the second study confirmed what the first study had already shown – performance was actually lower for the highest bonus – but there was a clear difference depending on the type of task. When the task was physical, the higher bonus level boosted performance, but when the task involved cognitive resources, the opposite was true: higher stakes produced lower performance. The potential stress caused by the possibility of achieving a very high bonus was an obstacle to participants' achievement when the task was intellectual, but the same stress didn't generate the same disability when physical strength was required.

The organizers concluded that: "A lot of companies offer very large bonuses for performing tasks that require creativity, problem solving, and memory. Our results question the hypothesis that increased motivation leads to improved performance. For many different tasks (with one important exception), higher monetary incentives actually led to a deterioration in performance."

We have seen that employee engagement is a major variable in business competitiveness, but that it is not as easy or mechanical as we might think: in particular, the link between performance and pay is not as obvious as a conventional and widespread view of motivation would have us believe.

A compliment or a pizza is more powerful than a monetary bonus!

Going on with the engagement challenge, here is another experiment, again carried out by the very prolific and inventive Dan Ariely. This study[34] took place in Israel and involved Intel employees in a semiconductor production facility. Employees in the study were divided into four comparable groups whose members would be given a specific incentive, depending on their productivity:

- Members of the first group could receive a $30 bonus.
- Those in the second group could receive a voucher for a family-sized pizza to be delivered to their homes.
- Those in the third group received a text message from their boss saying "Well done!"
- Group four was a control and did not receive any special incentive, it was used to assess the level of basic productivity.

The incentive was offered on a day when employees would be returning to work after a break lasting several days, because it was thought to

----

34   Dan Ariely, *Payoff: The Hidden Logic That Shapes Our Motivations*, Simon & Schuster/ TED, 2016.

be a good way to motivate employees and stimulate them to achieve a high level of productivity. But the results were surprising in more ways than one. When the incentives had been in place for one day, the three systems had all boosted productivity, but the best performance was obtained from employees who had received the voucher for a pizza to share with their family, ahead of those who had simply received a "well done" message from their boss. The $30 bonus actually came in third place. So money isn't the best motivator. It's especially interesting to note that the cost-free boss's message performed better than the $30 bonus.

But what happened when Ariely's team measured productivity over the entire week is even more informative: the productivity of participants who had benefited from the $30 bonus on the first day nosedived when the opportunity to get a bonus on the following days was taken away: -13.2% on the second day; -6% on the third day and -2.9% on the fourth day. Over the week, productivity dipped by 6.5% compared to the control group. On the other hand, the increase in productivity after the "Well done!" text message from the boss that employees received on the first day did not see a rebound effect and so resulted in greater overall productivity for the week.

These small, simple experiments by behavioral researchers are useful to help us understand the complex engagement challenge. Yes, there is a strong link between engagement and corporate performance. No, generating engagement is not as straightforward as paying out higher wages or offering financial incentive schemes, and yet this is where most companies focus their efforts and as we know, still end up with disengaged employees.

Rookie mistake: using money for motivation

Will we never learn?

Professor Barry Schwartz writes: "For more than two centuries, we have absorbed, as a society and as individuals, some false ideas about our relationship to work. It is a long-accepted tenet of economics that if you want to get someone – an employee, a student, a government official, your own child – to do something, you have to make it worth his or her while. People do things for incentives, for rewards, for money."[35]

And along the same lines, Ariely questions: "Why are people so demotivated at work?"[36] and answers: "I think it is partially because of the persistence of an industrial-era view of labor that is largely accepted as truth. This view holds that the labor market is a place where individuals exchange work for wages (regardless of how meaningless the labor is) and that people typically don't really care what happens to their work as long as they are fairly compensated for it."

This vision began in the famous book *The Wealth of Nations* published by Adam Smith in 1776. In it, Smith describes the conditions required to achieve better productivity at work, using the example of a pin factory. Rather than getting each worker to perform all the tasks, he recommends that the tasks are divided into sub-activities, with specialized workers assigned to each: "One draws out the wire, another straighten it, a third cuts it, a fourth points it, a fifth grinds the top to receive the head." And that system works in an industrial world in which standardized mass production is the norm! Production efficiency is given a massive boost. But the vision, which then applies to everyone, is clear: workers have to follow the tasks assigned to them if they are to produce efficiently and receive remuneration, in exchange for uninteresting but paid work.

This initial vision of a mercantile exchange in which the main motivation is remuneration gradually took hold, first with Taylorism then at the beginning of the last century, with Fordism. Frederick Taylor considered a person at work as one component element alongside others, within a larger complex machine. If this machine – the business – is to work optimally, employees need to do the right job at the right time. So tasks must be precisely and rigorously defined, and employees need to perform them, with good behavior being rewarded and bad being sanctioned.

....

35   Barry Schwartz, *Why We Work?*, Simon & Schuster / TED, 2015.
36   Dan Ariely, *Payoff*, *op. cit.*

For even greater efficiency and performance, the work is divided again: we set out to move from disorganized and expensive artisanal pre-industrial work, left to each person's initiative, and with no control systems, to a scientific organization of work for mass production, starting with very precise processes that must be followed to the letter. In this vision, managers are not looking to create an attractive job for employees, but to design an effective system where individuals are merely performers. They are not asked to be creative, to make decisions or take initiatives. They are simply required to respect what has already been defined and to carry out specific tasks. The fundamental levers used to get the job done according to the rules are the stick and the carrot: threatening sanctions up to and including dismissal when the processes are not respected or become inefficient, and calling employees' attention to salary increases, bonuses when goals are met or exceeded and, ultimately, the promise of tantalizing career prospects.

An outdated but persistent vision

Of course, we all think that's yesterday's world, and that today's businesses don't adhere to this archaic view. But then why are so many people barely engaged at work? The reason is simple, yet essential: in spite of an underlying awareness that humans need to be valued, the reality within companies is very different, and still mainly geared towards a very functional view of human motivation. Amy Edmondson – a Harvard professor and business organization expert – believes that "As a society, we are still largely inured to a fear-based work environment. We believe (most of the time, erroneously) that fear increases control. Control reinforces certainty and predictability. In fact, many managers believe that without fear, people will not work hard enough."[37]

Our management systems are certainly less direct and less authoritative now than they once were. In the 1960s, businesses began

....

37   Amy Edmondson, *Teaming: How Organizations Learn, Innovate and Compete in the Knowledge Economy*, John Wiley & Sons, 2012.

moving away from historical patterns and gradually incorporated new practices, and figures such as Abraham Maslow and Douglas McGregor began to attract attention. With his famous triangle, Maslow helped to shed light on the greater complexity of individual needs. McGregor continued along this path, seeking to bring the new vision into companies. They both emphasized the importance of motivation, rather than external rewards and punishments. Companies have learned from their findings, and sought to incorporate more flexibility into the workplace, in terms of both hours and dress codes. Employee autonomy has increased and more motivation drivers, other than monetary systems, have begun to appear.

Nevertheless, despite these positive developments, the basic motivational and organizational set-up is still the same, but with a more attractive veneer. The handling of the stick and the carrot has become subtler, but it remains the foundation of managerial practices in most companies.

In his excellent book *Drive: The Surprising Truth About What Motivates Us*[38], Daniel Pink illustrates this fragile evolution with a computer analogy. If we consider that motivation 1.0 (trying to survive) stems from our human nature, that motivation 2.0 is based on a reward/punishment system, then evolutions derived from Maslow and McGregor are rather more 2.1 than 3.0. He writes: "We have configured our organizations and constructed our lives around its bedrock assumption: The way to improve performance, increase productivity and encourage excellence is to reward the good and punish the bad."[39] It's an improvement, but not a shift in the paradigm.

Today's business world still creates tension and fear; it's a short-term dictatorship: indicators are increasingly specific, and there are more of them to follow; quantified objectives must be achieved, monthly reports are becoming weekly; there is constant pressure to control costs when there is no clear requirement to reduce them; deadlines are getting shorter; employees are expected to be available and reactive at all times; there is a constant quest for perfect service and

....

38 Daniel Pink, *Drive: The Surprising Truth About What Motivates Us*, Riverhead Books, 2011.
39 *Ibid.*

an exceptional customer experience for increasingly fickle consumers who can browse a global offer from a multitude of competitors around every corner, including where we least expect them; and start-ups can render your precious business model obsolete in just a few years, or even months.

Companies have certainly changed, but the legacy of Taylorism and Fordism is still alive and well. It continues to permeate how we manage, often without our even realizing it. Fear is still there, even though it is now of a different nature, and studies show that it is particularly destructive both for engagement and for individual and collective performance. A vision of what a high-performing company really is – with processes and controls – and what generates individual engagement – material incentives and external rewards based on remuneration – is still the basis of most companies' policies. Laszlo Bock, former Vice President of People Operations at Google, believes that "Leaders always spoke of putting people first, and then treated them like replaceable gears."[40]

Harvard University Professor Raffaella Sadun ran a study[41] on 12,000 companies in 34 countries to see how they implement 18 basic everyday managerial practices, such as talent management or the clarity of objectives. And the results are clear: on a scale of 1 to 5 for overall performance, only 15% of companies in the United States and 5% in other countries achieved a score of 4 or more. On the other hand, no less than 30% of US companies and 70% of companies surveyed in China, India or Brazil scored 3 or less. The conclusion is clear: "According to our criteria, many organizations throughout the world are very badly managed."

The main repercussions from this widespread mismanagement are not only poor economic performance and development difficulties, but disengagement on a massive scale. Barry Schwartz believes that "The way their work is structured means that there really is little reason to do these jobs except for pay."[42]

---

40 Laszlo Bock, *Work Rules!*, *op. quote.*
41 Nicholas Bloom, Raffaella Sadun and John Van Reenen, "Does Management Really Work?" *Harvard Business Review*, November 2012, hbr.org.
42 Barry Schwartz, *Why We Work op. cit.*

Disengagement is all the more problematic now, if only in terms of efficiency, than during the era of mass production, which was characteristic of the twentieth century economy. Our current knowledge economy with its key success factors expects completely different things from its employees. In the knowledge economy, humans are the key to success. In more and more sectors, the performance of a company no longer depends on its ability to have employees who scrupulously perform rigorously defined tasks to maximize productivity. Rather, it requires employees to bring their knowledge, intelligence and creativity to the company, so it can be more innovative in the products and services it offers to its customers, to constantly adapt to technological changes, and to keep on learning from both its environment and its mistakes. If we want to avoid becoming obsolete, and if we are to be creative on a daily basis despite constraints and challenges, we must focus on the magic trio: quality, cost and time.

The knowledge economy makes employee engagement even more crucial. But if remuneration and, more generally, rational and material incentives can't generate this engagement, what *can?*

Chapter 3

What really generates engagement

Human motivation has long been seen as an exclusive outcome based on two fundamental mechanisms: a biological motivation – the drive to survive (eating, drinking, reproducing, etc.) – and external motivation brought about by rewards or punishments.

The last forty years of research into behavioral science has turned this vision on its head.

What's important to realize here is that motivation actually derives from a whole host of factors. Human complexity involves various influences. As Dan Ariely so beautifully puts it: " Motivation is a forest full of twisting trees, unexplored rivers, threatening insects, weird plants, and colorful birds. This forest has many elements that we think matter a lot, but in fact don't. Even more, it's full of unusual details that we either ignore completely or don't think matter, but that turn out to be particularly important."[1]

This is not to say that the idea of someone reacting to material incentives is invalid, but rather to emphasize that on the one hand, this motivational mechanism is, as we have already seen, often very complex and has potential negative effects. And most importantly, other mechanisms can be much more powerful.

Employee engagement is generated by factors that can be grouped into four main themes, as illustrated in Figure 3.1:

- Fairness;
- Sense of personal achievement;
- Friendship;
- Mission.

....
1   Dan Ariely, *Payoff*, *op. cit.*

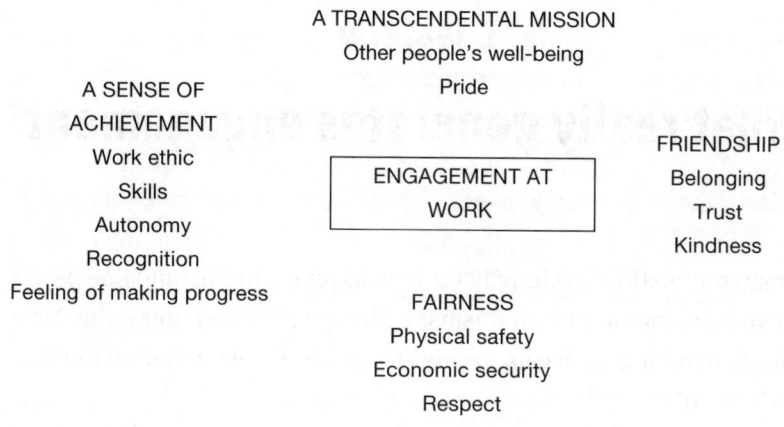

FIGURE 3.1: The four pillars of engagement at work

Fairness, the baseline

Being treated fairly, not only in terms of the work we do but more importantly as a human being, is the basic condition for building engagement among employees. We have already seen how humans are social animals, and how fairness is a key requirement and has a huge influence on behavior. When people go to work, they need justice to be done.

Nothing else matters more than this, and no other advantage can compensate for an individual feeling that he or she is being treated unfairly. In the most extreme cases, a perception of injustice can even be conveyed by harmful behavior from the person who experiences it. So the basis of employee engagement must be fairness. But that's not the complete picture.

Fairness leads on to three major themes:

- Safety at work;
- Economic security;
- Respect.

Safety at work is the bottom line. If they are to be engaged in the workplace, most people need to feel like they aren't taking risks when they do their job. The only exceptions to this rule are those who have consciously chosen an occupation where their lives are at risk.

Soldiers, for example. All employees need to feel that their company is doing everything possible to limit the occurrence of risk in the work environment. If they feel that risks are being taken on a daily basis, this results in both stress and impaired performance.

Fortunately, safety at work – in most countries – is an important concern and is now taken into consideration by the majority of businesses. But it's still a vital foundation for building engagement.

Economic security is the second pillar of fairness. It can be split into two sub-sections: one relating to job security, and the other to equal pay.

Job security is of course extremely important. The psychological environment of a workplace must not constantly remind employees that they could lose their jobs at any time. Job security is about not feeling threatened. At the very least, employees want to feel like they are paid and treated fairly by the company that employs them. The risk of losing your job is therefore not only extremely stressful from an economic standpoint, but also proof of unfair treatment given the effort and time employees expend at work.

And in view of the economic climate over the last forty years, especially in Europe, this challenge is not to be taken lightly. Employees in private companies know that their jobs are only safe as long as their company achieves a satisfactory level of economic performance. Businesses shouldn't try to hide that fact, which would actually be impossible to do, but rather refrain from pointing it out regularly, which will probably have the opposite effect: a drop in motivation and performance caused by the resulting stress, rather than a hike in motivation when employees feel they are in danger. It's all about striking a balance between the inevitable pressure of working in a private company, and an excessive level of paralyzing fear.

The second dimension is about the perception of fairness with regards to remuneration. Earlier we looked at the impact of salary on job satisfaction and how there is a positive but relatively low correlation compared to the other elements that we're learning about now. But while income does play a role in this perception of equity, income *in comparison to others* is what really matters. Numerous studies have shown that satisfaction with your own remuneration is strongly influenced by how much other people are earning. The same wage is seen as satisfactory if it is ranked among the highest in a professional circle, and unsatisfactory if the opposite is true. It's not so much the compensation in absolute terms that counts, as its relative amount in relation to your colleagues. So if you want to be sure that your employees perceive their salary as fair and satisfactory, then pay scales need to be made common knowledge.

In combination, job and economic security are not factors for engagement in absolute terms, but can be a source of disengagement if the company doesn't meet those expectations. They do not generate engagement, but if they are lacking, it's difficult for employees to move on to the next stage of engagement.

And the next stage is how we perceive the *respect* we are shown by the company. Ego is something we all have in common. We all need to feel valued, and how strongly we feel valued is hugely influenced by the respect we believe we are shown by other people, and how they behave towards us. A lack of respect is an attack on our ego and the image we have of ourselves. And it's even more relevant if this lack of respect is shown in public, or in the collective framework of a company. Criticism of a specific action or behavior may be accepted, but a lack of respect for an individual person certainly is not. Conversely, signs of respect are rewarding and therefore help to build the foundations for engagement. But here we are still dealing with the foundations for building engagement, without which it is not possible. And now let's venture into what generates the genuine motivation people feel when they give their very best to their company.

Achievement, pillar No.1

The second major dimension of engagement is the personal satisfaction that employees gain from working for a company. It is that overall feeling of success related to our own work that comes from the combination of five main factors:
- The meaning behind the work;
- The perception of competence and control over the task;

- Autonomy;
- Recognition for performance;
- The feeling you are making progress.

Meaning

The first element that develops a feeling of achievement is the meaning that employees give to the work they are doing. Is this work just one of many tasks, or is it perceived as a link in a bigger chain related to a more significant goal? There is a famous metaphor about a stonemason and a cathedral. If a stonemason only sees his work as sculpting individual stones, he can't possibly consider it to be an achievement: it becomes routine and boring. That's the kind of work we do with no motivation, and only for the money it provides. On the other hand, if the stonemason can see his work as part of the spectacular cathedral he has helped to build, then the meaning behind it is totally different, and his engagement is different as well. Contrary to how things may appear, it is not the intrinsic and objective characteristics of work that create meaning. In his outstanding book[2], Mike Rose shows how people doing what might be considered "entry-level" jobs – waitresses, hairdressers, plumbers or electricians – can develop high levels of specific expertise and intelligence in their lines of work, and above all, feel a very strong sense of purpose when going about their tasks. And this is because the meaning we find in our work doesn't stem only from what we are doing, but from the contribution we feel we are making to something that matters to us. It's not about changing the world. It may simply be that you feel your work matters to your colleagues, your manager, your company or your family. Our contribution is important: our work counts for something or someone that counts for us.

But this perception has its flaws. Remember Dan Ariely's Lego experiment? When the work is undone in full view, it doesn't matter how much people are paid, their motivation crumbles. It is neither the nature nor the sophistication of the work that gives it meaning, but a

....
2   Mike Rose, *The Mind at Work: Valuing the Intelligence of the American Worker*, Penguin Books, 2014.

state of mind and an external environment that makes it possible to develop that work.

Thinking that your occupation counts and has meaning is a fundamental intrinsic motivator.

Control

The second element relates to the skill and control we have, and how we feel about what we do. If we are to find a sense of achievement, we first need to be sure that we have the right skills and can master the task in hand. Otherwise, there is a high risk of stress, when we imagine we are unable to perform to expectations. Conversely, a feeling of competence actually enhances self-confidence. Developing this perception of control involves both technical expertise and support from the company (in terms of making resources available, especially time and money), but also from colleagues. Having the skills to perform your tasks and feeling supported by those around you create the right conditions for success.

Autonomy

However, even if an employee finds meaning in their work and feels in control and competent enough to perform their tasks, there can be no engagement if they are not given autonomy. In order to develop pride in our work, we need to feel that we are not merely a technical performer of a task but that we have taken it into our own hands, and shaped it, given it our own personal added value. And that's what helps to develop a feeling of personal success. There is no shortage of studies showing the importance of autonomy both in the satisfaction it provides and in the performance it generates, compared to centralized work structures. In a study of employees at a US investment bank[3],

3   Paul Baard, Edward Deci and Richard Ryan, "Intrinsic Need Satisfaction: A Motivational Basis of Performance and Well-Being in Two Work Settings", *Journal of Applied Social Psychology*, vol. 34, No.10, 2004.

Paul Baard, Edward Deci and Richard Ryan demonstrated the strong link between autonomy and job satisfaction, but also performance.

The more employees feel able to make their own decisions about how to reach their objectives and carry out their tasks, the more autonomous they feel. In parallel, being able to come up with a finished product and seeing tasks through to their conclusion help to create autonomy and encourage employees to feel like they bring added value. And this develops a sense of achievement in the work they have done. However, the more segmented the tasks, the more difficult it is to understand the importance of a single person's contribution.

Being autonomous in how they do their work, and being able to identify the usefulness of their work are the conditions required for people to feel like they are making a contribution, which then brings about a feeling of personal success.

Recognition

Being recognized for your contribution to the overall performance of your company is a central element in the perception of success. Earlier we looked at humans as social animals. Other people's perceptions of us and our community are a key factor in establishing a feeling of well-being. We need to feed our egos in order to develop a good self-image.

So if all the characteristics that we have just reviewed – the meaning of our work, our competence and perceived control in its realization, and the autonomy from which we benefit – only exist in our own minds, it is difficult to feel successful at work. Recognition from other people, especially managers, is very important. It's a kind of catalyst that affirms our perception of success. And recognition and ignorance don't need to be expressed profusely to have a huge impact on how we behave. The wonderfully creative Dan Ariely showed this once again in another study of his.

The basic task required of participants was relatively simple: it involved working on a sheet of paper showing several figures, and identifying which pairs of figures could be added together to make 1, for example 0.89 plus 0.11. Each time a participant completed a sheet, he had to hand it over to the examiner, who then suggested that the participant continue their work with another sheet in exchange for a gradually declining fee, and so on until the participant decided to stop. The objective of the experiment was to evaluate the participants' performance depending on three specific behaviors on the part of the examiner:

- The examiner for group 1 took the sheet from the participant and looked at it saying "ah ah" with a positive intonation (recognition).
- The examiner for group 2 took the sheet without looking at it and said nothing, then placed it on a pile with the other sheets that had been handed in (nonchalance).
- The examiner for group 3 took the sheet and put it straight into a shredder (destruction).

The examiner for group 1 showed minimal recognition; the one for group 2 expressed a neutral attitude to the work that had been done; and the examiner for group 3 destroyed the work.

So how did the participants perform? Rationally speaking, there should have been no difference, because the pay was the same for each group. But as you've probably predicted by now because we're dealing with human beings, that wasn't the case. The examiner's behavior changed the participants' behavior and in turn, the remuneration they eventually received. When the examiner destroyed the work, the number of completed sheets was almost 28% lower than it was for group 1 (in which the work was acknowledged). Seeing their work being destroyed – just like in the Lego study – brought down the participants' performance. But in a much more surprising turn of events, nonchalance produced the same effect. Group 2's participants, whose work was not even looked at when it was handed in, gave up almost as quickly as those in group 3, whose work was immediately destroyed. Neutrality causes almost as much damage as destruction. And while we can probably be fairly hopeful that any work done by an employee is rarely actively destroyed by his or her manager, how many managers are guilty of nonchalance? Not acknowledging an employee's achievements probably has more serious consequences than we realize.

Recognition is therefore a fundamental element that can give employee engagement a huge boost, and has the advantage of being very easy to implement on a daily basis. A simple gesture or a brief chat may be enough, but choose not to acknowledge performance and there may be enormous consequences.

Making progress by setting achievable challenges

Routine leads to boredom and disengagement. Even when your work does have meaning, when you think you have the right skills to do it well, and when you have a feeling of autonomy while still being recognized by your manager and your colleagues, none of the successes you achieve will satisfy you indefinitely. When everything seems to be going well, it's actually going too well. You are too far into your comfort zone, and that can lead to a feeling of monotony. Being too in control of everyday work can be detrimental to employee engagement. To have a lasting sense of accomplishment from the work we do, we need to push ourselves out of our comfort zones. This is what generates new excitement and forces us to make an effort, and in doing so achieve a key objective: constant progress.

Because efforts lead to rewards, the ability to go beyond what you have done before, and face a new challenge – big or small – reinforces pride and nurtures the human sense of accomplishment.

Even if we find something very hard to do, the effort we expend makes the achievement even more valuable. That's why new challenges requiring specific effort – as long as they don't seem impossible – help to value the work we do and bring new interest and excitement into our daily tasks.

Managing new tasks and facing new challenges bring progress. And the feeling of moving forward through daily success stories, whether big or small, is considered by one of the world's leading experts on professional engagement – Harvard University Professor Teresa Amabile – to be the most important factor in having a good day at work. Along with the psychologist Steven Kramer, Teresa Amabile created a fantastic study[4] that takes a look at daily realities at work.

......

4   Teresa M. Amabile and Steven J. Kramer, *The Progress Principle: Using Small Wins to Ignite Joy, Engagement and Creativity at Work*, Harvard Business Review Press, 2011.

The two researchers were able to monitor the daily working lives of 238 employees divided into 26 project teams in 7 different companies from three industries. Every day, these employees were asked to fill out a journal about the work they did. They had to describe the basic characteristics of their working day (number of hours, tasks performed, contact with colleagues, etc.), but they were also asked to evaluate the work they did and the motivation they felt, how their project was evolving, how they perceived their environment and autonomy, or the time pressure they felt, as well as the emotions they experienced during the day. They also had to describe what they thought was the most important event on each day. In the end, researchers received survey material from nearly 12,000 daily reports describing participants' lives over an average period of four months. A researcher's gold mine.

The purpose of this study was to identify and understand the factors that create what the authors call the "double nirvana": company performance and employee well-being. Their conclusion was clear. The researchers reported back: "Inner work life influences people's performance on four dimensions: creativity, productivity, work commitment, and collegiality."[5] And the key element that has a positive influence on this inner life is the perception of progress and success in what we do each day. Among all the events the researchers identified over the course of an exhaustive analysis of the employees' diaries, when they reported progress or success it had the most impact on their impression of having had a positive day. It influenced performance and motivation, and generated positive emotions. Of all the events that occur on a daily basis, the one researchers call the "progress principle" is the most powerful. Wins, whether small or big, nourish the sense of accomplishment that is so important for building engagement. Astoundingly, this key influence driver is mostly ignored by managers. In a study[6] conducted alongside their main research, Teresa Amabile and Steven Kramer interviewed 669 managers, asking

....

5   *Ibid.*
6   Teresa M. Amabile and Steven J. Kramer, "What Really Motivates Workers", *Harvard Business Review*, vol. 88, No. 1-2, January-February 2010.

them to rank five different factors that influence employee motivation in order of importance: recognition, incentives, interpersonal support, clarity of objectives and support for making progress at work. Managers rated the last factor on the list as the least influential. And not only was it rated least influential by some, the ranking applied to the vast majority: only 35 managers put it in first position. The study suggests that supporting employees every day as they strive to make progress is not perceived by managers as being important for employee motivation, well-being and, ultimately, performance!

But the challenge of engagement isn't just personal. Other people are important too!

Friendship, pillar No.2

In our personal lives, our family, friends and loved ones play a fundamental role in the happiness we feel. Being supported, and feeling like we belong to a community, knowing that we are important for other people and that they are important for us, are all essential to our happiness.

One of the world's leading experts on this key issue, or we could say THE key issue – Professor Martin Seligman from the University of Pennsylvania – made relationships with others one of the five dimensions of his famous Perma model[7] which deals with well-being. In his book *Flourish*[8] Seligman writes: "Everyone needs someone. We enhance our well-being and share it with others by building strong relationships with the people around us, family, friends, coworkers, neighbors."

What applies to our personal lives can also apply to well-being at work. And not just well-being, individual and collective performance are also affected, as shown in a study by researchers at the University

....

7   See "Positive Psychology Theory", authentichappiness.sas.upenn.edu/learn.
8   Martin Seligman, *Flourish: A Visionary New Understanding of Happiness and Well-being*, Atria, 2012.

of Pennsylvania.[9] They set out to test what impact there is on performance when friends are placed together in working groups. Participants were asked to carry out two types of tasks: one requiring collaborative work and the other involving repetitive manual work. For each task, the groups with friends working together performed better than those in which the individuals knew each other but were not friends. Analysis of the groups showed that the best final results produced by the groups of friends were brought about as a result of greater involvement from the beginning of the project, more intense communication within the group and stronger support between individuals at each stage of the project's development, as well as more critical assessments of the ideas as they were discussed. The presence of friends also strengthens the group's motivation to make the project a success. If the project we're working on does well, it means our friends also do well, which is a source of motivation in itself.

The importance of friendship at work is also shown in Gallup's research[10] on identifying the key characteristics of companies that achieve especially high results in the following four dimensions: employee retention rate, customer scores, productivity, and profitability. It identified twelve dimensions that are strongly correlated with these performance scores. And one of them was "I have a best friend in the company." This element is key to very high productivity in working groups within companies. Another study, conducted on people who responded positively to this statement, demonstrated these beneficial effects on many other dimensions: compared to other employees, 43% considered that they had been better appreciated in the last seven days; 37% found that they had received more encouragement; 35% that the commitment of their colleagues was of better quality; 28% considered that in the last six months, someone in the office had pointed out progress they had made; 27% that their company's goals helped them to understand the importance of their own work; 27% that their opinion seemed to count more at work and

....
9   Don Clifton, *First, Break all the Rules: What the World's Greatest Managers Do Differently*, Gallup Press, 2016.
10 "The Twelve Key Dimensions That Describe Great Workgroups – Item 10: I Have a Best Friend at Work", *Business Journal*, May 26, 1999, news.gallup.com/businessjournal.

21% that they had the opportunity to do what they do best, every day. The presence of friends at work means that doing your job is seen in a much more positive light. Conversely, studies show that when an individual feels isolated within a company, both their health and the quality of their experience at work are at risk. In those cases, individuals feel more stress, they may lose sleep, have more difficulty communicating with others within the company, and ultimately there will be a negative impact on their work.

In her book *The Power of Meaning*[11] Emily Esfahani Smith reports on a very striking study that was carried out by René Spitz in 1945, which shows how harmful a lack of relationships with others may be. The purpose of this study was to compare two groups of disadvantaged children: the first group was made up of orphans living in an orphanage and the second group were children living in New York State prisons where their mothers were incarcerated. In the orphanage, the primary goal of the institution was to prevent the children contracting diseases and subsequently, reduce their mortality. The instructions were very clear: the staff had to wear gloves and masks to touch the children, the children weren't allowed to play together, and their beds were placed at a specific distance from each other. Overall, the children were very isolated. The children in the prison lived in a very different environment. There were many forms of interaction – including with their mothers – because it was impossible to isolate the children in the sick bay. In the first group, the mortality rate reached a frightening level of more than 25% during the study alone. In the second context, no child died. The researcher's analysis led to the following conclusion: the difference is due to the children not feeling loved, and this had an effect on their health. Contemporary studies have confirmed René Spitz's analysis, and have suggested reasons for it. Chronic solitude results in a weakening of the immune system but also in major psychological difficulties. All told, in an extreme situation, the absence of bonds with other people drives up mortality rates.

Relationships with others in companies also play a key role in our well-being, but we don't need to experience the extreme ends of the

....
11   Emily Esfahani Smith, *The Power of Meaning: Crafting a Life That Matters*, Crown, 2017.

spectrum – having your best friend with you or feeling totally isolated – to understand that social interaction is essential. It begins with a simple but powerful feeling: belonging to a community.

Belonging to a community

A feeling of belonging is crucial for our physical and psychological well-being. It develops around two main elements:

- First, we need to have relationships with other people who we care about and who care about us. If we are important in the eyes of people we value, then we are worth their esteem. The existence of social relationships reinforces the image we have of ourselves. And we need to feed our ego to feel good. As we saw earlier, we are social animals and "we become fully ourselves only through the ever-richening interplay of our networks. We seek, more than anything else, to establish deeper and more complete connections."[12]

- The second element relates to how often we are involved in positive interactions. This frequency is key, because that's what prevents us from feeling isolated. The more positive contacts we have with our coworkers, the more we develop a strong sense of belonging.

The nature of our connections with others is of course important for developing an overall sense of belonging and well-being. University of Michigan specialists Jane Dutton and Emily Heaphy talk about "high quality connections"[13] to characterize the interactions that create genuine links between individuals. These interactions do not need to last for a long time, but they do need to be intense, and demonstrate the reality of each person's interest in the other. They can be simple, everyday encounters that prove you feel empathy and express genuine interest in the person you are talking to. A simple hello can

12 David Brooks, *The Social Animal*, op. cit.
13 Jane E. Dutton and Emily D. Heaphy, "The Power of High-Quality Connections", in Kim S. Cameron, Jane E. Dutton and Robert E. Quinn (dir.), *Positive Organizational Scholarship*, Berrett-Koehler Publishers, 2003.

create a quality connection in the same way that ignoring someone can destroy a sense of belonging.

A fascinating study[14] was carried out in a U.S. hospital involving a cleaning team. It looked at how actions are perceived and how they can destroy and nurture a feeling of belonging. The researchers showed that the simplest behaviors can have the biggest consequences. For example, crossing paths with a doctor in the hallway who does not even say hello can create a very strong feeling of discomfort in the other person. This behavior is perceived as negating the person's value. One cleaner pointed out that she feels she is "invisible": "I think it shows that they don't care about the cleaning staff." On the other hand, another member of the cleaning team says how a simple "thank you" from a patient after their room has been cleaned is enough to create a lovely feeling of gratitude: "They don't have to say thank you. But I appreciate that sort of thing." What's important is that contact – however short and superficial it might be – creates a sense of existence and respect. Another cleaner interviewed by the researchers underlined the satisfaction he felt when a doctor asked how he was doing after finding out he had been under the weather earlier that day: "Hey, Ben, how are you doing? Are things any better?" This question showed that the doctor was interested and helped to develop that sense of belonging. Of course, it's even stronger when you are directly invited to play a role in the life of the team. Another cleaner said how pleased he was to be invited to some department events: "When they have drinks or dinner together, or even donuts, or snacks or whatever, or coffee, they invite me along. It makes me feel that they like me and that I'm a good person." Small gestures like that, and interactions with colleagues on a daily basis create the conditions for this perception of belonging to a community.

But the feeling is even greater when members of the community, be it a business or any other form of organization, share a common goal that goes beyond their own interests.

14   Jane E. Dutton, Gelaye Debebe and Amy Wrzesniewski, "Being Valued and Devalued at Work: A Social Valuing Perspective", in Beth A. Bechky and Kimberly D. Elsbach (eds), *Qualitative Organizational Research: Best Papers from the Davis Conference on Qualitative Research*, vol. 3, Age Publishing, 2016.

The icing on the cake: a transcendental mission

From job to calling

We can perceive our own work in many different ways, and there can be fundamental consequences on our engagement.

Amy Wrzesniewski, Clark McCauley, Paul Rozin and Barry Schwartz[15] have established that people's relationship to their work can be characterized by one of the following three statements:

- The work is seen as a *task to be performed in exchange for pay*. In this case, there is a perception of necessity without choice and no pleasure is felt. The basic motivation to get up each morning is the need to make a living. It's just a job.

- The work may also be seen as a *career we pursue with the aim of making progress*. We have a destination in mind: a higher position or a more important role. Motivation therefore depends on obtaining a higher status, with its inherent benefits. In this case, our attention is mainly focused on the recognition that we get from others, including from managers. It's a race towards a goal, to reach the highest possible position within a company, or a move from one company to another. Engagement can be high, but it is self-focused and there is a risk of not finding real meaning while we are blinkered by the chase.

- Finally, the work may be *a calling*. And that changes everything – from the power of our inner motivation to how we perceive the tasks we need to perform. It's no longer a day's work for a day's pay, nor is it about being appointed to the highest status as quickly as possible. It's about completing a mission that is bigger and more important than we are.

....

15   Amy Wrzesniewski, Clark McCauley, Paul Rozin *et al.*, "Jobs, Careers, and Callings: People's Relations to Their Work", *Journal of Research in Personality*, vol. 31, No.1, March 1997.

A mission that transcends

A mission that transcends is something between the icing on the cake and the cornerstone of a cathedral. The icing on the cake is that one detail – a detail that may appear to be of secondary importance – that changes everything. It makes the whole mission special and beautiful. Without the icing, the cake may be good to eat, but it stops there. Without a transcendental mission, an individual may indeed feel engaged if he or she benefits from a certain number of the dimensions described above. But the intensity of the commitment, the feeling of well-being at work and the resulting performance are heavily, and positively, impacted when we feel that the mission goes beyond our own interests and contributes to society in a way that really matters. And without the cake – in our case, everything we have seen above – the icing is useless. If employees don't feel they have the skills to carry out their tasks, if they don't benefit from any sort of autonomy and struggle to find a sense of personal pride in achieving their goals, or if they don't have the resources they need to finish what they begin, it's much more difficult for them to perceive a transcendental mission and appropriate it for themselves.

A transcendental mission is also a cornerstone in the architectural sense of the word: a single element that can "bring cohesion to the collection of elements that surrounds it." When a mission set by a company has meaning for its employees, this meaning permeates everything the employees do. Even if the tasks are basic or mundane, the end goal transforms how they are perceived. They take on meaning in themselves. In a very interesting study[16], researchers Catherine Bailey from the University of Sussex and Adrian Madden from the University of Greenwich in London present an account from a garbage collector who explains the strong sense of purpose he feels at work when he collects waste to be recycled. He sees his work as being a contribution to the well-being of the planet. And that's the key characteristic for an engaging mission: it goes beyond our own interests and

....
16 Catherine Bailey and Adrian Madden, "What Makes Work Meaningful – Or Meaningless", *MITSloan Management Review*, summer 2016.

is linked with a bigger ambition; the mission has a global purpose. This perception creates the will to go beyond simply performing our daily work. We know why we are working.[17]

As emphasized by Dan Ariely, engagement is brought about by a huge variety of factors that go well beyond the monetary and material incentives designed to appeal to rational human beings, which don't consider our social and emotional dimensions. Most employee disengagement stems from an inability to truly and effectively not just talk the talk, but really walk the walk, and build engagement in a business environment. And yet engagement is an excellent performance lever with unrivalled ROI. So, how can a company create engagement using what we know about behavioral science?

---

17   Wikipedia definition.

Part 2

Creating the pillars for personal effectiveness and performance

Experiments conducted over the last forty years by behavioral experts have demonstrated how our decisions and behaviors – both individual and collective – are influenced by factors that have nothing to do with rationality: System 1 is basically in the driving seat. Emotions drive our decisions, and our relationships with others have a considerable impact on our own actions, all within an environment that also shapes how we perceive the various options involved in a choice.

This brand new vision of the human decision-making mechanism throws up some very big challenges for the business world, in terms of how decisions are made, what triggers individual effectiveness, and how to generate the essential behavior required for collective success. And that calls traditional – and ineffective – managerial methods into question. Despite trumpeting the importance of employees in mission statements, the reality on the ground often tells a different story. Perhaps less so over the last few decades, but still in the vast majority of cases, tools for motivation are based on a mechanical and functional vision with two pillars: the carrot and the stick. Behavioral science has shed light on a much stronger engagement that can be achieved by calling upon a range of levers to create powerful intrinsic motivation among employees, which benefits both the company and the employees themselves.

With the in-depth knowledge acquired from behavioral science, we can now design a powerful ecosystem within a company that creates the conditions for personal well-being, engagement and collective performance through a system of incentives that I call Nudge management.

The second part of this book describes the fundamental pillars of Nudge management: how to be more effective as an individual, and how to create a physical and psychological environment within a company that promotes personal and collective success.

Chapter 4

Being effective at work: from organization to state of mind

When we're striving to achieve personal effectiveness, we often come up against some difficult challenges, as we've now seen: limited attention spans, infinite distractions that break our concentration, decision fatigue that leads to poor quality decision-making, multi-tasking which reduces overall productivity, and procrastination which drives us to put off doing the things we don't enjoy. Our state of mind can also be either a hindrance or a catalyst for effectiveness and well-being. The barriers can vary from person to person, because everyone is different, but they affect us all. So if we want to break through those barriers, we need to put effective actions into place. Because they not only have a huge negative impact on productivity at work, but also on perceived employee well-being. Being ineffective leads to feelings of stress, linked to the fear of not being able to meet our goals. We experience a loss of control, and spend longer working on our tasks in order to complete them. Companies and employees all have something to gain from being more productive. Boosting effectiveness at work means improving collective performance and enhancing individual well-being.

Sounds great. But how can we do it? As is often the case in Nudge management, all it takes is a little clear guidance in people's daily lives, based on a good knowledge of the challenges to be met:

- Find out
- Prioritize
- Maximize potential
- Think positive
- Get motivated

Spotting effectiveness traps

We can build better personal effectiveness at work by being aware of all the threats to productivity that we might encounter.

Our default setting is to react to their negative influence: we go ahead and just read the text message; we do the most enjoyable tasks first and put the others off until later; we give in to the temptation of making the simplest choices as the day progresses and our willpower dwindles. These spontaneous reactions need to be stopped in their tracks by knowing about the harmful influencers and how they work.

Train and experiment

This knowledge can be shared through an internal training program for all employees: from managers to less experienced employees, because everyone is influenced by effectiveness traps. And like all good training, individuals must be made aware of the issues themselves. Before explaining how these obstacles to individual productivity operate, everyone needs to experience how their own behavior is affected. And that's really important, because it's one thing to learn about something, but entirely another to really experience it. The training should start with real-life experiences as told by employees. You could also run some small experiments before talking about the theory behind them. For example, before explaining the negative effects of multitasking, the trainer can ask everyone to perform the following exercise inspired by Caroline Webb in her wonderful book *How to Have a Good Day*.[1]

- Say: "a, b, c, d, e, f, g" then say "2, 3, 4, 5, 6, 7, 8", timing how long it takes you to say both;
- Now combine the two sequences and say "a2, b3, c4, d5, e6, f7, g8" and time yourself again.

....
1 Caroline Webb, *How to Have a Good Day*, Currency, 2016.

It should take you much longer to say the second sequence, and yet the actual work you are asked to do is the same. This type of exercise is a fun and simple way to understand and remember a more complex mechanism. You can then talk about more fundamental experiments and share explanations about why the phenomenon occurs.

But behavioral science has largely demonstrated that learning and remembering information is not enough to generate the desired behavior, even when an individual is very determined to succeed. Creating the intention to act – in this case countering the negative effects of cognitive biases – is only the beginning of the process. Employees need constant reminders of these pitfalls and best practices if they are to maximize their positive effects.

The right Nudge at the right time

Experiments in behavioral economics have highlighted the importance of what is on our minds when we make our decisions. We're not super-computers with unlimited memory banks, so we base our decisions on what we are thinking about when we make them. This is the "mental availability" we looked at earlier. We can't possibly take every single factor involved in a decision into account. This might be why one time when I was deep in conversation with a friend while walking along the street, and he was kind enough to offer me a piece of candy, I threw the paper onto the sidewalk instead of throwing it into the trash can just a few yards away. I wasn't thinking about "cleanliness" when I made that wrong, yet mechanical, decision. Obviously I know that I shouldn't drop trash, and I didn't set out to do it. Simply intending to do the right thing isn't enough. We need to reactivate our intention when we make the decision if we are to transform it into effective behavior. A friend of mine, and a professor at the university of Roskilde – Pelle Hansen – was able to do just that, simply by placing green footstep-shaped stickers onto the streets of Copenhagen, pointing towards the nearest trash cans. This initiative led to a 46% reduction in the amount of waste on the city's streets during the experiment. The green footsteps drew public attention to a specific fact – a trash can was available nearby – and people felt encouraged to behave in a certain way.

For your training to be effective, it must be part of your employees' everyday experiences, and its teachings must spring to their minds right when they are likely to be victims of one of the traps. The good intention needs to be activated when the decision is being made. And the right Nudges need to be invented for each effectiveness trap.

Decide on your daily priorities with an inspiring to-do list

The ability to prioritize is a key strength for top performers. It's demonstrated in a wonderful study by Morten Hansen, who was at that time a professor at INSEAD and is now at Berkeley. In this analysis of 5,000 managers and employees, the results of which are presented in his fascinating book *Great at Work*[2], the researcher showed that individuals who were able to channel all their effort into a handful of high priorities performed 25% better than other participants. This is what Morten Hansen calls "do less, then obsess" and, based on his research that takes all the factors that influence performance at work into account: "Do less, then obsess affects performance more than any other practice."[3]

But obviously it's not easy to put into place. Tasks are becoming broader and more complex, there are more and more distractions and solicitations from other people and the pressure from direct supervisors on employees to fall into the multitasking trap can be incredibly strong. So we need some rules to know how to cope in this environment where effectiveness can be severely hampered. We need to be able to choose priorities and then be strict in how we make our choices: eliminate any task that is not completely

----

2   Morten T. Hansen, *Great at Work: How Top Performers Do Less, Work Better, and Achieve More*, Simon & Schuster, 2018.
3   *Ibid.*

necessary and concentrate on what will make a difference. The key is to focus on the tasks that bring value to your colleagues or end customers. Then try to perform these tasks in the most efficient way and to the highest possible standards. Less is more. Here again, Morten Hansen's study shows that top performers don't work long hours, but manage to select their priorities carefully, based on how they will benefit others, and then focus on doing high quality work to complete their tasks.

The first trap that we face every single day is deciding just what must take priority. Our System 1 – under the influence of the present bias and procrastination – tends to steer us toward the most enjoyable tasks. Remember? It says that effort can wait until tomorrow, and it wants rewards as soon as possible. We need to counter this natural tendency to avoid doing the most important tasks – which are often the most difficult – late in the day. Because doing them at that time is doubly risky: the tasks may be put off until the next day because of an unplanned emergency that took longer that we thought, and doing them in the late afternoon means that our faculties are greatly reduced, because they have been used up. In the first case, an important task might be delayed due to an emergency, which is often less important in the medium term. In the second case, the quality of your work when you do go ahead with the task may be lessened, because of how tired you are when you do it.

So each morning, decide on your top priority tasks, and keep in mind the general selection principles that I mentioned above. Of course, you might think that simply knowing about the traps is enough to counteract their effects. But in Nudge management, we believe that people need a little help to take action, to make life easier and create efficient routines. To-do lists may help to prioritize tasks if they include a certain number of features.

First of all, your to-do list must be designed as a simple standard document that cross-references two criteria: the importance of the tasks and how urgent they are. This produces a matrix with four quadrants.

important but not urgent	**important and urgent**
neither urgent nor important	**urgent** but not important

FIGURE 4.1:   To-do list matrix

This kind of to-do list can help you prioritize the tasks that require immediate attention by forcing you to think rather than starting an action simply because System 1 makes you believe it is important.

The way we list our tasks also has an impact on how productive we will be. The more we write in 'behavior' mode, the more action-oriented we are. For example, "write a memo", "organize a meeting with so-and-so", "call customer X" all set an action in motion. When you go back over the list at the end of the day, you'll see what has been done and what hasn't.

But the traps are still out there, including how we decide to put a particular task in a box and in the number and type of actions we assign to a given day.

The confirmation bias can make us assess the various tasks badly, giving priority to the ones we want to do rather than those we know we should do. To avoid falling into this trap, experiments show that a good way of doing things is to think about the expected benefits of carrying out the various tasks: an increase in profit and a feeling of accomplishment and progress. By imagining the satisfaction you will feel when you have completed the tasks, you reinforce how important they are right now. Future benefits become more tangible, you can feel them, and that reinforces motivation.

Another bias must be controlled when we set about dealing with to do lists: the overconfidence bias. Its effects may lead us to overestimate our ability to work efficiently, which can give rise to a feeling of failure at the end of the day if a significant number of the actions we had planned to do are not completed. And if this is a daily occurrence, the feeling of failure can be transformed into both a feeling of overall incompetence and daily stress. A to-do list should not be as long as possible: it must only include the tasks you really think you are able to do. And your goals must be set with a clear understanding of your abilities; to counter the natural overconfidence that drives us to think we are more productive than we really are. A reasonable to-do list is one that our System 1 will spontaneously appreciate, both in the morning by noting that the objective is achievable and at the end of the day when it has been reached. This will have a two-fold benefit: more energy and motivation at the outset and a boost of pride in our accomplishment and a sense of progress when we're done. Our brain reacts very differently when it performs all seven of the seven tasks we initially planned, rather than when it only achieves seven tasks out of the ten we had set for ourselves.

But to achieve this, the number of tasks is obviously not the only key factor. The expected difficulty and time we need to complete each task must be taken into account as well. And one of the dangers of writing a to-do list is the risk of including overall tasks – for example, a complete project – rather than subdividing them into a series of mini-projects. In the first case, your overall project may stick stubbornly at the top of your to-do list and leave you feeling that you are achieving nothing, because you can't cross it off, despite all the progress you might be making. Here again, System 1 spontaneously perceives a lack of efficiency. If your project is subdivided into various small tasks, the effect is very different, because you will be able to strike off those subtasks more regularly – as and when they are done. And each time you'll be rewarded with a little extra feeling of accomplishment, and a corresponding boost of pride.

A simple and well-written to-do list can clearly identify priority objectives while reinforcing a sense of control, competence and pride in your achievements, and that enhances personal satisfaction.

Maximizing your potential

So now we've got a clear set of daily and overall objectives. They've been carefully selected by focusing on the benefits to be reaped, and intelligently written, taking our talents into account, so that we are motivated from the minute we arrive at work. They've also been designed to send us positive messages throughout the day so that we finish up with a feeling of achievement and satisfaction. But obviously, that's just the starting point for a successful day. While the beginning of the day is more important than we might think, because it creates a positive state of mind that maximizes our chances of achieving our objectives, getting into a task also throws up some very specific traps that we must learn to avoid: the gradual exhaustion of our resources, multitasking, and the effect of distractors.

Managing internal resources

We are not superhumans. We gradually become exhausted when we use up our resources, whether they are energy, attention, determination or our decision-making abilities. And this gradual exhaustion can and must be managed in order to make the most of these limited resources to maximize the quality of our work and our lives.

So where do we start? First we need to acknowledge that not all working hours are equal. There are times when we are firing on all cylinders, and others when everything is a struggle, times when we need to make much more effort only to achieve less than we wanted. As we have seen before with the example of the Israeli judges, the quality of the decisions we make evolves during the day and depends on our energy, as well as our physical and mental resources. For example, I am definitely at my most productive during the first two hours of the morning after I wake up: at that time everything feels easier and I know I'm at my best. On the other hand, unlike friends or colleagues who can be very effective during the evening, that's when I'm at my worst: it takes me a lot of effort and determination to start working or keep on working; I am sluggish and my work is of a lower quality.

In his wonderful book[4] which seeks to shed new light on the secrets of perfect timing, Daniel Pink confirms that there are three main chronotypes: for most of us (60 to 80%), the pace is characterized

....
4   Daniel H. Pink, *When: The Scientific Secrets of Perfect Timing*, Random House Large Prints, 2018.

by a gradual increase in capacity during the morning with a peak in the late morning, a gradual decrease from there to reach our lowest level in the middle of the afternoon, then a gradual but only slight improvement during the late afternoon through to bedtime. Two other chronotypes exist, with individuals whose cycle is shifted towards the earlier morning and others towards the end of the day. And all the many studies cited by Pink demonstrate that our performance is directly affected by our chronotype. He writes: "We are smarter, faster, dimmer, slower, more creative, and less creative in some parts of the day than others."[5] Not only is our performance affected, but it is even more greatly affected than we might think, with a difference of about 20% for cognitive tasks depending on the time of day.

Along with these differences in the quality of our working hours, the difficulty of the tasks we have to perform may also vary. Some are very routine and others much more demanding. If I take my role as a manager, thinking about the structure of the business plan next year for the company (yes, I'm writing this in November and it's time to think about the business plan) is very different to simply answering basic e-mails.

So first we need to identify our chronotype and then organize our working day so as to match the maximum level of performance with the nature of the tasks to be performed. If, like me, you work best in the early morning, schedule the "important and urgent" tasks of your to-do list at that time. You'll maximize your chances of being productive while minimizing your effort and producing quality work. And plan to read your e-mails or go for a walk to meet your colleagues at times when your energy is beginning to ebb.

Eliminate distractors before giving in to them

Let's continue our journey into the world of greater personal efficiency. Our objectives are now clear and we have organized our tasks so that we perform them at suitable times. Now let's get down to the nitty gritty,

5   *Ibid.*

actually doing the tasks. Here again, there are traps to avoid: distractors – minor interruptions from everyday life that as we've already seen, cause us to lose our concentration and stop us from being efficient.

And here the rule is clear – and has been demonstrated by a great deal of research conducted by Professor Walter Mischel[6]: don't trust your determination! It will quickly run out and you will give in to temptation. You'll end up opening the e-mail that has just popped up on your desktop, or you'll read the text message that has just pinged on your cellphone. There is no shortage of studies to prove it: we are helpless in the face of temptation. If we do manage to resist for a certain amount of time, it doesn't last for long, and we give in after a while. If, like me, you are unfortunately (slightly) overweight, you will know that you can refrain from munching on a chocolate bar in your cupboard on several occasions, but you also know that at some point, the temptation will be too strong and you will cave. The only solution is to build an environment that shields you from temptation, so you have no more need for resistance!

Basically this means that you have to temporarily eliminate all potential distractors from your immediate work environment. So first you need to identify them and secondly you need to put them at a psychological and physical distance. We all know what distracts us: our cellphones, with their multitude of temptations and the links they provide with the outside world; computers for the same reasons, especially if they're used to perform your main tasks; desk phones, maybe even your desk itself if it's in a noisy environment; and perhaps colleagues who interrupt you. Depending on different work environments and your own personality, there may also be other potential and more personal distractors.

Eliminating temptation mostly means setting distractors to silent mode. The idea behind distractors is to attract our attention either by their mere presence – for example when I see my phone, all I want to do is check it, to see if I have received a message – or by emitting a sound whose purpose is to distract us from our main task. The first

6   Walter Mischel, *The Marshmallow Test: Understanding self-control and how to master it*, Corgi, September 2015.

way to eliminate temptation is simply to turn off all notifications, both sounds and pop-ups, which might catch your eye: put applications on silent, forward your calls or set your phone to voicemail, and deactivate your internet or telephone connections. However, this way of doing things is not ideal for at least two reasons: even though it might be quick, it's not instant and we know that as soon as we have to make an effort – even a slight effort – there is a psychological price to pay that can stop us from doing what we know we should. In short, the price we pay acts as a micro-barrier, with the consequence of not working as we would like it to: in this case, we don't actually bother to cut the connections with the outside world.

The best way to perform a task effectively and avoid the negative effects of distractors is to design your workplace specifically for that purpose. We will come back to this later when we discuss how to tailor your environment to what we know about behavioral science. But the basic idea is to provide spaces dedicated to the main tasks that employees must perform by designing these spaces in a way that maximizes performance: for individual tasks, employees must be alone and left to focus; for meetings, the rooms need to be designed and equipped to promote discussion and, where appropriate, creativity. In this case, the energy we need to protect ourselves from distractors is minimal: it is only a question of going to the space in question, without taking your smartphone or other potential distractors with you.

Small boosts and effective routines for difficult tasks

The most important tasks are also often those we find most difficult to get started. We know we have to do them, but we tend to lose heart. Procrastination drives us to find plenty of false good reasons to do something else first. To break this mechanism, a ranked to-do list as well as a good sense of timing can be an effective aid, but you can also give yourself an extra boost. All it takes is the first step, a simple task which is easy to perform, and which triggers a more general mechanism leading towards the completion of the task. As far as

I'm concerned, writing my book is a task that is both important and urgent, especially when the deadline for the manuscript is looming, but it's a very difficult task. It's a real challenge to get up and sit in front of my computer to write a few pages every day. One way that helps me is to turn on my computer and open my Word document to start reading what I wrote the day before. I then start correcting my mistakes, edit some sentences and gradually continue my writing. Not having to start writing straight away acts like a decompression chamber, so I don't have to dive right in, which always feels like a challenge, and is a task I often find myself putting off until later. When faced with tasks that seem difficult, you can help yourself by identifying the first step, the one you find easy, but which goes some way to achieving the entire task.

When you have to do an important task, not just a specific project but a daily chore, creating a routine is also a good way to prevent procrastination. Following a routine means that you won't wonder how essential it is to perform the task. To continue with the example of how I have been writing my book, my routine is to work on my writing every morning for two hours as soon as I wake up. I don't have to remember to get down to the task at any other time during the day. I get up, shower, and I do my two hours of writing. Creating a habit means that I can go into "autopilot" mode. I don't need to make decisions every day; I just need to follow my routine.

And Charles Duhigg's excellent book *The Power of Habit*[7] points out that when we establish a routine, the existence of a final reward helps us to stick to the habit. If you want to keep going with something, associate it with a final reward. When the task is over, treat yourself to a break, a coffee, a chat with a colleague, etc. whatever you want, it just has to be something you like that will make the task easier.

....
7   Charles Duhigg, *The Power of Habit: Why We Do What We Do in Life and Business*, Random House Trade Paperbacks, 2014.

One hour of concentration is better than two hours floundering

So now we've made sure the conditions are right for productive work: the aim of the task has been identified, we're mentally available to start work, a small reward awaits and potential distractors have been put to one side. It's time to get going, but also time to watch out again for the overconfidence bias, in terms of our own abilities. Remember, we're not robots with infinite energy. Yet that's how we tend to think of ourselves when we schedule work sessions or meetings that are simply too long. Experiments show that after one or two hours of continuous work, the quality of that work, and especially the quality of our attention and concentration, takes a nosedive. Tests carried out to find what differentiates top performers from ordinary mortals highlight the ability to be truly focused on a task. Anders Ericsson is one of the world's leading performance experts. He has conducted many different studies aimed at identifying and analyzing the specific behavior of those who achieve outstanding performance in very different fields. And his findings are clear: top performers don't work any more than others, but they are totally devoted to the tasks they perform, when they perform them. They are 100% focused, they don't multitask or yield to distractors, and they set a clear goal for each work session. And that intense concentration makes the difference between average and exceptional performance.

To be effective, it is vital to be thoroughly focused on the task in hand, but also to consider your limited abilities. Because we simply can't stay focused for a long period of time. Anders Ericsson's research has also shown that top performers can't maintain this intense level of concentration for longer than two hours, and generally work for periods of time lasting between an hour and 90 minutes. Forcing yourself to keep working for continuous periods longer than two hours makes you considerably less efficient. You gradually lose concentration by being more and more sensitive to distractors.

The remedy is simple but imperative: schedule work sessions on a given task to last no longer than an hour and a half so that you can concentrate intensely and achieve a clear goal.

And, before moving on to another task, take a break to regenerate.

Regular breaks and a short nap for greater productivity

Here again, studies are unanimous. Breaks don't mean less effi-ciency; they are actually an investment for greater productivity over an extended period of time. In line with Anders Ericsson's research, a large-scale project was carried out by DeskTime, which has developed an application to improve employee productivity. The tools developed by DeskTime were used to analyze how a company's top performers organized their working hours, and the results were compared with those of its other employees. The outcome was striking: a company's top performers alternate work cycles lasting an average of fifty-two minutes with breaks lasting seventeen minutes. These breaks help to physically recharge and boost emotional and cognitive resources, resulting in better concentration, improved creativity and enhanced decision-making. These periods of rest are not really designed to give our brains some time out, because they are actually still busy consoli-dating and memorizing the information we have just collected and processed. However, as the brain has already had chance to complete this process, it is then more efficient in performing the next task. By analyzing participants' brains during periods of rest after carrying out specific learning tasks, neuroscientists Saber Sami, Edwin Robertson and Chris Miall[8] demonstrated that the performance of participants who had rested was better than the performance of those who did not receive breaks but had specific brain work to do during these periods of down time. Participants performed better in later tasks after a break, because during rest, the brain develops new connections to enhance the ongoing learning process. When we are resting, our brains are not dormant, they actually go on working to make us more efficient without our having to make a conscious effort.

During breaks, it is best to take a walk, if possible in a garden or park. Again, studies show that proximity to nature has even more

8   Saber Sami, Edwin M. Robertson and Chris Miall, "The Time Course of Task-Specific Memory Consolidation Effects in Resting State Networks", *The Journal of Neuroscience*, vol. 34, No.11, March 2014.

positive effects on future performance. We will come back to this later when we talk about innovation and creativity, but breaks really do enhance our ability to find creative solutions to the problems we have to tackle. In a study carried out by two Stanford researchers whose title says it all: *Give Your Ideas Some Legs: The Positive Effect of Walking on Creative Thinking*[9], the creativity of participants who took a six-minute walk outside the office was 60% greater than that of participants who sat on their chairs during the same rest period. So breaks not only have the mechanical effect of recharging our physical abilities, they also improve the quality of our thought process. So if you can, get back to nature for fifteen minutes.

In addition to breaks, research on performance at work has also highlighted the importance of an afternoon nap. NASA conducted research to evaluate the impact of a twenty-five minute nap on astronauts' performance. And the results are impressive: 35% improvement in judgment by astronauts and a 16% improvement in vigilance. But the nap should not exceed thirty minutes, because experts show that we then fall into a deep sleep and if it is interrupted before its natural end (which is around an hour and a half), our bodies find it difficult to get going again. It's counterproductive: we wake up feeling groggy so it takes some time to return to a normal state and work efficiently.

Alternating intense work cycles and breaks is the key to greater efficiency but also to improved quality of life at work. We should be in control of the work to be done, rather than the work controlling us. And as a result we feel like we're in the driving seat. The quality of both the task in hand and our experience of doing it are improved.

Meditation to improve stress control

Another type of break is also very beneficial: taking time out to meditate every day. All you need to do is sit in a comfortable position, close your eyes, breathe deeply through your nose and focus

---

9   Marily Oppezzo and Daniel L. Schwartz, "Give Your Ideas Some Legs: The Positive Effect of Walking on Creative Thinking", *Journal of Experimental Psychology: Learning, Memory and Cognition*, vol. 40, No.4, April 2014.

on that breath, and whatever sensations you may be experiencing in your body. Studies[10] have shown that regular meditation brings about structural changes in the prefrontal cortex, increasing gray matter and improving your ability to control stress. It's like being a spectator of your own body, reacting less spontaneously and taking control of your emotions. When we get into difficulty, our brain triggers defensive mechanisms that generate stress. Whether it is a memo that we are struggling to put together, a particularly important customer meeting we're planning, or an internal appointment we think will be difficult, we experience a type of stress that, if it overwhelms us, creates a general feeling of discomfort and brings our cognitive abilities crashing down. Meditation helps to control stress by recognizing it, then taking a step back in order to control the situation. Meditation should be part of a daily routine, but is particularly useful during times of intense pressure.

Better quality sleep, and more of it

Breaks and meditation improve the quality of our work because they generate a boost in our resources, which gradually decline as the day goes on. But that brings us to a key point: our ability to rest, and sleep. Again, many studies have shown that the amount and quality of the sleep we get have a massive impact on our performance at work. According to the National Sleep Foundation[11] most of us need seven to nine hours of sleep per night. In reality, most people sleep much less, and it is reaching crisis point. Opinion polls and direct measurements of how many hours we sleep demonstrate this reality. In a Gallup study[12], an incredible 40% of Americans reported sleeping less than seven hours. Jawbone, a fitness tracking app, has also reported a

---

10 Sara W. Lazar, Catherine E. Kerr, Rachel H. Wasserman *et al.*, "Meditation Experience Is Associated With Increased Cortical Thickness", *Neuroreport*, vol. 16, No.17, November 2005.
11 See "How Much Sleep Do We Really Need?", sleepfoundation.org.
12 Jeffrey M. Jones, "In U.S., 40% Get Less Than Recommended Amount of Sleep", 19 December 2013, news.gallup.com.

sleep deficiency issue in many parts of the world: five hours and forty-five minutes in Tokyo, six hours and three minutes in Seoul, six hours and thirteen minutes in Dubai and six hours and thirty-two minutes in Las Vegas.

What's behind this sleep crisis? In her book on the subject, Arianna Huffington suggests, "Today much of our society is still operating under the collective delusion that sleep is simply time lost to other pursuits, that it can be endlessly appropriated at will to satisfy our increasingly busy lives and overstuffed to-do lists."[13] Our insatiable appetite for activity has made sleep a variable we can manipulate to devote our time to more leisure or professional occupations. If we need to stay up late to finish an urgent task, or if we just feel like going out to see friends, we cut back on our sleep time.

The problem is that we seriously underestimate the effects of sleep deprivation on our overall health and performance on subsequent days. In terms of the link between sleep and health, medical experts all agree: a lack of sleep has serious consequences. Dr. Judith Owens, Director of the Center for Pediatric Sleep Disorders at Boston Children's Hospital, believes that "Having proper sleep is quite simply just as important as eating a balanced diet, getting enough exercise and wearing a seatbelt."[14] The consequences are extremely serious, ranging from increased risk of heart disease, depression, a weaker immune system and the associated risk of contracting all kinds of illnesses, and of course accidents of all kinds caused by reduced vigilance, including road accidents. Sleeping less in order to do more is therefore a very bad idea, and we're only barely aware of it. As is often the case, the double influence of the confirmation bias and the overconfidence bias convinces us that all these potential negative consequences apply to other people, but not to us.

Of course, a lack of sleep also has a severe impact on performance at work. Arianna Huffington quotes the staggering figure of $63 billion[15] in terms of cost to the US economy due to lack of sleep,

---

13   Arianna Huffington, *The Sleep Revolution: Transforming Your Life, One Night at A Time*, Harmony, 2016.
14   *Ibid.*
15   *Ibid.*

caused by absenteeism and what it calls "presenteeism" (when an employee is physically present but not able to be mentally effective). Professor Ronald Kessler from Harvard Medical School believes that "Americans are (...) accomplishing less because they're tired. In an information-based economy, it's difficult to find a condition that has a greater effect on productivity."[16]

The negative effects of sleep deprivation on performance can be explained by the fact that sleep is not just rest. Scientific studies run by experts on the matter show that sleep is vital for the brain. Harvard Medical School Professor and Neuropsychiatrist Allan Hobson says in no uncertain terms: "Sleep is of the Brain, by the Brain and for the Brain."[17] It is busy dealing with key functions: regenerating cells and eliminating toxins, as well as memorizing and learning. And, as well as temporary consequences the day after a night of insufficient sleep, the effects can also cause irreversible damage to the brain, as recent studies have shown. The theory that a few long nights of sleep can compensate for a few short sleeps is therefore wrong. A study conducted by the NUS Medical School at Duke University[18] showed a link between brain aging and sleep: the less we sleep, the more quickly our brain ages! A good night's rest is therefore essential to our overall health, and our performance at work in particular.

Beyond the statistics that recommend humans sleep for an average period between seven and nine hours, it is important to pinpoint your own personal needs, and that's certainly not difficult. All you need to do is to pay attention to two elements for a two-week period: in the late evening, note down what time you start yawning. In the morning, note down what time you wake up naturally. You can also identify the times you feel sleepy during the day. The purpose of this exercise is to find out the duration of your rest cycle. It is usually somewhere around 90 minutes, but varies from person to person. For a good sleep, you need

....

16 aasm.org/insomnia-costing-u-s-workforce-63-2-billion-a-year-in-lost-productivity-study-shows/
17 J. Allan Hobson, "Sleep Is of the Brain, by the Brain and for the Brain", *Nature*, vol. 437, No.7063, October 2005.
18 June C. Lo, Kep Kee Loh, Hui Zheng *et al.*, "Sleep Duration and Age-Related Changes in Brain Structure and Cognitive Performance", *Sleep*, vol. 37, No.7, July 2014.

to go to bed at the beginning of a cycle, and get up at the end of a cycle. For instance, if your cycle is one and a half hours and you first noticed you were yawning at 10:30 pm and then again at midnight, you have two options: you need to sleep for five cycles (seven and a half hours), so either you go to bed at 10:30 pm and get up at 6 am, or you go to bed at midnight and wake up at 7:30 am. There are two benefits to this process: you will fall asleep easily because you are consistent with your natural cycle, and you will wake up fresh and feeling good, because you won't be in the middle of a cycle.

And if you want to get more sleep, just go to bed a little earlier. Like any change, it isn't easy and it does take long-term effort. Start small, Arianna Huffington suggests. Begin in ten-minute increments following a routine that suits you, before you reach at least the essential seven hours. To get motivated in the evening, consider the benefit of a good night's sleep and waking up fresh. And gradually train yourself to respect your natural sleep cycle.

Breaks during the day – and a brief restorative nap – are important as well, but the ability to sleep for at least seven hours is an essential asset for your performance at work.

While effectiveness depends on how you organize your daily life – from defining your priorities to the quality of your sleep – it also depends on something subtler: a specific state of mind.

Thinking positive: when happy means effective

We look at the world around us through our own eyes at all times. There is not one single reality, only our perception. We build and interpret the world in a unique way, based on our own perceptions. And these have a huge impact on how we behave.

We have seen that it is the role of our System 1 to interpret the world at all times to make sense of it, using the immediate clues it finds in the environment as well as past experiences. As Daniel Kahneman has observed, without any specific effort on our part, System 1 will guide our decisions and our behaviors. But we can also influence our state of mind, to become both happier and more effective. This groundbreaking discovery was made by experts of what is now known as positive psychology. We can take action to put a "positive spin" on how we perceive the world. As noted by one of the world's leading specialists – Professor Barbara L. Fredrickson from the University of North Carolina at Chapel Hill – in her book *Positivity,* "The new scientific discoveries about the importance of positivity are stunning. Your mild and fleeting pleasant states are far more potent than you think. We know now that they alter your mind and body in ways that can literally help you create your best life."[19]

So let's now take a proper look at this concept of positivity, to understand what it covers, how it can lead to a better life at work, and a better life generally, and how we can all learn to be proactively positive.

Experiments carried out by researchers in positive psychology, including those conducted by Barbara Fredrickson, have identified ten forms of positivity: joy, gratitude, serenity, interest, hope, pride, fun, inspiration, reverence, and love.

We're all familiar with the feelings that these emotions trigger. But what we need to understand is that they don't wholly depend on what is happening around us. We can use our own willpower to maximize our chances of feeling these emotions. Our circumstances are not the only factors that shape our moods. They can also depend on our determination. At any time, we can decide to "think positive" and choose to see the world around us in a positive light. When we have an upbeat attitude, not only does it enrich our lives, but it also makes us more open, more creative, and generally more efficient. And the science is there to back it up!

In a study by Barbara Fredrickson and Christine Branigan[20], researchers found that ideas came less freely when participants experienced fear or anger, compared to when they were relaxed and calm. After bringing about positive or negative emotions in each group of participants by having them watch various films, they were asked to write

---

19 Barbara L. Fredrickson, *Positivity – Top-Notch Research Reveals the 3 to 1 Ratio That Will Change Your Life*, Three Rivers Press, 2009.

20 Barbara L. Fredrickson and Christine Branigan, "Positive Emotions Broaden the Scope of Attention and Thought-Action Repertories", *Cognition and Emotion*, vol. 19, No.3, May 2005.

a list of things they wanted to achieve after the experiment. The list was significantly longer for participants who had experienced positive emotions. Another experiment generated some entertaining and surprising results. As in the previous study, participants were split into two groups and shown three geometric shapes. These shapes could be perceived in two different ways: either they were identified as three different shapes that could be put together to make up another shape, or they could be perceived as three individual shapes, with no larger shape. When participants had just experienced positive emotions, more of them identified the larger shape. This supported Fredrickson's previous hypothesis that "positive emotions –by broadening people's mindsets and building their enduring resources– can alleviate human languishing and see human flourishing."[21]

A study by researchers at Brandeis University[22] shows that this capacity for attention that is enhanced by a positive state of mind has a physiological explanation. The study used the eye-tracking technique, which involves following where the eyes move and what captures the gaze. We may believe that our eyes are relatively still, but in fact they are in constant motion. The mechanism is activated at a very early stage of the perception process, so we are unaware of it. During the experiment, two groups of participants were asked to look at three images: the first group had previously been subjected to negative stimuli and the second to positive stimuli. For the second group, eye-tracking analysis revealed that participants' eyes were wider, and more attention was being paid to peripheral areas. A positive state of mind changes how we perceive our environment. And that changes how we behave, including at work.

Many other experiments have shown the same thing. A study carried out in the medical field[23] by researchers at Cornell University

....

21 Barba L. Fredrickson, "The broaden-and-build theory of positive emotions", *The Royal Society Publishing*, vol. 359, No 1449, September 2004.

22 Heather A. Waldinger and Derek M. Isaacowitz, "Positive Mood Broadens Visual Attention to Positive Stimuli", *Motivation and Emotion*, vol. 30, No.1, March 2006.

23 Alice M. Isen, Andrew S. Rosenzweig and Mark J. Young, "The Influence of Positive Affect on Clinical Problem Solving", *Medical Decision Making*, vol. 11, No.3, July-September 1991.

showed that physicians who received a small gift (a bag of candy) before making a diagnosis related to liver disease were more thorough and more careful in how they entered their patients' information. Another study, led by researchers at the University of Berkeley, gave the same type of result, but was based on the behavior of managers. The results of this study were that those with the highest level of positivity are also those who make the most appropriate decisions and are the most effective in their interpersonal relationships at work. This last point is very important: not only does positivity enhance our individual capacity making us more open-minded and creative, it also generates greater empathy towards others. So we're better at negotiating, bringing others into a project and building strong relationships. Barbara Fredrickson concludes: "As positivity broadens your mind, it shifts your core view of people and relationships, bringing them closer to your center, to your heart."[24]

If positivity is as beneficial personally as it is professionally, how can we develop it on a daily basis? Scientific studies show that not only is it possible, but that there is a process by which it can be achieved, as long as people keep in mind that the rules are different for each individual.

First, you need to assess your basic level of positivity. This can obviously change from day to day depending on what happens to you, but we all have a more or less positive personality. Barbara Fredrickson has designed an open access questionnaire that allows you to assess yourself, and you can find it at www.positivityratio.com. This will give you an objective starting point.

The next step is realizing that there are attitudes and behaviors you can adopt or strive towards in your daily life, based on the essential objective of being more open-minded. From this basic orientation you can build and develop positivity: be open to your senses, be open to others – their questions, problems, and ideas – in order to be open to the opportunities that life can offer. Open-mindedness is a constant challenge because we have convictions, beliefs, goals

----

24 Barbara L. Fredrickson, *Positivity – Top-Notch Research Reveals the Upward Spiral That Will Change Your Life, op. cit.*

to achieve, problems to solve, and cognitive biases that tend to draw our focus back to ourselves. In *Twilight of the Idols*, Nietzsche writes: "Convictions are prisons." And we have plenty of convictions that keep us shackled. Striving for more openness is a constant challenge, but a catalyst for greater positivity.

Research into positive psychology shows that the following two behaviors reinforce positivity:

- Create high quality connections with other people;
- Be kind.

Opportunities for high quality connections

Jane Dutton is a professor at the University of Michigan and co-founder of the Center for Positive Organizational Scholarship. She is one of the world's leading experts on research into interpersonal relationships. We have already discussed her work – especially her views on "high quality connections" – in the chapter on belonging to a community. But effective connections are also the basis for positivity. An ability to build positive connections with others strengthens our personal well-being, other people's well-being, *and* our cognitive performance. And building high quality connections is not a question of hours, days or years, but state of mind. Jane Dutton highlights the importance of four main behaviors[25] in our relationships with other people if we want to create these opportunities. The first behavior is genuine engagement in our interactions. Making the other person feel that we are really with them. Really listening. And we all know that it's possible to talk to someone or be with someone without really being there. Listening can be superficial, we think of something else that matters to us more; and it shows. There are lots of signs that reveal this lack of interest. We might glance at our smartphone while we are listening, or just ask mundane questions or ones that only need an automatic

....
25   Jane E. Dutton, "Build High-Quality Connections", in Jane E. Dutton and Gretchen M. Spreitzer (dir.), *How to Be a Positive Leader: Small Actions, Big Impact*, Berrett-Koehler Publishers, 2014.

answer. There is more than one way to ask "How are you?" The tone, look, and posture of the person asking you the question implicitly reveals the type of answer they expect. In the vast majority of cases, all we're looking for is "Fine, you?" But not a full answer to that question. Sometimes, the way we express the same question can show that we expect a full answer, that we are interested. We can let the other person know we have time for a real conversation by asking questions that lead to those genuine answers. It is an active presence, empathy, underscored with a real physical and psychological commitment that demonstrates to the other person that we care and respect them. This behavior brings about a high quality connection. It changes everything. And studies show that both of the people involved benefit from these connections.

The second behavior that brings about high quality connections involves helping other people to succeed. We'll come back later to what companies and managers can do to help their employees succeed. But now we're looking at supporting your peers on a daily basis, and finding ways to acknowledge how your colleagues support you. Of course, everyone has their own roles and tasks, but here we're talking about informal support that can be expressed by giving a word of encouragement, a brief chat to let someone vent and release their stress, or even lending a hand to find a solution. It's about providing emotional support by expressing empathy or feedback about what they are going through. Again, this type of behavior makes the person who benefits from it feel that someone cares. And often that's all they need. In turn, the person providing the support also feels good, and experiences the benefits of positivity.

The third behavior that helps to build high quality connections is the trust we have in each other. Because in the workplace giving your trust is neither easy nor without risk. Most of the time, trusting someone also means putting yourself in a vulnerable position of risk. It means believing what you are told without the need for proof, without the need to control or verify what has been done or said. Our default setting is to trust. And by putting ourselves in danger this way, we show the other person that we respect them, and that they are valued, so these strong connections are formed.

Finally, the fourth behavior that helps us create these connections involves playing together and having fun! Yes, it can be done in the workplace, and in addition to specific team building exercises there are plenty of opportunities to have fun with colleagues, from going out for drinks to more organized activities. But the more a company encourages this behavior, the more opportunities there are for intense connections between employees, and this benefits everyone, as well as the company itself.

And that brings us naturally to another fundamental behavior that creates positivity: kindness.

Be kind, it'll make *you* happy and boost *your* business!

The word kindness may seem slightly out of place in a professional setting. At the very least, it may be considered inappropriate to talk about kindness in an environment where the watchwords are competitiveness, performance, efficiency and productivity. At worst, you could even say that it's a waste of time, or that kindness is naive or weak, and goes against a company's drive for constant efficiency. People may think kindness encourages unreliable emotions where rigor and rationality should reign supreme. Well, science actually proves that the opposite is true. Kindness – which of course has nothing to do with weakness or low standards – is a quality, and also applies to the work environment. An international leader in happiness research, Professor Martin Seligman, believes that "Doing an act of kindness produces the single most reliable momentary increase in well-being of any exercise we have tested."[26] And neuro-scientists confirm the impact of kindness[27]. When we show kind-ness, the same parts of the brain are activated as when we receive

....
26 Martin Seligman, *Flourish*, op. cit.
27 Jorge Moll, Frank Krueger, Roland Zahn *et al.*, "Human Fronto-Mesolimbic Networks Guide Decisions About Charitable Donation", *Proceedings of the National Academy of Sciences USA*, vol. 103, No.42, October 2006.

kindness. Being kind – from the brain's standpoint – feels as good as receiving kindness.

Being kind in a work environment helps to build a sense of belonging and strengthens solidarity among employees. Kindness breeds kindness, so if someone is kind to you, they create a social debt. You "owe" them kindness, which brings about a sort of positive contamination throughout the company.

Sonja Lyubomirsky – author of *The How of Happiness*[28] – recommends doing five acts of kindness every day. But even without going after a set number of goals, it is possible to live your life in this way every day. Being kind in the workplace is not only possible but preferable. And beneficial for your personal well-being, the overall performance of your company, AND your career!

That's what Professor Adam Grant of Wharton University demonstrates in his wonderful book *Give and Take*[29] In companies, individuals can be classified, depending on their behavior, into three different groups that the author calls the "takers", the "matchers" and the "givers". "Takers" seek to get as much as they can out of their relationships with others; "matchers" strive for a balance of give and take, while "givers" help others without expecting anything in return. And these behaviors have a huge impact on people's individual success. Studies led by Adam Grant show that while some "givers" are exploited by their colleagues, the greatest leaders with the most glittering careers come from this category. Because giving appears as a sort of investment in relationships, to create an outstanding network of supporters who, when the time comes, will be there for you and help you.

Kindness isn't just a good deed, it's also a way to boost your chances of a good career, and we can all decide to be kind just as we can all decide to be something else that is essential: motivated.

----

28 Sonja Lyubomirsky, *The How of Happiness: A Scientific Approach to Getting the Life You Want*, Penguin Books, 2008.

29 Adam M. Grant, *Give and Take: Why Helping Others Drives Our Success*, W&N, 2014.

Motivation is also a choice

It's generally accepted that our motivation at work stems from the intrinsic interest of the task in hand and derives from what is happening within the company. But studies show that this is only partly true. We have an important role to play in our own motivation. It's not just something that comes to us; we can also help to generate it. Charles Duhigg writes: "Motivation is more like a skill, akin to reading or writing, that can be learned and honed. Scientists have found that people can get better at self-motivation if they practice the right way."[30] And of course, being more motivated by our day-to-day tasks makes us perform them better and boosts our well-being.

So what can we actually do to get ourselves motivated? There are two main ways: the first involves the meaning of our work, and the second our ability to feel in control of it.

First of all, the meaning we give to our work doesn't derive from what the work actually is, but from how we look at it. Studies show that regardless of the occupation, individuals may feel motivated if they believe their work is useful to society. John Coleman – one of the authors of *Passion & Purpose*[31] – explains that "You don't find your purpose, you build it." But how? By focusing on what our work might mean to someone else. When we realize how much what we do can benefit other people, we can start building the meaning we are looking for. A study led by Adam Grant[32] shows that a direct connection with a person who will benefit from our work is a very effective way to find meaning in our tasks. In his experiment, when fundraisers from a university call center had been introduced to a student whose education was funded by the money raised by the call center's work, the fundraisers were much more efficient than their colleagues who

30 Charles Duhigg, *Smarter, Faster, Better: The Transformative Power of Real Productivity*, Random House, 2016.
31 John Coleman, Daniel Gulati and W. Oliver Segovia, *Passion & Purpose: Stories from the Best and Brightest Young Business Leaders*, Harvard Business Review Press, 2011.
32 Adam Grant, Elizabeth M. Campbell, Grace Chen *et al.*, "Impact and the Art of Motivation Maintenance: The Effects of Contact With Beneficiaries on Persistence Behavior", *Organizational Behavior and Human Decision Processes*, vol. 103, No.1, May 2007.

had not met the student. So we can proactively seek out usefulness, rather than waiting for that interest to come to us, which is the general belief, as Yale University Professor Amy Wrzesniewski so aptly puts it: "Students think their calling is under a rock, and if they turn over enough rocks, they will find it."[33] If it helps, we can also take our company's mission statement into account to further strengthen the meaning we find in our daily tasks.

The second key to self-motivation is having a feeling of control over what we do. Many studies, including an interesting one by Professor Mauricio Delgado of Rutgers University, demonstrate that a feeling of being in control and having the power to decide are two ways to find well-being and satisfaction. And we can do something about that, because it doesn't only apply to high-stake decisions. In fact the simple process of making a decision, even a minor one, is enough to generate a feeling of being in control. So we can purposefully become more aware of the decisions we make, and value them. We can also search actively for a connection between what we have just learned, how useful we might be to others and how that might relate to a bigger project.

You can also try to redesign and tailor what you actually do, with a view to becoming more productive and having a better time at work. Morten Hansen's study showed that top performers aren't those who work the most, but those who are constantly trying to improve the way they do their job by troubleshooting, not just to benefit themselves, but to benefit other people too. These top performers are constantly optimizing, and are not victims of their automatic routines or the status quo bias. And Hansen offers these words of wisdom: "Don't just see yourself as an employee – see yourself as an innovator of work. Hunt and cure pain points, ask stupid questions, and zoom in on how you can redesign and create value for others."[34]

....

33 Quoted in Emily Esfahani Smith, "How to Find Meaning in a Job That's Not Your True Calling", *Harvard Business Review*, August 3, 2017, hbr.org.
34 Morten T. Hansen, *Great at Work*, op. cit.

So we can be instrumental in getting – and staying – motivated, as well as being productive, without sitting around waiting for someone else to do it for us!

So there you have it. You're now ready to work efficiently for your own personal benefit, the benefit of your colleagues and the benefit of your company. You've found out how you need to organize your time so that you can focus on real priorities, allocate resources and attention, avoid the pitfalls of distraction and keep going all day long, to be more efficient, for longer. You've also learned how to keep your mind focused on looking at events and other people in a positive light, which keep your energy, well-being and performance levels high. In short, you are in a position to perform your best work, feel in control, and enjoy it!

However, while the ability to be personally effective is a major advantage for individuals and businesses, it still depends on their physical and psychological environment.

Let's now look at the fundamental theme of the working environment, and ask ourselves an essential question: how can we create and encourage a workplace setting that brings out the best in employees by supporting them and encouraging them to behave positively as a group to benefit the company?

Chapter 5

First key incentive: a workplace geared towards well-being

We know from behavioral science that we are contextual beings: our decisions and our behaviors are very strongly influenced by our environment. And it's often our environment that wins when our personal intentions clash with the structural ecosystem around us.

Many recent studies have revealed a set of surprising influences showing that everything matters: ceiling height, desk color, ambient sounds, a visual proximity to nature, etc. and we're often unaware of any of it. Without knowing how much these factors count, it's difficult to anticipate them, and so it's hard to design an environment that triggers the behaviors we want to encourage and the well-being we'd like to incite. One of the world's top experts on how our environment influences our behavior demonstrates this particularly well: Paul Dolan, Professor of Behavioral Economics at the London School of Economics, and former colleague of Daniel Kahneman, winner of the Nobel Prize in Economic Sciences in 2002, assisted by Chloe Foy, devised an acronym to summarize research in this area: SALIENT[1] *"Sound"*; *"Air"*; *"Light"*; *"Image"*; *"Ergonomics"*; *"Nature"*; *"Tint"*.

Each of these characteristics has a proven and sometimes unexpected influence on how we perceive the world around us and behave within it. Let's explore the effects of the physical environment on our well-being, our perceptions, and our daily individual and collective decisions and practices.

....
1   Paul Dolan, Chloé Foy and Sophie Smith, "The Salient Checklist: Gathering Up the Ways in Which Built Environnments Affect What We Do and How We Feel", *Buildings*, vol. 6, No.9, May 2016.

Color me happy: how external factors influence how we think and behave

Suitable sounds: calm yet stimulating

Let's start with the letter "s" as in "sound". Nobody would argue the point that a noisy environment stops you from concentrating well: it's an attention distractor that reduces efficiency. Many studies have shown how noise brings about fatigue or loss of concentration. And that's what is often criticized about open spaces at work where individual concentration can be a real challenge. So interior designers try to create quiet environments using partitions or specific furniture. But as is often the case with human behavior, the reality of how sound influences what we do is somewhat more complex.

For example, a study carried out in 2012[2] by a team of American and Canadian researchers demonstrated that a moderate level of noise (70 decibels) is better for creativity than a lower level (50 decibels) or a higher level (85 decibels). As expected, the moderate noise slightly distracted participants but encouraged them to process the information in a more abstract way and led to a boost in their creativity. Too much noise kills creativity, but a lack of noise is just as bad. As often applies to environmental issues, the fundamental point is to start from the main tasks that have to be performed in a specific space, and to design the space according to what else needs to be encouraged. For creativity, a total absence of noise is undesirable, while the same level of noise can be a hindrance for someone working on a complex individual task. There's no such thing as the perfect space, but specific environments can be tailored to suit different purposes.

And not all noise is created equally. Different noise has different effects. If a noise is surprising and unusual, it can create a sudden loss of concentration, while a moderate but constant hum in the background is much less harmful.

....
2   Ravi Mehta, Rui (Juliet) Zhu and Amar Cheema, "Is Noise Always Bad? Exploring the Effects of Ambient Noise on Creative Cognition", *Journal of Consumer Research*, vol. 39, No.4, December 2012.

In addition to whether or not we expect to hear a certain noise, the type of sound we hear can also be disruptive or beneficial. For example, the music that is played in a space can have very powerful effects, especially on emotions. A study by Stefan Koelsch[3] shows that the music we listen to has a powerful effect on our state of mind. So it can be used in specific spaces – such as in the context of certain therapies – to encourage rest or meditation, and bring about a sense of calm.

Lastly, the sound environment must generally be of moderate volume to allow the concentration required to perform complex tasks, and reduce possible distractions, but most importantly it must be tailored to the activities being undertaken.

Fresh air and the right temperature

Air – in its broadest sense, i.e. its source, temperature and possible odors – also plays an important and often unconscious role. The main conclusions of studies carried out on this issue show first of all how good ventilation is very important: an investigation carried out in 2000[4] proves that effective ventilation in an office generates many benefits both in terms of perceived well-being – a better perception of air freshness, less dryness of the lips and throat – and efficiency at work through a greater ability to think clearly, and a measured increase in productivity.

Temperature is also an important variable that has an impact on employee well-being and productivity. An experiment[5] by a team of researchers testing the effect of three temperature levels (63°F, 70°F and 82°F) showed that the two extremes generated not only less well-being but also a dip in motivation and a greater difficulty in maintaining

3   Stefan Koelsch, "Towards a Neural Basis of Music-Evoked Emotions", *Trends in Cognitive Sciences*, vol. 14, No.3, March 2010.

4   Pawel Wargocki, David P. Wyon, Jan Sundell *et al.*, "The Effects of Outdoor Air Supply in an Office on Perceived Air Quality, Sick Building Syndrome (SBS) Symptoms and Productivity", *Indoor Air*, vol. 10, No.4, December 2000.

5   Li Lan, Zhiwei Lian and Li Pan, "The Effects of Air Temperature on Office Workers' Well-Being, Workload and Productivity-Evaluated with Subjective Ratings", *Applied Ergonomics*, vol. 42, No.1, December 2010.

participants' efforts to complete everyday tasks. These effects are not only psychological, since the study also revealed that the lowest and highest temperatures brought about physiological changes as well. It's no great surprise, but confirms that temperature affects our well-being and productivity. However, it's interesting to note that this drop in productivity, observed in many of the studies, can be explained not only by personal discomfort, but also by changes in collective behavior, in particular by less cooperation between people working in the same office.

Temperature is important, and a setting of around 70°F would appear to be optimum.

Dominant natural light, with tailored artificial lights

There is also no shortage of studies on how light impacts perceptions and behaviors at work, and two key factors are important: the source of the light, and how intense it is. Natural light appears to be better than artificial light. A study carried out by Antal Haans[6] from the University of Eindhoven shows that this preference is linked to beliefs about the positive effects of natural light on health and concentration. But in addition to these beliefs, experts think that exposure to natural light has an impact on how our bodies work, which includes serotonin and melatonin secretion, and also determines sleep quality. A 2013 study[7] showed that employees working in an office with a window slept an average of forty-six minutes more per night than those whose offices had no windows. And productivity is also affected. Another study, carried out at a telephone call center, showed that when employees worked near a window, their productivity was higher by an estimated $3,000 per year. So exposure to natural light is beneficial.

In terms of electric light intensity, behaviors differ; low intensity boosts creativity while greater intensity improves alertness, increases

6   Antal Haans, "The Natural Preference in People's Appraisal of Light", *Journal of Environmental Psychology*, vol. 39, September 2014.

7   Amanda L. Chan, "Windows in the Workplace Linked with Better Sleep", *The Huffington Post*, 6 December 2013, huffingtonpost.com.

concentration and ultimately, perceived employee well-being[8]. Here again, workplace light intensity should be adapted to the purpose of each space.

The benefit of a connection with nature

Before talking about the role of the images, which comes next in Paul Dolan's acronym, I would like to jump directly to the letter N of "Nature", which links up to what we have just learned about how natural light and proximity to a window can increase well-being and efficiency.

Because it's all part of a much broader and fundamental process: many studies show that elements from nature can bring about improved perceived well-being, as well as a decline in the number of work-related problems. A study carried out in 2012[9] demonstrates that an extended period spent surrounded by nature enhances a group's creative abilities by more than 50%. That's not just a slight improvement, it's a real creativity boost, and helps to improve mental availability: because our mind is no longer occupied or solicited by the countless distractions presented by our excessively technological environment.

But significant positive effects can also be achieved without having to move your desk to the middle of a forest. Adding a plant to your office can be a step in the right direction. A 2011 study showed that employees randomly assigned to offices containing indoor plants, compared to other colleagues in offices without plants, performed significantly better on tasks requiring concentration and sustained attention, and experienced a reduced level of perceived stress. First of all, plants have a beneficial effect on air quality inside offices. A study

8   Karine C. H. J. Smolders and Yvonne A. W. de Kort, "Bright Light and Mental Fatigue: Effects on Alertness, Vitality, Performance and Psychological Arousal", *Journal of Environmental Psychology*, vol. 39, September 2014.

9   Ruth Ann Atchley, David L. Strayer and Paul Atchley, "Creativity in the Wild: Improving Creative Reasoning through Immersion in Natural Settings", *PLoS One*, vol. 7, No.12, December 2012.

by researchers at the University of Technology, Sydney[10] established that there is a 75% reduction in indoor pollutants when plants are present, with a similar effect in an air-conditioned environment, depending on light intensity. So plants do have a physiological benefit as well.

But plants also have a beneficial psychological effect on individuals' own perceived well-being. Another study[11] confirms that there is a specific regenerating effect when people are in contact with nature, rather than in conventional urban environments. Nature replenishes our energy and restores our mental faculties. Employees surrounded by nature observe that their health is better – they experience less stress, fatigue, colds or headaches – and that their energy is enhanced by the presence of plants. But plants aren't the only things that can bring these benefits; plenty of other things can remind us of nature. A fun experiment[12] showed that when people are near an aquarium they feel more relaxed and more open to interacting with their colleagues. Other studies show that the mere presence of posters featuring scenes from nature also has a positive effect.

All told, being in natural surroundings has major benefits for both the well-being and psychological health of employees, and has a positive knock-on effect on productivity.

Images that tell a story, or how to send out the right message at the right time

Picking up Paul Dolan's acronym again, we now come to the letter I for "Image", but I'd actually like to expand the theme to how our indoor work environments are designed. Because while images are important, and do have a role to play in our perceptions and behaviors, the

....

10 Jane Tarran, Fraser Torpy and Margaret Burchett, "Use of Living Pot-Plants to Cleanse Indoor Air: Research Review", *Proceedings of Sixth International Conference on Indoor Air Quality, Ventilation and Energy. Conservation in Buildings – Sustainable Built Environment*, October 28-31, 2007, Sendai, Japan, vol. III.

11 Marc G. Berman, John Jonides and Stephen Kaplan, "The Cognitive Benefits of Interacting With Nature", *Psychological Science*, vol. 19, No.12, December 2008.

12 Mary M. DeSchriver and Carol Cutler Riddick, "Effects of Watching Aquariums on Elders' Stress", *Anthrozoös*, vol. 4, No.1, January 1990.

overall design of the spaces where we work should also be taken into consideration. Regarding the notion of image, studies come to two fairly intuitive conclusions: first, images can have a beneficial role on perceived employee well-being, especially if they depict scenes from nature. So adding images to a work environment can be a potential asset. Paul Dolan himself demonstrated in a study[13] with Robert Metcalfe that artistic visuals in creative environments reinforce participants' perceived well-being.

Second: there needs to be a balance in the number of images and visuals that are used in the work environment. Choosing not to display images of nature (paintings, posters, photos, etc.) means depriving yourself of a tool that can promote action and communication and have a huge impact both on perceived well-being and on encouraging specific behaviors. But put up too many images and there can be a negative effect on how well tasks are performed, because there is too much distraction. So it's important to strike the right balance, using visuals sparingly to boost well-being but avoiding distractions, and selecting images that are appropriate to the tasks being performed in each area. Visuals and images can be provided by the company, but why not ask the employees themselves to provide visuals too? A wall could be set aside for staff members to post photos of themselves at private events or group activities. It could be a fun and inspiring way of personalizing your workspaces.

But in addition to the emotional well-being they can provide, visuals within companies can be used more directly to communicate specific messages. And as well as visuals, words.

More and more businesses are now using walls, especially in common spaces, to post keywords that reflect their values, or the behaviors they want to encourage. Rooms can also be named proactively. Rather than giving them impersonal names such as 1, 2 or 3, a branding strategy could be implemented to spark creativity. For instance at BVA we give rooms used for creative meetings names such as "Ideas" or "Andy Warhol". Many experiments show that small

....
13   Paul Dolan and Robert Metcalfe, "The Relationship Between Innovation and Subjective Wellbeing", *Research Policy*, vol. 41, No.8, October 2012.

triggers of this type unconsciously get participants into the right state of mind and encourage positive behaviors.

Many different types of spaces have huge potential for effective communication with employees. Most companies look no further than "official" bulletin boards. But many other places can also be used, for example the staff washrooms. At Google, press articles are made available in the bathrooms so that employees can read them at a time when their attention is not required elsewhere. The backs of stall doors can also be a great place to capture employees' interest. It's a very "Nudge" way to communicate: clearly, easily, and at the right moment, when people's attention is potentially available.

Corridors and common spaces, such as coffee machines or dining rooms, also have great potential for sharing information – and as always, keeping in mind that information only ever reaches its target when that target wants to receive it. The nature of the information must therefore be tailored to the mindset of employees when they are in that space, and presented in a way that suits both the setting and your target's state of mind. It's not advisable to share the same amount of information in the same style in a corridor, lift and toilet stall. The time people spend in each of these spaces is different, and the strength of your message ultimately depends on your ability to take these factors into account.

Ergonomics: from practical to influential

For decades, occupational ergonomists have highlighted the importance of good workstation ergonomics to ensure that employees are kept effective and healthy. The set of interfaces employees use to do their jobs plays a fundamental role in their health, well-being, and efficiency. But this is already common knowledge, and is put to use by most companies.

However, other mechanisms such as the choice of office furniture and how it is arranged often have unknown and badly neglected effects. Furniture plays a role both in terms of a perceived image, but also more surprisingly – and unconsciously – behavior. A study by researchers at Yale, Harvard and MIT[14] showed that seat comfort has an influence on behavior during negotiations: people sitting on hard wooden chairs are less inclined to compromise than people nestled in armchairs with plump cushions. Another study carried out by professors Rui Zhu and Jennifer Argo[15] highlighted that when chairs are arranged in a circle rather than in an angular shape, it reinforces the feeling of belonging to a group and people are more open to new ideas. This is well known to organizers of qualitative studies and creative sessions. Ultimately, there is no good or bad office furniture, only furniture that is more or less consistent with the attitudes and behaviors we would like to encourage.

Research on the general theme of interior design however does have something important to teach: while the various themes that we have discussed so far can be applied to many different disciplines, the same is not true of interior design. English researchers have concluded that: "People's emotional responses seem to vary depending on their generation, social group, nationality and culture."[16]

What's important here is to avoid applying irrelevant information, and to keep in mind that interior design has an important role to play when attempting to take employees' aspirations into account.

Colors that suit the space

Behavioral science has demonstrated that color plays an important role in individual mindsets. As our brains are constantly looking out for risks and opportunities, we process all the stimuli we encounter. We see the signs and adopt a posture that is either defensive or receptive. And from this point of view, our brains are particularly adept at processing colors. "Color" information, unlike words and sentences,

....

14 Joshua M. Ackerman, Christopher C. Nocera and John A. Bargh, "Incidental Haptic Sensations Influence Social Judgments and Decisions", *Science*, vol. 328, No.5986, June 2010.

15 Rui (Juliet) Zhu and Jennifer J. Argo, "Exploring the Impact of Various Shaped Seating Arrangements on Persuasion", *Journal of Consumer Research*, vol. 40, No.2, August 2013.

16 Oya Demirbilek and Bahar Sener, "Product Design, Semantics and Emotional Response", *Ergonomics*, vol. 46, No.13-14, October 2003.

requires no specific attention for it to be understood. As such, colors are often used in companies to convey instant messages. Red is often associated with danger or energy. Black in some societies may be a symbol of death.

As it is processed very quickly and used to convey messages, there is huge potential for color to be used to influence our immediate perceptions and behaviors, including in the work environment. For example, studies have highlighted the particular effects of red and blue. An experiment showed that participants took red to be a warning sign, and were more likely to show caution, fearing that a task would fail. Red triggers greater vigilance and an enhanced state of alertness. Another study[17] revealed that individuals performing tasks requiring attention to detail did better when exposed to red before they started. On the other hand, being exposed to blue enhances creative performance in tasks requiring imagination.

Here again, color can be used intentionally depending on the behavior the company wishes to encourage and the tasks to be performed in specific spaces.

The key takeaway is clear: all the elements combined in the acronym SALIENT are subtle influences that can be used to design a physical work environment that can in turn encourage and facilitate the desired behaviors, for greater efficiency and well-being. They aren't mere details, but elements that really do impact overall performance.

We've now come to a central theme: how to organize your space.

Organizing space: how to achieve the winning combination of flexibility, cooperation and personalization

Separate offices, open spaces, shared offices or working from home: what have scientific studies shown about the influence these configurations have on perceptions and behavior? And there's a

---

17   Ravi Mehta and Rui (Juliet) Zhu, "Blue or Red? Exploring the Effect of Color on Cognitive Task Performances", *Science*, vol. 323, No.5918, February 2009.

fundamental question behind this specific question: from a behavioral science point of view – what is an ideal working environment?

Over the last few decades, they have evolved from closed offices to open spaces, which are now the norm. Lauded for allowing better communication between individuals compared to the isolation of closed offices, the open space concept has enjoyed huge popularity because of its low cost and greater flexibility when shake-ups happen. Less space is needed per person, and building, maintenance, and re-organization costs are much lower. For example, in the United Kingdom, the average area allocated to an employee dropped from 179 sq. ft. in 1997 to 127 sq. ft. in 2009 (British Council for Offices).

Countless studies have been carried out all around the world to assess the effects of open-space working.[18] There are a number of concerns, and obviously these depend on how the open spaces themselves are designed. We have already seen the distraction and concentration challenges presented by a noisy environment. These distractions are provoked not only by background noise, but by interactions with colleagues, which can be too frequent or unsolicited. They result in both a loss of productivity in the tasks performed and greater fatigue due to the additional effort spent on trying to focus in an atmosphere that isn't conducive to effective work. The drop in productivity is even more striking when there are more people occupying the open space, and when these negative effects aren't mitigated with soundproofing furniture.

The lack of privacy is also an inherent difficulty in an open space, compared to separate offices. Plenty of studies have shown that this point is a key factor in employees not being satisfied with open spaces, particularly because they do not allow private conversations or confidential business discussions. Jacqueline Vischer – founder of the research group on work environments and professor at the University of Montreal – writes: " One of the most consistent findings from user surveys is that office workers are dissatisfied with the 'open plan'

---

18   Matthew C. Davis, Desmond J. Leach and Chris W. Clegg, "The Physical Environment of the Office: Contemporary and Emerging Issues", *International Review of Industrial and Organizational Psychology*, 2011.

office, whether this is due to noise levels, distractions, lack of privacy or the sameness of 'cubicles'."[19]

In terms of advantages other than financial benefits, the goal of an open space is better collaboration among employees and better sharing of information, so that interpersonal relationships and individual well-being can be improved, team spirit encouraged and overall productivity increased.

When weighing up a company's difficulties with open spaces and their real and potential financial and behavioral advantages, the key question remains: can we design an office that solves problems and encourages individual productivity and perceived well-being while creating the structural conditions for better cooperation between colleagues and rising to the individual efficiency challenges we highlighted earlier?

Two promising solutions have emerged:

- A work environment that combines open spaces with areas set aside for specific tasks based on employees' needs.
- Encouragement for working from home.

Open spaces and specific spaces: a winning combination

The combination of an open space structure with the provision of areas designed for specific purposes is a new organization adopted by the most advanced (and best performing) companies. It's a simple idea: if certain tasks performed within an open space – phone conversations, a confidential discussion, concentration on a complex task, meetings, and rest periods – are difficult while other people are working within the same workspace, why not transfer them to an area set aside for that purpose? People who need privacy for important calls can use "telephone booths", individual work cabins free of distractions can be occupied for complex tasks requiring concentration, and of course, meeting rooms of various sizes can be booked depending on

....

19   Jacqueline C. Vischer, "Towards an Environmental Psychology of Workspace: How People are Affected by Environments for Work", *Architectural Science Review*, vol. 51, No.2, June 2008.

employees' needs. And beyond these spaces for day-to-day activities, more specific spaces – areas to unwind, whose importance we have seen above – complete the ideal set-up: rooms where employees can disconnect for a few moments or take an afternoon power nap; reading and learning spaces that demonstrate the company's ambition to promote constant employee development; meeting areas (especially around the coffee machine) so that employees can talk to each other informally when they take a break; gyms to give employees a chance to get some exercise for their physical and mental well-being, but also because the link between health and effective performance is no surprise to anyone.

But these spaces shouldn't just be allocated and furnished. The elements mentioned above (light, sound or color environment, images, visuals and physical proximity with nature, etc.) can all be used to ensure that each space reaches its maximum potential for stimulation. For example, a rest area with soft music, a subtle fragrance such as those used in spas, and relaxing natural images can help employees benefit fully from the space. A gym with beautiful pictures of sports events, jerseys pinned to the walls, a screen showing games, posters with tips for using a particular piece of gym equipment or an exercise, etc. Each room may be a source of useful inspiration to visit specific spaces outside the workplace: for example, a local spa for the relaxation rooms, a library at a university for training rooms or a sports bar for exercise areas. This may also be applied to meeting rooms, which as we have already suggested, could be given specific names depending on their purpose. The room might also be decorated in a style that matches the chosen name. The Pop Art meeting room could be decorated with original works by Andy Warhol... Okay, I'm getting carried away, but it was just to check that you were keeping up, and still retaining your grip on reality! So, let's say posters of Andy Warhol's works!

Behavioral science tells us that context influences how we behave on a daily basis, and what decisions we make: a work environment with rooms we can use to work out, rest or relax gives employees an incentive to use them. The space also conveys the values and behaviors the company wants to encourage. For instance, if a company provides learning and reading spaces, it values its employees' development. A space that shows how well the company has understood its employees' needs, both in terms of effectiveness and enhanced well-being, is also a demonstration of its interest, and proof that the company respects and values its employees. As we have seen, this is a key factor in engagement: I feel like I play an important role in my company because my interests are catered for. I'm not just a performer or a producer, and my company wants to take care of me. A space designed in this way is daily proof that the company is focused on human beings: not only during its annual speeches and in its literature, but in the reality of its work on the ground.

It goes without saying that this work environment strategy, one that seeks to combine the benefits of efficiency and well-being – which reinforce each other – has a certain price tag, compared to conventional open spaces where the vast majority of tasks must be performed in the same area. It really isn't about setting aside a few symbolic rooms as a token favor; that wouldn't be a practical solution for the people who used them. And there's the trap. Evaluating employees' real needs for specific spaces and not being overly influenced by brilliant and money-conscious financial directors (a nod to my friend Jean-Bernard, BVA's administrative and financial director) resulting in a dead end, and everyone going back to square one: work mostly done in open spaces with all of their inherent problems, and more employee resentment for this potentially useless advantage.

In fact, the extra cost is a way to show employees just how committed the company is to meeting their needs. It's the ultimate way of proving to employees that they are worth the additional investment. What's important is not simply providing the basic equipment and resources, but investing in the non-compulsory and the unexpected. Because that's what employees, and people outside the company, will notice: gyms, relaxation rooms, learning spaces, and cafeterias that aren't just functional and reduced to minimal space, but attractively designed. And in the end, these facilities and approaches will be a competitive advantage compared to more conventional companies; they will provide a *living space at work*. Because the quality of life at work in a space designed this way improves daily efficiency while securing internal loyalty and attracting external talent. What could be easier than showing an attractive candidate around the company and demonstrating to them in a real way how the company values its employees? Humans are important, and in this type of working environment, it shows. Remember that in our dominant System 1, visual stimuli are what generate emotion, and they are much better at convincing us than words and arguments. To finish, I'd like to share the advice given by Professor Ron Friedman on space organization in his outstanding book on the subject: "The model for the modern workplace is no longer an evolved version of the factory floor, but a modified version of the college campus."[20] What does Friedman mean by this? That American universities offer students a goal and provide them with the means to achieve it. Their goal is to pass exams in order to obtain a degree. The means to achieve that goal is the provision of a campus offering various resources. And the bottom line is that everyone will use the resources available however they want, to maximize their effectiveness and well-being. Friedman also writes: "What can companies learn from a college campus? How to create an environment that fosters self-direction, for one thing. Within a college setting, students receive a set of expectations at the beginning of the semester. How they approach their work is up to them. If they succeed, they are rewarded with good grades and the propspects of a better future. If they fail, they may be asked to leave... The campus serves as a tool"

A well-designed workspace is an environment that encourages good behavior every day, from all employees. From a behavioral economics perspective, the major benefit of the "default" structure is constant daily encouragement. Whether concentrating, working alone or as part of a team, meeting, resting, having fun, or learning, a good space must be sufficiently adaptable and diverse to accommodate all these behaviors, because they have all been anticipated.

----

20 Ron Friedman, *The Best Place To Work: The Art and Science to Create an Extraordinary Workplace*, TarcherPerigee, 2014.

Anticipate needs by involving users of the space

Good results require good planning. And to get good results, the people who will use the spaces should be able to give their input on how they are to be designed. Because even managers who work very closely with their employees can't be as familiar with all the ins and outs of their daily tasks as the employees themselves, they can't know what little details could make it easier or more difficult to perform their tasks. But sadly genuine employee involvement in the design of workspaces is still far from being the norm. It's not just about superficial consultation on a few major or minor issues; it takes real co-creation. It means involving the employees in how the workspaces are designed to maximize the chances of understanding their real needs, while making sure those needs are being evaluated as objectively as possible to avoid the risks of insufficiency and excessiveness: meeting rooms, specific areas, individual spaces, etc.

Co-creation shouldn't be limited to general organization, but how people really work on a daily basis. Because the idea isn't just to find the right features for effective day-to-day work, but to involve everyone in coming up with ideas to meet the company's behavioral goals. A company I know well – my own – is actually right in the middle of this phase. BVA is planning a move for the end of 2019 (I hope that by setting this date I'm not going to fall victim to the famous over-confidence bias and its associated corollary: the planning fallacy). Caroline Michel – our dynamic and dedicated employee experience director – has just launched an intranet site entitled "BVA Home", which describes the project's goals and gives employees a chance to share their ideas on the various key initiatives we have selected. The project is called "BVA Home: bienvenue chez vous !" (BVA - Welcome home!). After defining our objective to create an "inspiring work environment to live and work together better", here's what Caroline said about it: "The move is an opportunity to reinvent how we work, but not only that. It's also a way of taking a fresh look at our lifestyles, all together. We want to start this initiative with you because this space will be yours, and we want you to play a part in it, whether in terms of interior design, layout, atmosphere, pathways, furniture, lifestyles, how it works, etc. We need to reinvent everything!" In the end, we presented all our employees with a proposal. They could take part and share their ideas on seven main projects ("Working and living together", "A sustainable project", "Flexiworking", "Teleworking"; "The visitor experience at BVA", "Healthy BVA" and "Conviviality and fun"). Beyond the expected benefits in generating ideas, the process itself is crucial: we need to show each person that they count, that the company values its employees' contributions, that together we form a team, and so on. In short, it is about seizing the opportunity of this move to demonstrate the consideration and respect the company has for its employees. And again, not through words, but through actions in the spirit of Nudge management – tailoring the company's values to its employees' real-life experiences, rather than spouting a lot of hot air –obviously keeping in mind that taking their ideas into account during the final design process for the spaces will be the ultimate proof of the company's esteem for its employees. The process is not simply the company's humanist vision of relations in practical form. It really is a performance and efficiency drive. And there are studies to prove it: when employees are involved in designing their workspace, they are more efficient. For example, a study by Craig Knight from the School of Psychology at the University of Exeter and Alexander Haslam from the School of Psychology at the University of Queensland[21] has shown that employees who personalize their workplaces are both happier and more successful. And this extra performance is not to be sniffed at: +32%. Personalizing our environment gives us a sense of control and autonomy, which are important factors in engagement at work. Involving employees in creating their professional living space is an investment in performance.

Investment in an attractive and effective space to encourage good practice isn't just a bonus, or worse, an inconsequential expenditure: it is a powerful and relevant management decision because it boosts business performance through increased employee engagement,

21 Craig Knight and S. Alexander Haslam, "Your Place or Mine? Organizational Identification and Comfort as Mediators of Relationships Between the Managerial Control of Workplace and Employees' Satisfaction and Well-Being", *British Journal of Management*, vol. 21, No.3, September 2010.

greater employee efficiency in day-to-day tasks (both from an individual and a collective point of view), more lasting loyalty and an additional benefit in the fundamental struggle to attract the best talent. However, your workspace may not be shared with other employees, it may also be your home. Is it a good idea to encourage working from home?

Working from home? Yes, but sparingly, and only by choice

The combination of lots of people working outside the office in some categories of employees – sales representatives for instance – and the opportunities presented by new digital technologies such as smartphones, the Internet or Skype business, make working from home an attractive option, one that may be perceived as beneficial for employee well-being and productivity, because of the physical and psychological comfort provided by the home environment, in addition to the time saved (and the lower level of stress) by avoiding long commutes. When encouraged by companies, this flexibility can also be a way for employers to show their trust in their employees and increase engagement. So naturally, employees' perception of control and autonomy is greater.

But decisions made by some of the top business leaders such as the CEO of Yahoo! Marissa Meyer call this into question: when Ms. Meyer arrived at the helm, she decided to cut out the option of working from home, after her experience at Google. She seemed to consider teleworking as the wrong choice. But what have we learned from experiments and behavioral science about this appealing practice?

As is often the case, the key to the results is found in how the working conditions are applied. For example, a study carried out in China[22] on a travel agency with 16,000 employees showed that productivity can be given a real boost when employees work from home. In the experiment, employees at a call center saw their performance grow by 13%

---

22 Nicholas Bloom, James Liang, John Roberts *et al.*, "Does Working from Home Work?: Evidence from a Chinese Experiment", *The Quarterly Journal of Economics*, vol. 130, No.1, February 2015.

when they were permitted to work from home, in comparison to their colleagues who traveled to the company's call centers. There were two main reasons for this improvement: fewer break times at home, and less sick leave, as well as more calls per minute. But this type of work is very specific, and involves very few interactions with other people on a team. And yet it's actually the norm for a great many companies. That's the key point raised by Marissa Meyer: working from home isn't better or worse in itself, but depends on the tasks that need to be performed. When formal and informal interactions are key to a project, working from home presents a major disadvantage: despite all the technological tools available to us, communicating with collea-gues properly becomes more difficult. And behavioral science shows that making it easy for people to behave the way we want them to is a very important condition for success, as outlined by Richard Thaler. Making it more difficult to connect with other people means that we do it less often and that our interactions are of lower quality. And when it is crucial for a mission, or simply essential for creating those impor-tant opportunities for intense connection that we mentioned earlier, it has become a real obstacle. Jacqueline Reses – People Director at Yahoo! – underlines this point to explain her superior's decision: "In order to become the best place to work, communication and collabo-ration are very important, so we need to be working side by side."[23]

Working from home also presents a huge personal challenge. It depends on people's individual ability to resist the many temptations of the home environment. A comfortable bed, the television, social media, the refrigerator, or simply other people are all sources of temp-tation at home. Relying on our own willpower may be the overconfi-dence bias in action. Professor Dan Ariely points out the importance of self-discipline at home to avoid giving into temptation: "We need to create rules for ourselves about how we work at home."[24] And he goes on to say: "For example: I sit at my desk every day by 8:30 a.m. I don't get up for anything aside from bathroom breaks, coffee and tea until

---

23 Kevin Smith, "Here's The Confidential Memo Yahoo Sent Employees About Working From Home", *Business Insider,* 23 February 2013, businessinsider.com.
24 Iliana Strauss, "A Behavioral Scientist's Guide to Working from Home", *From the grapevine*, 13 July 2017, fromthegrapevine.com.

12:00 p.m." The revered professor from Duke goes on to say: "The same rules that are very effective for work are even more important for home." Not only are interactions with colleagues much more difficult – with negative effects on creativity, team spirit and personal relations – but it's not easy to be productive at home, because it requires the conditions for improved performance: a specific isolated area where you can concentrate, control over potential distractions and self-discipline rules so that you stick to routines including intense periods of work and proper breaks. It's important to ensure that the work doesn't suffer a never-ending cycle of interruptions without colleagues to check over your shoulder, which may in fact encourage better concentration.

And in addition to performance at home, the benefit we instinctively feel in terms of enhanced well-being has not been backed up by studies. Gallup[25] showed that only employees who work from home part of the time are more engaged and more satisfied than their colleagues who work full time at a company. If the time spent working from home is lower than 20% of the total time spent working, employee engagement is higher than average.

The equivalent of one day out of five seems to be the tipping point: more than this and the benefits perceived by employees themselves would appear to be reduced, and feelings of isolation may arise. Vinton Cerf – Vice President and Chief Internet Evangelist at Google – gives his thoughts on these results and highlights the existence of a point that should not be passed: "There's a limit to the utility of remote work, and I think your statistics suggest that. You're seeing a positive response up to a point because people see that flexibility as a benefit, and then beyond that, you start to have less utility. So it's not a black-and-white situation."[26] Studies have shown that working from home is an opportunity to provide employees with a more flexible schedule, more autonomy and freedom in how they organize their time, and it's also a sign of the company's trust in

....
25 Steve Crabtree, "Can People Collaborate Effectively While Working Remotely?", *Business Journal*, 13 March 2014, news.gallup.com.
26 *Ibid.*

their abilities. But it's more about offering employees an occasional opportunity than it is about systematically working from home, which gradually erodes the feeling of belonging, relationships with others, team cohesion, and ultimately individual and collective performance. And Vinton Cerf concludes: "Establishing relationships is really important and one of the ways you do that is by face-to-face meetings, sharing a meal, or doing some other activity together. The fact that you establish some kind of human contact is important because then the remote meetings – or the collaborative but not co-located meetings – are reinforced by these personal experiences."

As is often the case, the flip side of the coin may be that behind the official announcement for increased freedom for employees, the company might actually be attempting to reduce the cost of office space. If more and more people are working from home, the company requires less communal space, because those areas are replaced by employees' homes. But this quest to save money by encouraging employees to work from home can mean that flexibility is a poisoned chalice: it becomes almost compulsory to work from home because there is simply not enough space at the office. And then the desire to save money, more than the desire for employees to enjoy greater flexibility, leads to a reduction in available space, with the harmful outcome that "less" becomes "not enough".

Calculating a percentage of remote working – based on employees' genuine needs up to a maximum of this 20% tipping point – is key for successful flexible working hours to establish a suitable business environment. This flexibility for employees will then be meaningful, and bring about greater engagement, better performance, and an intelligent reduction for the business in terms of office space.

Shared offices: a deceptively beneficial solution?

This ability to strike a smart balance paves the way for a new trend now being seen in how corporate spaces are laid out, with workplaces becoming shared offices. A study conducted at 400 multinational companies shows that two thirds plan to adopt this type of workplace arrangement by 2020.[27] Here again it may be implemented for a very noble and well-meaning reason, first to adapt to new and more nomadic work practices and to benefit from new communication technologies, and on the other hand to encourage the development of interpersonal relationships within the business. Shared offices are supposed to encourage people to get to know each other better, through the very fact that workspaces change every day depending on what is available, or employees' personal determination to discover other locations and other colleagues. In addition, sharing office space can be a financial saving based on an improved "occupation rate" for workspaces, because regular work station occupation sometimes only reaches 60% in some companies.

So the benefit is two-fold: financial savings and an improvement in interpersonal relations within the company, which we know are very important for enhancing employee well-being, engagement, and ultimately, individual and collective performance. But here again, traps are emerging behind these potential advantages as many studies evaluating the consequences of this type of organization have shown. One study looked at a sample of 1,000 Australian employees[28] and identified a great many complaints about shared office spaces: rather than achieving the desired goals, employees experienced a loss of confidence when faced with others, more untidiness, an increase in uncooperative behavior, and negative relationships. Another study[29], carried out by Alison Hirst from the University of Bedfordshire and based on ethnographic observations and interviews, highlights other difficulties, especially the marginalization of employees who are constantly travelling and don't have a specific office space, as well as greater indifference toward other people, increased social tension and a loss of identity.

Beyond the attraction of shared office space, in reality it is very difficult to improve relationships within a company, break down silos

....

27   Libby Sander, "The Research on Hot-Desking and Activity-Based Work Isn't So Positive", *The Conversation*, 11 April 2017, theconversation.com.
28   Rachel L. Morrison and Keith A. Macky, "The Demands and Resources Arising from Shared Office Spaces", *Applied Ergonomics*, vol. 60, April 2017.
29   Alison Hirst, "Settlers, Vagrants and Mutual Indifference: Unintended Consequences of Hot-Desking", *Journal of Organizational Change Management*, vol. 24, No.6, October 2011.

and generally improve collective performance. Because in seeking out financial savings, which is often the reason for establishing shared office space, the number of available stations is often underestimated. As a result, new difficulties crop up such as the time employees waste looking for a free station, or the tension and conflict that is created when employees vie for the best spots. The very absence of an office space to call your own also goes against the basic human aspiration for a protected territory, a cocoon in which we can indulge in our habits that generate well-being. The inability to personalize our workspace is a significant point of weakness that is intrinsic to the very concept of shared offices, and results in people feeling out of control and less autonomous. The strength of this aspiration is such that shared office space might actually lead to employees always occupying the same spaces and sitting with the same people they know and like, which ends up going against the original intention.

In addition, new management issues may arise, such as difficulty finding team members at any given time, and the need for additional tools to cope with these challenges.

Ultimately, behind its apparent contemporary sparkle, shared offices present a great many challenges that may not be resolved if the arrangement is widespread throughout a company and compulsory for its employees. It is more preferable that areas with shared office space should be established for certain roles in which employees travel on a regular basis.

From general knowledge to adaptation

Everything we have learned from behavioral science with regards to designing a workspace that promotes individual effectiveness, employee well-being, productive behavior and improved collective performance, can be collated into four main ideas:

Start with what you know: workspace science

It's my belief that we can now talk about workspace science; we can move from space management that is still too driven by intuition or channeled by functional or economic imperatives for most companies, to a strategy based on established scientific data.

It's important to be aware of the potential impact of all the factors we have studied – sound, light, temperature, colors, proximity with nature, and of course the organization of the space itself – and come to a conclusion: everything has a meaning and sends a message to employees, and encourages them – whether intentionally or otherwise – to behave in certain ways, to experience more or less well-being, autonomy, recognition, and to work more or less effectively.

Adapt your knowledge to the specific features of each space, its users, and the company

You have almost certainly noticed that on many occasions, I have pointed out that a characteristic of a space is not simply good or bad in absolute terms, but with regards to a certain task or a specific behavior.

Each space must be doubly personalized depending on how it is to be used – what is to be done within that space, who is using it, what needs to be achieved as a result – from a set of specifications applied to each space that define:

- The main task that will be performed there;
- The psychological and functional characteristics required to complete that task effectively;
- The users of the space and any specific expectations they may have;
- The activation variables and a precise description of each.

Let's look at an example of a room designed for employees to use during periods of rest:

- Main task: rest;
- Psychological and functional characteristics: encourage employees to unwind by establishing a relaxing atmosphere and making it easy for them to rest with the right furniture;
- Users: all employees;
- Activation variables:
    Gentle lighting;
    Colors: soft pastels;

Sounds: soothing music or individual earphones;

Scents: a discreet aroma of some kind;

Images: peaceful images of nature;

Furnishings: comfortable seating with rounded edges, etc.

This type of process means that each variable will be adjusted to ensure that the spaces are designed optimally and have the best chance of achieving their objectives.

But all of that must fit into the company's overall strategy.

Define the values and behavioral practices the company wants to encourage

The workspace provided by a company must convey its values and facilitate the behavior it wants to encourage.

Here again, behavioral science provides a framework for thinking about and designing the values and behaviors to be encouraged: as we saw earlier, these are the key factors that make employees feel engaged and comfortable, and lead them to work effectively. I suggest that these values should be split into four main categories:

- Fairness: economic equality and respect;
- Pillar No.1, achievement: attitude to work, skill and competence, recognition, autonomy, a sense of progress;
- Pillar No.2, friendship: belonging, trust, mutual support;
- The icing on the cake: a transcendental mission and the feeling of pride that goes along with it.

In addition to these values, there are other collective behaviors that are key to the success of a business today:

- Cooperation among employees so that the company benefits from their collective intelligence;
- Innovation so that it stands out from the crowd with offers and services that appeal to its customers;
- Ongoing training for its employees in a constantly and quickly changing world.

And it's the management team's job to define the central values and main behaviors that the company wants to focus on, based on the ideas I set out above. Because the specific nature of each company depends on its market, competitors, history, positioning, organization, the profile of its employees and especially of its managers, as well as its current values and operational context.

After selecting its priorities, a company needs to decide how to implement them, and in Nudge management, that's at least as important. Take each of the priorities – the values and behavioral practices – and call into question what can be done to firmly root these elements in employees' daily lives, through their workspace.

Design and co-create an employee experience within the workspace using all available contact points

We'll get back to the methodology of Nudge management in the final part of the book, but I think now is a good time to share an inspiring analogy about customer experience.

When designing an impactful customer experience – one of the major strategic goals for many companies – you need to start by identifying and understanding all the contact points between the customer and the brand. From this information, we can try to think about how to maximize the customer experience and the quality of the perceived relationship at every point of contact. Of course, customer satisfaction is the number one goal, but the type of satisfaction required is very different for a customer at Chanel or Apple than it is for someone shopping at IKEA or Lowe's.

To design an employee's experience in the workspace we need to establish a detailed and clearly laid-out itinerary of their typical day: the "employee's journey", from when he or she arrives in the morning to when it is time to leave at the end of day. The idea is to chart this experience in the workspace, focusing on every single micro-step (I arrive and push a door to enter the building, I walk into the lobby, I press a button to call the lift, I walk into the lift, I get out at my floor and walk down the corridor, etc.) All these elements are points of contact that we may or may not activate by seeking to communicate a specific element or perception. For instance, the doorbell outside my own office has an arrow next to it, and the following message is displayed: "Enter the world of the future." This is a simple little gimmick that we wanted to use for a bit of fun, but also for meaning, it seeks to create an initial impression of the company through the eyes of the visitor. I use this example to show that each micro-point of contact can be activated to give more meaning to the world.

Using this mapping system – by team type or role – we can look at the kind of experience it is possible to have in the various spaces that are occupied, with an objective in mind: maximizing the quality of the experience in the space while using its potential to convey the most appropriate messages or values.

While all points of contact can be used in this way, they don't all play the same role in how the experience is perceived. Some occasions mean more than others: the first contact, the end of an experience, and peak times that may be magical or tragic. This is what many experiments in behavioral economics have demonstrated, the first of which were carried out by the 2002 Nobel prizewinner Daniel Kahneman and gave rise to the famous "peak and end" rule.

But before we go into more detail about the rule, let's look at the first point of contact we have with the company, because that's going to set the tone for the day. If the first contact is negative, our overall state of mind will be negative for a certain amount of time; however if the first contact is positive, our starting point will be a temporary good mood. And in behavioral science that's what's known as the priming effect: our behavior is unconsciously influenced by stimuli that have affected us beforehand, even though they may have no direct link with our current experience. For example, in a study[30] during which participants were exposed to words associated with seniors in the United States – "old, lonely, Florida, gray, polite, stiff, retired, etc." – which they had to use to make a sentence, their walking pace over the 9.75 meters they covered when leaving the experiment room was much

30 John A. Bargh, Mark Chen and Lara Burrows, "Automaticity of Social Behavior: Direct Effects of Trait Construct and Stereotype Activation in Action", *Journal of Personality and Social Psychology*, vol. 71, No.2.

lower than the speed of a control sample who did the same exercise but with neutral words. The mental presence of words associated with a slow pace (without actually using the word "slow" itself), changed how people behaved. Of course, the effect is temporary, but starting off with a positive boost for your working day is not without its benefits.

In addition to the importance of this first contact, two periods of time also have a special role, these are the "peaks" and the "ends". The end is a key step in any process for a simple reason known as the freshness or novelty bias. This bias refers to the fact that our brain tends to memorize what is near to us better than what is further away. The end of an experience is therefore disproportionately important in our overall perception of it. But other periods are also fundamental: ones that have generated powerful emotional intensity, whether in a positive (magic moments) or negative (tragic moments) way. If we experience an event with a fairly average emotional intensity, but at a certain moment something very positive or negative happens, our perception of the experience overall will be modified by the event in question. The entire event will be remembered as positive or negative. Here again, this phenomenon can be explained by taking a look at how our brain functions: we remember intense emotional events more strongly and for a longer period of time.

This basically means that the perception of an experience can be enhanced, without trying to make it exceptional all the way through, but by making sure that its key moments – the end and the peaks – are as positive as possible. In the workplace, this does not mean that you have to think up magical moments and memorable evenings every day, but it can be food for thought about the opportunities that may be available to create surprising experiences that will enhance life at work and have a positive impact. My friend Caroline Michel, who I mentioned earlier when I referred to her co-design process for the new BVA premises, also created a memorable emotional peak experience for employees at our Boulogne-Billancourt site: a bus – decorated with the words "BVA Circus" – appeared in the street in front of the building, megaphone blaring, with music, colors and confetti – to announce our forthcoming annual party: a huge circus-themed evening event. And the wonderful and noisy circus performers then burst into the building, occupying each of its seven floors, singing, dancing, making music and handing out glasses of champagne to everyone, creating a party mood to enhance the experience that was planned for two months later. Now that's an emotional peak! And I can assure you that everyone was delighted with this extraordinary surprise. Every face lit up with smiles. That particular working day was, for many of us, hugely brightened by this emotional peak. Of course, make no mistake, one peak does not constitute improved quality of life at work, but behavioral science shows that the role of such events is much less insignificant than it might seem to rational beings... because we are all deeply emotional.

So now you have the knowledge to design a physical working environment for employees that will help them adopt the behaviors the company wants to encourage, while conveying its key values. Obviously, building new premises is a relatively rare event in the life of a company, but all the influential factors can be gradually integrated to develop the quality of the workspace.

However, just as individual motivation is practically powerless in an ecosystem with a current that flows in the opposite direction, a workspace is only able to produce the desired behavior if there is a psychological environment to match. The physical environment is a receptacle, a facilitator and an incentive. If the values advocated through physical workspaces are developed, and the behavior they encourage becomes the norm within the company, it is essential that the company's management team and its executives – from the highest ranks down to direct supervisors – create the psychological conditions that promote the practices they expect.

With insight from behavioral science and through the fundamental vision of Nudge management, let's now look at the role of company managers and executives in creating the psychological conditions for engagement, promoting individual effectiveness, encouraging winning collective behavior, and ultimately, establishing the conditions for optimal collective performance in which everybody works to the best of their ability, to the benefit of everyone in the company.

Chapter 6

An engaging psychological environment: inciting through leadership and progressive management

How can leaders optimize the performance of their teams using what we know about behavioral science? How can they generate engagement as well as individual and collective effectiveness while optimizing the quality of their strategic decisions? What is the role of direct supervisors in achieving objectives? Those are the main questions we're going to raise and try to answer in this chapter.

The leader of a company has two roles:

- Communicate with the company's internal audience (its employees) and its external audience (its clients and ecosystem) to both inform and convince them that their strategy fits the decisions it is making, while bringing value to the company's products and services.

- Make decisions about how the company is organized internally and the strategy it should follow externally, and how it should go about achieving that strategy to create the conditions for sustainable performance, taking into account the interests of the shareholders and the nature of the company's ecosystem.

In terms of behavioral science, these main tasks work in two completely different dimensions, and that presents a huge challenge to any manager. The challenge involves being able to distinguish between Daniel Kahneman's System 1 and System 2 through leadership, but not at the same time and not in the same contexts:

- A great leader needs to communicate using System 1 to be inspiring and persuasive.

- But needs to think using System 2 to make fair and intelligent decisions.

So what does that involve? And how can it be achieved?

Leaders that communicate using System 1: inspiring and persuasive

You now know from what you have learned in the first part of this book that "most of what we think and do is driven by System 1."[1] This is one of the most important discoveries made over decades of research into human behavior.

For all leaders, being inspiring and persuasive in front of any type of audience, whether they are employees at a company, investors or customers, means addressing "System 1" people, in other words individuals who hear the information and interpret it using the specific filters that this system engages, and the main human characteristics we saw earlier. These people are more than just an audience listening to a presentation by a leader, they are human beings who perceive, process, interpret, understand and remember information with varying degrees of success, and in the end are left inspired, convinced or bemused by that information. Leaders shouldn't communicate or try to convince using logical, rational and statistical arguments – which are often boring and soulless – from System 2, but rather focus on attention-grabbing elements and spark the audience's interest using System 1.

With the objective, in any business communication, not just to inform for its own sake, but to encourage and generate the specific behaviors that will benefit the company: in this case to get employees to behave in a way that meets the expectations that have been laid out, and to ensure that they feel engaged by setting objectives that they have clearly understood and taken on board. Shareholders need to be convinced of the strategy's merits, and where appropriate,

---

1   Daniel Kahneman, *Thinking Fast and Slow, op. cit.*

provide their support to the board of directors or devote new financial resources to the strategy. Potential customers are encouraged to become effective customers, those who are already effective are driven to become even more loyal and, ideally, proud ambassadors of a brand. Potential external talent is attracted by the messages that are delivered, and candidates send applications in droves. Suppliers go above and beyond the call of duty to play a bigger role in their customer's success, and new potential investors strengthen the company as it grows. A great leader must be able to persuade the company's entire ecosystem to adopt the specific behaviors that will contribute to its success.

A leader's role isn't just to share information, but to incite and inspire. At least that's how it should be: leaders should share a vision that is clear and rousing, and should make each person to want to do their bit in achieving the company's objectives. But that's a huge challenge, because it goes against established belief systems. A business leader is supposed to be studious, rigorous, a hard worker, intelligent, with impeccable self-control. Basically a rational human being with all the external signs of logical sense that makes the individual responsible and right for the role. This vision was developed and upheld as the norm for company managers throughout the twentieth century. With just a few exceptions, a good business leader used to be a model of System 2, and that image still persists today in many companies, and has a very strong influence on the style of communication presented by leaders and on their daily behavior: rigor and rationality rule supreme. In this vision, which for a long time dominated and was encouraged by business school teachings in all countries, communication by leaders was – and often still is – based on the desire to convince through well-laid out logical arguments peppered with facts and figures to prove their accuracy. The underlying problem here is that according to behavioral science, that's not how people are convinced or inspired. And it's not how to go about changing behavior. Because once again, using System 2 to communicate – logic, reason, cold hard facts – to persuade System 1 individuals – instinctive and emotional humans – is a fundamental mistake.

But what does it mean to be a System 1 leader, and how can we really change people's behavior?

In behavioral science, there are four types of leadership that have proven to be essential:
- The inspiring leader
- The behavioral architect leader who conveys values
- The emotional leader
- The leader who multiplies talent

The inspiring leader: sharing a vision

In our analysis of what generates engagement, we have already highlighted the specific role of a transcendental mission. When employees feel that their company is seeking to achieve success and productivity not only in their market, but also to achieve a bigger objective that contributes – even modestly – to making the world a better place, they feel greater pride, and are more engaged.

The ability of a business leader – often the company's own founder – to define, bring to life, and share the mission is required to generate this pride within each employee, so that even the most mundane task becomes a link in a chain that is connected to a much bigger, much stronger and ultimately more inspiring ambition. When employees can really get a mental hold on the overall mission and feel how it really links up to their own work, their engagement and motivation to make a contribution using their personal skills are much greater. Each person seeks to do more than their best, because they find purpose in what they are doing. They can make a little more effort and though it may be difficult or even painful, it generates a genuine feeling of achievement. To illustrate this apparent paradox of painful effort and the intense pleasure it can bring about, Dan Ariely gives the example of a mountaineer reaching a summit. Granted, there is certainly a lot of effort and pain involved, but it also creates a wonderful feeling of accomplishment that can become a lifelong memory. We don't all have to climb mountains, obviously, but it illustrates the motivation we can muster when we set about focusing on a goal we want to achieve.

In his best-selling book *Start with Why*[2], Simon Sinek – a great expert and contemporary leadership guru – talks about the ability of top-level leaders to inspire, through the mission he calls "the why" of a company, and explains: "WHY: Very few people or companies can clearly articulate WHY they do WHAT they do. When I say WHY, I don't mean to make money – that's a result. By WHY I mean what is your purpose, cause or belief? WHY does your company exist? WHY do you get out of bed every morning? And WHY should anyone care?"

So as you'll have gathered, company managers find this type of mission extremely difficult to achieve, and it also goes beyond what is usually expected of employees. What's needed is a mission that inspires the majority of employees and is simultaneously aligned with the company's business. It's not what Sinek calls the "what" of the company, nor "how" the company does it, but its genuine reason "why".

Some large corporations have managed to achieve that – funnily enough, they are the best performing companies in the world – and Sinek holds up Apple as an example. Its founder Steve Jobs believed that Apple's mission was to "make a contribution to the world by making tools for the mind that advance humankind."[3] Its famous slogan "Think different" is also quoted. I have never worked for Apple, but I personally believe that this suggestion would make an employee of the company glad to come into the office every day. If my work involves helping to make the world a better place through the tools I am designing, then yes, I feel more motivated on a daily basis. If my goal is to put computers together, it's a job. Even though I may find it fascinating, it's still just a job. But if it involves making the world a better place, then the ambition is completely different.

Another global giant – Google – states that its mission goes beyond its business objective: "to organize the world's information and make it universally accessible and useful."[4] Here again, if an employee's mission is to design ultra efficient algorithms for collecting and

....
2   Simon Sinek, *Start With Why: How Great Leaders Inspire Everyone to Take Action*, Portfolio, Reprint edition, 2011.
3   economist.com/news/2009/06/02/mission-statement
4   google.com/about

reproducing information, engagement may be relatively high, but when you add the idea that they are organizing the world's information so that everyone has universal access to it in order to be more useful, then these three qualifiers enhance the ensuing perception and motivation of the person doing the task even further.

In comparison, the mission of another big company, Microsoft, seems to me less aspirational: "to enable people and businesses throughout the world to realize their full potential". There is a desire to create ambition that explains the "what", and the "how" with the terms "to enable people" and "full potential", but by putting the words "businesses" and "people" in the same sentence, the mission's aspirational dimension is to my mind somewhat limited. As Ariely emphasizes, combining the social dimension with the market dimension is often a bad idea because each upholds different values. Microsoft may genuinely want to enable businesses to realize their full potential, but in saying so, it presents a self-serving aspect to its mission, which then loses some of its altruism. The weight of words can also transform how a statement is perceived, and that's what behavioral economists call "framing": how situations are presented can change how we behave in them.

Making a mission aspirational depends on three elements: the intrinsic quality of the proposal and how it relates to the company and employee aspirations; the words used to describe the mission; and of course the character of the person conveying the message, most importantly the passion and authenticity that radiates from that person when they explain and promote the mission.

But that's nothing compared to the importance of behavior within a company. To be truly engaging, a mission must be relevant to the daily reality of each employee's work.

The Nudge vision: be part of your employees' daily experiences

I mentioned the missions of very large corporations because everyone is familiar with them. But this ability to find meaning in your company isn't just for big global businesses. Each company can design and express its own transcendental mission and develop an attractive culture. Before they became giants, Google, Facebook and eBay were start-ups with founders who already had a powerful vision, and that vision still exists. When a company is small, the challenge is less about defining a mission than about preserving it and keeping it alive as the business develops, and the number of employees grows.

But the real challenge for all company leaders – if the vision is aspirational enough – is to make sure that the vision becomes part of their employees' daily lives. Because many "visions" are simply words that appear in annual speeches, on the home pages of corporate websites, or in business reports.

In order to illustrate how a vision applies to employees' everyday realities, I would like to talk about my childhood friend Laurent Dumas, founder and chairman of the real estate promotion company Emerige who has just been awarded the Businessperson of the Year prize for the Île-de-France. This charismatic leader designed and shared an inspiring mission with his employees, and it permeated the company's entire ecosystem: his personal fascination with contemporary art. In his own words, "My fascination with art applies to the entire company... I love to say that we're not only creating buildings, we are creating the cities of our dreams."[5] And Laurent goes on to say: "The programs we deliver help to improve the urban environment and how we live as a community... It is our firm belief and my personal conviction that art can changes lives, and is a wonderful weapon against injustice."

Did you spot it? That's the transcendental mission: it doesn't focus on business objectives, but on how to make the world a better place by designing buildings that create well-being for everyone. And what I find interesting about Laurent Dumas and Emerige is not so much the vision but the way Laurent shares it with his employees in their daily lives.

In an interview for *Les Échos* about bringing his fascination with art into the lives of his employees, Laurent answered: "Sharing and

----

5   (In French) Martine Robert, interview with Laurent Dumas, "Les artistes nous font entrer dans le monde de la liberté et de la création", *Les Échos*, October 14, 2017, business.lesechos.fr.

encouraging artistic creation are the pillars of our business culture. A work of art such as painting or a sculpture is displayed in every office and common area. We also organize visits to exhibitions for our employees, which gives them an opportunity to enjoy an artistic experience with their coworkers and a chance to talk about something other than what they are working on every day." And it also allows Laurent to underscore the connection between art and his employees' daily work: "Being around art stimulates creativity. A work of art is the culmination of the creative process. What we want to do is open up other fields of vision and help our employees to understand what the creative process is really about. So we invite various artists to visit the company and explain more about their approach and their work to all our employees. Understanding more about the creative arts is incredibly helpful. It enhances the quality of the dialogue we have with our architects, designers, landscapers and artists."

Art is part and parcel of his employees' daily lives: canvases hang on office walls, which links back to the role of the physical space that we looked at earlier. In addition to exhibition visits, and discussions and debates with artists, tangible actions bring the company's vision to life. Art isn't just a policy, but a genuine everyday experience.

And it doesn't stop there. The vision is also brought to life through many other initiatives outside the company. For example, Emerige created the annual Révélations Emerige grant, which is awarded to young contemporary French artists. It's designed to give them an opportunity to display their works at some of the country's leading galleries, and gain recognition from the rest of the art world. Similarly, Emerige has also built an arts center on the Île Seguin in Paris to support young artists, house exhibitions and host artists' residencies. The company is also the driving force behind the "1 building, 1 artwork" (1 immeuble, 1 oeuvre) charter, which was signed by the French Ministry of Culture. The charter is a commitment by companies to order or acquire a work of art from an artist for every construction or renovation project they undertake. This initiative, spearheaded by Laurent himself, goes beyond his company and involves the entire profession, with signatories including Bouygues

Immobilier, Ogic, BNP Paribas, Real Estate, Eiffage, Accor, and Vinci Immobilier.

The idea isn't just to support the development of French contemporary art, but also to bring art to more people – to "bring art where it doesn't exist", in the words of Laurent Dumas. In this case, apartment block residents, because works have been displayed in more than fifty Emerige real estate projects. But that's not all. Another Emerige initiative in partnership with the Château de Versailles and local councils from the suburbs of Paris also illustrates the company's intention. In the summer of 2017, Emerige treated almost 6,000 children aged 6 to 13 from in and around Paris who weren't able to go on holiday to a day visiting the Château de Versailles when it would normally be closed to the public. In addition to this visit to the palace and its gardens, the children got a chance to meet the contemporary artist Olafur Eliasson, who gave a presentation on his work. In its press release, the Château de Versailles explained the goal of the project: "The aim of these days is to give children a chance to familiarize themselves with part of their heritage, and with contemporary art, through a learning-based artistic and cultural project on an outstanding scale."[6]

Laurent Dumas brings his vision to his employees through their daily experiences, and through memorable events that convey that vision to the outside world, giving meaning to his desire to make the world a better place, and ultimately, creating pride and engagement among his employees. And the amazing thing about his vision is that it has significant benefits on how employees behave and work at Emerige. Laurent Dumas sees interaction with artists as having three main advantages.

The first is the openness and creativity generated by being around artists. When you come into contact with contemporary artists, you naturally look for meaning in their work. You may be surprised, shocked, and often curious, which helps you to move away from conventional ideas and the established beliefs that can blinker your view. Studies have actually shown that there is a close link between

---

6   (in French) "Une journée de vacances au château de Versailles pour près de 6 000 enfants grâce au soutien du groupe Emerige", 21 July 2006, presse.chateauversailles.fr.

open-mindedness and innovation, including the ability to find solutions to everyday problems at work.

The second element involves something that might be less obvious about the work of an artist: its intensity, and the extremely high standards that creativity requires. These high standards are an implicit lesson in success, and Laurent Dumas believes that his employees take inspiration from that in their work.

The final element is about the debate that art can trigger. The founder of Emerige points out, "Art encourages interpersonal relationships, and therefore discussions among employees." We'll look at this in more detail later on when we discuss cooperation among people who work in a company, but talking about something to do with life outside the office is definitely one of the keys to establishing strong personal relationships inside the workplace.

The Emerige example shows that bringing the vision of a company director to life is a challenge, and yet we can rise to that challenge in a strong and effective way so that the vision is a genuine trigger for employee engagement and performance.

Leaders must not only nurture their vision, but also create the conditions for that vision to be propagated among their employees.

The behavioral architect leader who conveys values

A company's culture is rooted in its values. My goal here isn't to rehash an already well-known topic, but rather to emphasize the key role of directors in defining their mission and values, and most importantly, in sharing them and making them relevant to their employees' everyday lives.

Because defining a specific business culture is only one of the conditions for an employee to achieve the ultimate objective; they also need to be inspired and guided by it on a daily basis. The culture needs to permeate their behavior and motivation and act as an invisible yet constant guide. And in order to succeed, these values need to be reflected in how they live their lives at work. Just like a vision, values are merely words in the mouths of directors if there is nothing explicit or implicit to allow employees to genuinely experience this business culture.

The role of a leader or any business manager is once again essential for two reasons:

- A leader must be instrumental in building a structure that encourages the behavioral practices he or she wishes to promote.
- A leader must behave in a way that conveys these values on a daily basis.

Let's take another look at these two points.

The first role, which I call the architect leader, mainly involves what I described in the previous chapter. Of course, leaders can play a key role in organizing the physical space of the company, on the condition that they understand its strategic relevance and want to be a part of it. And we already know how much influence the physical organization of a workspace can have on encouraging and facilitating specific behaviors. If a company wants to emphasize the importance of cooperation among its employees, the space can be designed to stimulate contact points by creating meeting rooms or areas for communal activities such as sports.

Leaders can then design the workspace like an architect, while taking behavioral economics into account, driving the behaviors they would like to encourage in that space.

The second role leaders need to play is even more essential in bringing about the desired behavior. And that role depends on the entire management team. Because while a workspace can encourage employees to behave in certain ways, it is still only a receptacle, an environment: its potential power can be catalyzed or annihilated, depending on how the company's managers behave within it.

For instance, if the spaces set aside for informal chat and relaxation are designed to encourage employees to get to know each other better, learn more about each other and share their experiences, and then a manager walks by a group of people having a chat and booms: "Working hard or hardly working?!" or something equally amusing, there is very little chance that the physical environment will successfully foster interpersonal relationships. By criticizing the employees' behavior – even jokingly – the manager creates a psychological environment that goes against the potential created by the physical setting.

So leaders are behavioral architects by virtue of the impact they have on how the space contributes to and facilitates the desired behaviors. But their ability to create a psychological environment that fulfills this potential is also fundamental.

Using what we have learned about behavioral economics, you won't be surprised to learn that what really matters is *how* people behave. In this case, the daily behavior of the leader and managers within the firm. A culture can only exist if it is nurtured from day to day. And leaders are vital, because they serve as examples for all the employees in the company. The way leaders handle major, strategic, and everyday decisions affects how employees react. Do they say hello in the morning? Do managers take a few minutes to chat with everyone they meet? These are the markers that establish company culture. But words are nothing without actions to back them up! Exemplary behavior by leaders is a very important, but very demanding challenge, because leaders are highly visible in companies. The way they travel, the size of their offices, the space they inhabit within the company, how they dress, what time they arrive and when they leave, the people they talk to (and those they never address), how they move around the building, their body language (are they always smiling or do they always look serious?); everything has a meaning when it comes from a manager. Everyone sees what managers do, and their movements are interpreted – or misinterpreted – by all employees. To use Nudge terminology, they are messengers whose implicit or explicit message – expressed through daily micro-behaviors – is magnified by their status.

The emotional leader

For System 1, a good messenger is a behavioral messenger, but also an emotional leader who is in tune with their surrounding environment, and especially in tune with their employees.

When leaders have an emotional connection with their environment it means they are aware of their ecosystem and can be inspiring and persuasive in how they communicate and behave.

This type of leader listens well and shows empathy, but can also express personal emotions while presenting a rational external message. Because behavioral science has taught us that to communicate successfully and get your audience on board – whether you're explaining a business mission, illustrating a firm's culture, presenting a company's results or laying out its forthcoming internal transformation plan, you need to integrate the System 1 dimension, and not depend solely on logic and reason.

Even though it is rooted in specific analysis and not the result of behavioral economics research, Professor Daniel Goleman identified in the mid-1990s that this emotional dimension is important in successful leadership, and popularized the concept of emotional intelligence.[7] His conclusions, which he drew after carrying out studies linking the behavior of business leaders with their company's performance, led to this concept of emotional intelligence that he defines as "the ability to manage yourself and your relationships with others effectively using four key skills: self-knowledge, self-management, social awareness and social skills." Daniel Goleman describes each of these fundamental skills:

- Self-knowledge is your ability to identify and understand your own emotions, as well as recognizing how they impact your work and your relationships with other people.
- Self-management is how you cope with your emotions and impulses, but also includes intellectual honesty and integrity, awareness about what you are doing, how you adapt to changes in your environment, how you are driven towards success and your ability to sense and grab opportunities.
- Social awareness is your ability to empathize and be interested in other people and their problems, how you perceive their emotions and how you interact with people and deal with politics in a community or internal network.
- Social skills are your talents for inspiring and influencing other people, how you communicate and listen, but also how you

....
7   Daniel Goleman, *Emotional Intelligence: Why it can matter more than IQ,* Bantam Books, 1995; "What makes a leader?", *Harvard Business Review,* November-December 1998, hbr.org.

develop their skills, forge ties between individuals, foster team spirit, incite collaboration and resolve conflict.

In addition to his analysis, what's interesting about Goleman's conclusions is that they are close to those of behavioral economics, but he arrives at them from a very different angle. Goleman demonstrates the importance of emotional intelligence in great and successful leaders; behavioral economics gives the basic foundation for this importance by revealing the highly emotional and social dimensions of human beings. Human beings are emotional, so their leaders must be emotional in order to be on the same wavelength.

When dealing with *Homo economicus*, the qualities of a great leader must focus both on reasoned explanations – facts, figures, and logic used to inform and persuade – and motivational systems – the carrot (remuneration, bonuses, and material advantages) and the stick (sanctions and redundancies). But real people are social and emotional, and these elements alone won't generate engagement or individual and collective performance: emotional intelligence is therefore the key success factor for a great leader.

Goleman also refers to another key concept from behavioral economics in the latest edition of his book, *Primal Leadership*[8]: the priming concept we covered earlier. As you may remember, this idea refers to the influence that previous experiences can have on individuals' attitudes and behaviors, as illustrated in the example where participants in a study were exposed to words to do with slowness and moved more slowly as a result. In his foreword, Goleman and his co-authors write: "The fundamental task of leaders, we argue, is to prime good feeling in those they lead. That occurs when a leader creates resonance – a reservoir of positivity that frees the best in people. At its root, then, the primal job of leadership is emotional."[9]

For Goleman, the key to emotional intelligence is an ability to prime positivity through how a leader behaves. And this positivity flows

8 Daniel Goleman, Richard Boyatis and Annie McKee, *Primal Leadership, With a New Preface by the Authors: Unleashing the Power of Emotional Intelligence,* Harvard Business Review Press, 2013.
9 *Ibid.*

down through the company to change employees' behavior and generate better performance. Because that's what it's all about: boosting the company's competitiveness by managing people more effectively. Goleman calls it "Good moods, good work" and demonstrates the link between "positivity" generated by the behavior of a leader, and the results that are achieved. Indeed, there are many studies to back up the findings[10]: there is a link between a benevolent, positive environment and good productivity. That productivity is brought about by the development of greater camaraderie among employees, enhanced creativity, open communication, less intimidation and more appreciation for the work people do. Here again we find the same elements that improve employee engagement. The role of a director is crucial in driving this "good mood culture". A study[11] on 62 CEOs and their top management teams in the United States showed that the more they fostered a positive and optimistic environment, the fewer internal conflicts were observed; the more they cooperated positively, the better the company performed.

While positive emotions are brought about through the emotional intelligence of a leader, they also act as a mental catalyst that strengthens bonds, creates cooperation, develops optimism and encourages employees to help each other.

Ultimately, a great System 1 leader – one who goes against a traditionalist vision based on an obsolete understanding of a rational being at work – is an emotional individual who inspires and guides employees by feeling affection for the company, by communicating and behaving in a way that calls upon that intelligence, and by expressing his or her own emotions positively and intelligently, to prime and create the conditions for a culture that will benefit their company.

....

10   R. Wilburn Clouse and Karen L. Spurgeon, "Corporate Analysis of Humor",
     Psychology: A Journal of Human Behavior, vol. 32, No.3-4, 1995.

11   Sigal G. Barsade, Andrew J. Ward, Jean D. F. Turner *et al.*, "To Your Heart's Content:
     A Model of Affective Diversity in Top Management Teams", *Administrative Science
     Quarterly*, vol. 45, No.4, December 2000.

The leader who multiplies talent

Designing a workspace that will incite individual effectiveness and good collective behavior; creating the psychological conditions for employee engagement by presenting an inspiring mission that is meaningful for daily life at work, and echoing the company's values through the words and actions of an emotional leader... all of these are great assets in creating the internal conditions for successful collective performance. But exceptional leaders, those who Professor Sydney Finkelstein – Director of the Leadership Center at Dartmouth College and world-renowned specialist in the study of business managers – calls "superbosses", have another quality that is of no lesser importance: they are incredible detectors, developers and diffusers of talent. And they can help their employees to accomplish more than they themselves could hope to achieve. Following a very comprehensive meta-analysis of leadership, Finkelstein writes: "The biggest discovery I've made over the course of studying organizations is also the simplest: it really is about people. Executives often prioritize strategy, assuming that if they get that right, everything else will fall into place. They think they can ignore their people or, at any rate, treat them as secondary. Bad idea. People are an essential part of any strategy, and regenerating the talent pool is the single most important thing any leader can do to survive and prosper. Superbosses understand this, and for this reason they're able to achieve unparalleled influence and business success in their respective fields."[12] And Finkelstein concludes: "The primary path to winning is via great talent fully immersed in creating value."

Another expert in the field of leadership – Liz Wiseman – comes to similar conclusions about the importance of this leadership skill in people she refers to as "multipliers", to ensure that future leaders can grow and develop within their companies.[13]

....

12   Sydney Finkelstein, *Superbosses: How Exceptional Leaders Master the Flow of Talent*, Portfolio-Penguin, 2016.
13   Liz Wiseman and Greg McKeown, *Multipliers: How the Best Leaders Make Everyone Smarter*, HarperBusiness, 2010.

Obviously, as is often the case in management, it's all very well having the knowledge, but what really matters is how you put it into practice. Three main lessons can be learned from how these exceptional leaders operate:
- They and their businesses are natural magnets for talent.
- They recruit by focusing on specific qualities using original methods.
- They manage talent by combining exceptional ambition and significant autonomy.

First and foremost, along the same lines as what Robert Cialdini calls "pre-suasion" in his latest book[14], companies with "superbosses" are a spontaneous draw for talent. Having helped to establish a motivational, effective and benevolent working environment in the form of an aspirational mission, and instilled motivational values in as many employees as possible, great leaders can attract talent to their companies because they are desirable employers. The inner workings of an organization are always visible from the outside. If employees feel proud to belong to the company, they are its own natural ambassadors. They talk about the company and become its unpaid advertisers, reaching out to those who are looking for a new challenge.

The leaders of these companies are "talent magnets" themselves, to use Liz Wiseman's expression. And that's actually the number one quality she attributes to these exceptional "multipliers", based on her analysis of 150 leaders[15]: "People are drawn to work with multipliers directly or indirectly, because they know they will grow and succeed." Great leaders are therefore an asset to their businesses, not only in terms of their leadership but also by dint of their very presence, which attracts other talents from outside. True talent – with the specific qualities that I will go over again later – attracts talent.

In addition, companies with these superbosses often perform well in their sectors, because as we've seen, there is a close link between

....
14 Robert Cialdini, *Influence and Persuasion,* Harvard Business Review Press, 2017.
15 *Ibid.*

internal characteristics, competitiveness, and collective performance. So these companies are often known for their success.

Finally, the premises of these companies – such as Google – are also a sort of constant advertisement for the company. The super-bosses create the fundamental conditions that make their businesses attractive to external talent.

Often starting out with a vast pool of potential candidates, superbosses use a recruitment method that Finkelstein considers "unconventional", which involves focusing their evaluation on three important qualities: intelligence, creativity and flexibility.

Intelligence is one of the qualities that superbosses look for. Superbosses obviously prefer a candidate's ability to understand the workings of a complex and unstable global competitive environment at the mercy of technological breakthroughs over their ability to focus on strategy. But exceptional leaders really seek out intelligence combined with creativity, flexibility and adaptability. This is closer to Goleman's theory about emotional intelligence, but really boils down to a candidate's potential to understand a company's ecosystem. It's their ability to listen carefully to their environment, implement innovative solutions from new angles, remain extremely open – especially to weak signals – and learn quickly by knowing how to manage inevitable surprises. Of course, a candidate's professional history certainly counts, but it's less about experience within a sector, the roles they have had in the past, or any qualifications, and more about a specific attitude that includes open-mindedness, imagination and flexibility.

As they are more focused on personal qualities, the recruitment process needs to be tailored to their objectives, which creates the need to avoid stereotypes and ask original questions to understand how a candidate's personality might offer the qualities the leader seeks to attract. Finkelstein uses the example of Ralph Lauren – founder of the eponymous global apparel giant – who questions the candidates he receives on the clothes they wear and why they wear them. The objective is to use a specific questioning style to pick out extraordinary talent regardless of their experience, while trying to evaluate the person's fundamental qualities; but we will come back to this later when we talk about recruiting well with the help of behavioral science.

Superbosses hire their best candidates by looking for specific qualities and by using appropriate processes. But while this phase is fundamental, the way they manage the talent they have recruited is also very important.

The first detail refers to how a role is defined: superbosses are able to redefine it, or even to reshape how the company is organized in order to create perfect coherence with the candidate's specific qualities. The role and structure is tailored to the individual as much as the individual must adapt to the role. Superbosses look for flexibility and imagination in the people they hire, but they also know how to use these qualities to create the conditions that bring out the greatest potential in the person. This calls traditional human resource practices into question. The same system cannot be used for all new recruits, because it's essential to be able to implement the optimum conditions for a new hire to succeed: structures must not be set in stone, but adapted to each individual's specific qualities.

The second detail about how superbosses manage their employees is in their incredibly high expectations. Finkelstein writes[16]: "Superbosses are bullish on what their teams can accomplish. They demand extraordinarily high performance; 'perfect is good enough' captures their attitude." But beyond this almost unachievable ambition, what characterizes a superboss is that they know how to convey the confidence they have in their employee's ambition and their ability to achieve the objectives the superboss has set. Speaking about his former boss Jay Chiat, the chairman of the TBWA advertising group Tom Caroll says: "Jay brought something out in people, and after working with him it was hard for them to go back to an ordinary manager. Once you felt it, you could never go back." Superbosses are able to both set very high goals for their employees and instill a powerful sense of confidence.

....
16 Sydney Finkelstein, "Secrets of the Superbosses", *Harvard Business Review*, January-February 2016.

But while the state of mind they want to instill is key, there is often a two-fold element that permeates the daily contact they have with their employees: they allow a huge amount of autonomy and back it up with plenty of support. Warren Buffett is one of those superbosses who practice to the highest degree what *The New York Times* – later taken over by Finkelstein – calls effective delegation. Once they have been recruited by superbosses, new hires benefit from an enormous amount of autonomy. If they are intelligent, imaginative, and flexible, totally focused on ambitious objectives that they believe in, what need is there for excessive control? Superbosses define the goal and allow their employees to decide how they are going to achieve it. They trust that the people they have recruited will feel completely invested in their roles, and responsible for their actions. And we know that autonomy is a key element in securing the engagement of all employees. Liz Wiseman talks about leaders who give their employees free reign to develop their ideas. This conscious delegation is not a lack of interest or involvement in employees' work. Great leaders are always available to give advice, support and feedback when needed. They are there to provide backup, and guide their employees to optimize their chances of success. But they don't do the job for them! Liz Wiseman's research focuses on this ability to invest in other people's success by providing the resources employees need and discussing key decisions, but allowing them to be the owners of those decisions and giving full responsibility for them. And that's the polar opposite of micromanagement. These superbosses firmly believe in what Carol Dweck – Professor of Psychology at Stanford University – calls a growth mindset.[17] Individuals can develop their basic skills and intelligence by working and learning. Here, micromanaging, deciding for other people, would be a big mistake. Supporting talents and allowing them to develop and flourish by giving them autonomy and providing support is a smart investment in the future.

This state of mind allows those recruited by superbosses to grow alongside them, while always giving their very best. Liz Wiseman says "multipliers establish a unique and highly motivating work

....

17   Carol Dweck, *Mindset: The New Psychology of Success*, Ballantine Books, 2007.

environment where everyone has permission to think and the space to do their best work. Multipliers operate as *Liberators*, producing a climate that is both comfortable *and* intense."[18]

Lastly, great leaders provide opportunities for their employees to grow and develop in a faster, more personalized and more consistent way than the average manager. They "compress" career moves.

Once an individual has achieved their first successes and learned from their role, they are offered new challenges that will push them to learn more, and give the best of themselves in order to succeed.

However, even though the ability to inspire and create engagement might be fundamental qualities, the most important goal for a leader is to make good decisions and drive the company along the road to success. And we have seen that humans in their state of nature – to quote the Enlightenment philosopher Jean-Jacques Rousseau – make decisions under the potential influence of many different biases that must be controlled to avoid their harmful effects.

Good leaders need to communicate using System 1, but rationalize using System 2. So how can they think clearly and decide fairly?

A leader who thinks using System 2: making fair decisions

How to avoid decision biases

All leaders are first and foremost human beings, individuals who are under the influence of System 1, and the main decision biases we've already learned about: overconfidence, confirmation, mental availability and present.

Remember that on the one hand, humans are unaware of the influence these biases may have on our decisions, and on the other hand, expertise is not an advantage but an additional burden because it aggravates the feeling that we are immune to the effects of the

....
18   Liz Wiseman and Greg McKeown, *Multipliers: How the Best Leaders Make Everyone Smarter*, HarperBusiness, 2010.

biases. And because all leaders see themselves as experts, they are even more at risk! Making good decisions is an even more difficult challenge than is generally admitted. So how can business leaders maximize the chances of avoiding those pesky biases that influence their decisions?

Knowledge, an essential prerequisite

First we need to be aware of how vulnerable we are. Even though behavioral science has clearly proven that knowledge itself is not enough to generate a desired behavior, as a starting point it is absolutely vital. To reduce the risk of making wrong decisions, we need to be aware of the underlying mechanisms that influence our behavior:

- The essential role of System 1, especially in terms of mental short-cuts that lead us to jump to conclusions from clues that may be misleading, or the huge importance of emotions.
- The cognitive biases that thwart our perceptions of a situation and make our analysis more subjective than that of a properly enlightened decision-maker.

In order to avoid these two potentially harmful influences, the very foundation of a good decision is a comprehensive knowledge, by virtue of proper training, of the factors that influence our behavior. And of course, this fundamental knowledge mustn't be restricted to business managers but made available to all employees who – within the confines of their roles – need to make decisions that impact the company's overall performance. I would go as far as to say that the insight we have obtained through behavioral science is so essential in helping people make the best decisions, both personal and professional, that the subject should be taught on school curriculums. Understanding what influences our decisions and behaviors is to my mind at least as fundamental as understanding mathematics, biology, or foreign languages. It's basic knowledge that is useful for everyone. But that's a whole other matter... Let's get back to decision-making in companies.

Even though in-depth knowledge of how we are influenced when we make decisions is essential, it's just the beginning and brings with it a huge challenge: how can we leverage this knowledge and make better decisions on a daily basis? How can we be sure that in each decision we make, we avoid the pitfalls and traps we described earlier?

Use a specific process to move from theory to practice

If we are to overcome this challenge, knowing the trap exists is simply not enough. Systematic processes must be implemented to help our brains move from theoretical knowledge to beneficial practice.

Because biases are like optical illusions: awareness of how they work isn't enough to release yourself from their grip. In the famous example where two identical circles are surrounded by circles of different sizes, even when we know that the two are the same size it doesn't stop us from seeing one as being larger than the other.

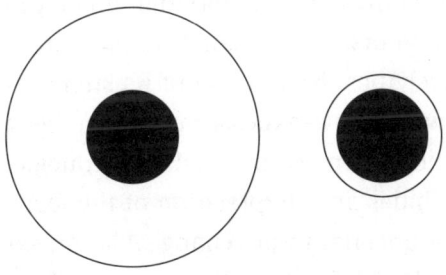

FIGURE 6.1:   Delboeuf illusion

Knowledge of the bias doesn't shield us from its misleading impact. In her wonderful book on gender equality[19], Harvard University Professor Iris Bohnet draws on analysis carried out by her colleague Frank Dobbin on more than 800 large American corporations running diversity training programs from 1971 to 2002[20] to show that there was no effect on diversity in the companies involved. Providing training means sharing knowledge, but is not enough to counteract the effects

....

19 Iris Bohnet, *What Works: Gender Equality by Design*, Belknap Press, March 2016.
20 Alexandra Kalev, Erin Kelly and Frank Dobbin, "Best Practices or Best Guesses? Assessing the Efficacy of Corporate Affirmative Action and Diversity Policies", *American Sociological Review*, vol. 71, August 2006.

of our unconscious biases, and in this case, gender stereotypes in particular.

It is of course useful to take step back and think about the potential effects of these biases when making decisions, so that we can try to avoid falling victim to them. But there is another risk: first that simply considering the effects of the biases might not be enough to resist them, and above all, that the pressure of daily life makes doing this much less of a reflex than it ought to be. That's why designing and applying specific processes might mean that we can make "unbiased" decisions more confidently.

Warren Buffett decided to establish processes like these to avoid the negative effect of one of the most dangerous biases for an investor: the confirmation bias. As you may remember, that's the bias that encourages us to collect, process and memorize information that confirms our original opinions. In investment terms, choosing to back a company based on an in-depth analysis of its situation may in fact be warped by the confirmation bias. A company's initial appeal may have generated an excessively positive opinion of its strengths and its ability to create value, while its weaknesses may have been underestimated. Because behind the most painstaking strategic, financial, fiscal or social audits hides an interpretation of the facts, and perhaps most importantly the uncertainty of a changeable context in which all companies operate. The confirmation bias can be lurking in the depths of even this kind of process.

So what was the process that Warren Buffett put into place in his attempt to invest as often as possible by avoiding the confirmation bias? First by recognizing its existence, even in a brain as well structured as his. Buffett writes: "Man's natural inclination is to cling to his beliefs, particularly if they are reinforced by recent experience."[21] This knowledge led the director from Berkshire to give his peers the following advice: "Doubt yourself." But as well as putting this doubt in his own convictions into practice, Buffett also uses another specific process: he asks his team to perform

....

21   Jason Zweig, "Lesson from Buffett: Doubt Yourself", *The Wall Street Journal*,
     5 May 2013, wsj.com.

systematic and comprehensive searches into the facts and elements that would *stop* him from going ahead with the decision he plans to make. He also encourages meetings with those whose opinions differ from his own, in order to test his initial feelings. His aim isn't to bring the other person around to his point of view, but to understand the logic and reasoning that led that other person to draw a different conclusion from Buffett himself. Buffett's final goal is easy to understand: evaluate the relevance of his own position by questioning it through the eyes of those who are best placed to do so: people who disagree with it. This process optimizes his chances of fighting against the potential effects of the confirmation bias and ultimately maximizes his chances of making the best investment decisions.

This specific process is based on some general rules that we can all follow. Not only for the confirmation bias, but for all the main biases we have described:

- Doubt ourselves while we are in the process of making a decision (so that when the project is in progress, we can take action rather than begin doubting).
- Collect data based on research into facts and arguments that call our initial thoughts into question (because those thoughts will naturally be favored).
- Listen to different points of view.
- Establish a psychological context that encourages criticism and debate.

As we have seen, "Doubt yourself" is Buffett's number one piece of advice. It is only possible when we are aware of the biases, but also requires inner humility on the part of the decision-maker. Doubt must not be debilitating, but rather helpful in the making of an enlightened decision. It must prevent us from jumping to the conclusions that System 1 naturally suggests, while making sure we question our initial feelings. Is the decision I am about to make a result of my analysis of the facts and the situation, or could it be influenced by one of the biases? This initial doubt means that the decision we eventually make will be of better quality.

Information generated by the data collection process is also a very useful tool in better decision making. By focusing on what calls the initial feeling into question rather than what confirms it, we are more likely to perform an exhaustive and rigorous analysis. The emergence of both big data and artificial intelligence are certainly promising for reducing bias in information gathering.

Juxtaposing different points of view is also a very useful approach. It has the advantage of examining what arguments may be presented by someone with opposing views. It may connect all the facts and present a story based on logical arguments generated by these facts to create a situation in which the final decision maker has a much broader and potentially more convincing overall position.

Lastly, none of this can work unless there is a fundamental basis: that each person invited to take part in the decision-making process in the leader's entourage feels free to express their opinion without it having negative implications for their image, or worse, the development of their career. Leaders often have strong characters, and convictions to match. And while that's often a quality – especially with regards to expressing their vision and their conviction – it may also significantly sabotage good quality decision-making. Because when confronted with a confident leader who pushes their initial feelings to the forefront, someone with an opposite point of view requires a healthy psychological environment for them to express an opposite opinion. The company and the leader must have created and encouraged a culture of listening and contradiction to ensure that debate and good quality decision-making are actively encouraged. While collective decisions are a way of limiting the negative effects of individual biases, behavioral science shows that this can only be true under certain conditions, because a group of individuals are all prone to major potential biases.

Collective decisions: a useful approach... but only under certain conditions

As well as co-creating Nudge and being one of the world's best experts on behavioral economics, Professor Cass Sunstein worked closely with President Obama and served as Administrator in the White House Office of Information and Regulatory Affairs from 2009 to 2012.

In American administrations, as in most businesses and companies, group decisions within a management team or as part of a team-based project are now standard operating procedure. Why? Quite simply because several heads and expertise in several fields are supposed to generate better decisions than a single person. That's what we would naturally believe. But behavioral science doesn't actually agree. In their book about how groups make decisions, Cass Sunstein and Reid Hastie write: "Do groups usually correct individual mistakes? Our simple answer is that they do not. Far too often, groups actually amplify those mistakes."[22] In fact, studies carried out to understand how groups make decisions show that in the absence of a certain number of specific rules, groups naturally operate under the influence of major biases that drive them to decisions that are often of a lesser quality than those an average individual from that same group would have made. The two-fold hope that a group would at least have the same decision-making ability as those of its best members, and ideally even better thanks to the positive synergy associated with sharing information and taking part in debate didn't hold water when researchers analyzed decisions made by several groups.

When they examined these studies, Sunstein and Hastie identified four negative effects of a group on decision-making quality:
- Amplification
- Cascade
- Polarization
- Information sharing

The amplification effect spotlights the fact that a group is collectively even more greatly influenced by the negative effects of individual biases than they are as individuals. For example, the group as a whole is even more prone to overconfidence in its vision and its decisions,

---

22 Cass R. Sunstein and Reid Hastie, *Wiser: Getting Beyond Groupthink to Make Groups Smarter*, Harvard Business Review Press, 2015.

or it is even more influenced by the framing effect and the way information is presented. Being in a group doesn't automatically reduce these individual biases. Quite the opposite, the group actually tends to amplify them.

The cascade effect stems from humans' social dimension that generates imitation and conformity with the society in which we live. In a group, the cascade effect lies in the impact an individual who expresses their opinion has on the individuals who speak next. There is an order in all debates, and that order has a huge impact on the decisions that are made. The manner in which the speakers that go first share a piece of information or an opinion, depending on their status within the company or the expertise they are supposed to have about the subject of the discussion, dictates how the speakers that follow react. Subsequent speakers may even be compelled to change what they say. A speaker may for instance withhold a fact if they are concerned that it may counter what other members of the group have said, or if they are afraid to appear incompetent after an expert has already given an in-depth presentation on the same subject. They may also prefer to keep their disagreement under wraps, because several other people have already expressed opposite opinions. A false consensus can then emerge after the first few opinions are expressed, if they appear to converge. The other members of the group then accept them not because they agree necessarily, but because they are victims of self-censorship. Ultimately, even though working as a group is supposed to mean that everyone benefits from the knowledge and points of view of all of its members, the cascade effect may actually go against the expected positive effect of making a decision as a group, and generate bad outcomes.

The polarization effect is characterized by driving the group to an extreme final position as a result of a discussion when individual participants did not go into the meeting intending to support the extreme position. This effect is particularly true in groups of individuals who respect and admire each other. When individuals in the group start out by being in favor of risk-taking, they are even more in favor of it by the end of the discussion. In contrast, when individuals favor a prudent option, they become even more cautious as a group. For example, if sales volumes or expected revenue for a new product or service are being discussed, a positive individual estimate by each member of a group will lead to a very positive estimate by the group as a whole at the end of the discussion, and conversely, a conservative individual estimate will lead to an ultra-conservative group estimate! The polarization effect can also generate bad final decisions.

Finally, the information sharing effect refers to a specific group bias known as the common knowledge effect. Initially, some information may be known by the majority of the group – common knowledge – while other information is only known by one or two people. In this case, the common knowledge will have a much stronger influence on the group's judgments than the information that is only known by some individuals. The importance of the information would appear to depend on the number of people who knew it before the discussion began, whereas the benefit of making a decision as a group is actually to gather more information to get a better outcome.

These various biases show that decisions are not necessarily better if they are made by a group. Here again, as with individual biases, the key is to set up a process that allows a group to avoid the negative effects of these biases and therefore to benefit from the potential advantages of collective decisions in comparison to individual decisions.

The beginning of wisdom is, of course, when the members of the group know about the biases that may be at work. But that's just the beginning. Applying the following fundamental principles can maximize the quality of the final decision making:
- Starting point: a diverse group
- Golden rule: a favorable psychological environment, a leader who encourages people to listen, ensures balanced participation, provides constructive criticism... and speaks last
- A reward for collective performance
- Examining opposite viewpoints

First, a diverse group is essential for avoiding the negative effects of the confirmation bias. A group of individuals with different backgrounds, responsibilities and personalities will generate potentially different points of view and offer a vast scope of knowledge. That's the fundamental advantage of a group, compared to an individual: being able to understand a situation with as much relevant information as possible in order to make an enlightened decision. But that's just the start, because as we have just seen, studies show that information and opinions may be withheld in a group situation.

The psychological environment and how the group normally functions – or doesn't function – dictate how its members express their views. The group leader needs to proactively foster the conditions for productive discussion. First by encouraging each participant to express themselves individually. The aim is to fight both the natural predisposition of some people to speak out of turn, and others to stay quiet, while giving space for "junior" participants to express their views as often as the more seasoned members of the group. If a participant has been fairly selected to participate in a group discussion, then that person potentially has a point of view and a stock of information that may be useful to the group as a whole. So each person should be encouraged to speak, and talk time should be distributed equally. If necessary, the most reserved participants should be solicited directly. The leader must also ensure that the group understands the importance of listening and an open-minded attitude, to counteract the possession bias that naturally draws us to our own ideas and makes other people's input appear less attractive. Constructive criticism is also the cornerstone for a successful debate. Expressing views is not enough if the speaker withholds information to avoid situations of conflict with another participant, or is frightened of appearing negative. Leaders must encourage criticism from all sources, while ensuring that the debate centers on ideas and not people. Finally, the leader of the group must only express their own opinion when everyone else has had a chance to express theirs. This is especially true in the very specific context of a board of directors. The views of a company director can generate such a strong leading message that when they are expressed at the beginning of a debate they can become a focal point for the discussion, and have a strong impact on the views of the other participants and how they express them. The best thing that a director can do for a group to encourage discussion and arrive at the very best decision is simply to keep his or her mouth shut... or at least speak last. And obviously, as well as emphasizing the importance of this method as soon as the meeting begins, the director and each member of the group must follow the rules: there must be no negative (or even positive) implications for individuals who have given their opinions during the discussions. Criticism can only be encouraged and useful if it is properly respected. Members of the group can only feel confident and make good quality discussions if they feel supported.

Giving rewards for collective group performance – through the quality of the decisions that are made – is another way to align each member's own specific interests. Some bonus or incentive systems may counteract the positive effects that the aforementioned rules may encourage. On a board of directors of an international company for instance, some members may be responsible for a specific region, country or offer. If individually they are only evaluated on the results generated from their own area of responsibility, they may be driven to fight a decision that would potentially be beneficial for the company as a whole, but not for them as individuals. If they are also evaluated on the company's overall performance, these members of the board will be motivated by a global vision, while being able to express possible solutions to improve the situation in their area.

Finally, the group's decision-making process can include systematic approaches that aim to take into account the specific risks and costs involved in a decision the group is about to make, before it is fully approved. For example, Dan Ariely suggests writing out in black and white all the reasons why the decision a company is about to make would end up being a failure. It's not about expressing a position, but working as a group to look for all the elements that may back up this point of view. It has a clear objective: to look at the initiative critically and with an open mind, to maximize the chances of making a good final decision, while identifying possible risks and thinking about what suitable measures could be taken to avoid them.

It's also possible to give the specific role of devil's advocate to one person, or a group of people to encourage them to be critical of the ideas that are being developed: explicitly attributing this role will prevent others in the group from seeing that person in a negative light.

The end goal is the same: to have an in-depth discussion that takes all points of view into account. Using a process like this helps a group benefit from the synergy it needs to avoid the traps of the biases we have mentioned earlier, by maximizing its chances of making good decisions.

A fair and meaningful balance

Professor Edgar Schein[23] did some work many years ago that is still very useful in understanding how a leader disseminates a company's culture. Schein identifies six key elements:

- What do leaders notice, what do they measure and verify on a regular basis?
- How do leaders respond to major incidents and organizational crises?
- How do leaders distribute the resources that are available to them?
- How do they direct, learn and coach?
- How do leaders allocate rewards and status?
- How do leaders recruit, select, promote and dismiss?

In fact, each of these elements is a way of understanding the company's culture. As behavioral economist Koen Smets points out[24] in a recent article, the judgments that leaders make in these particular situations are indicative of the company's culture in action.

A few simple questions put to a firm's leaders can quickly identify the true nature of its culture. Here are a few concrete examples that may give clearer insight into the reality of a company's corporate culture, beyond the words that are being spoken: on the board of directors' meeting agenda, are the financial results the first point to be examined and the one on which most time is spent? Are the bonuses and incentive systems usually only related to financial results or do they incorporate more behavioral elements such as participating in group projects, being recognized by your employees, or carrying

....

23 Edgar H. Stein, *Organizational Culture and Leadership,* John Wiley & Sons, 2010.
24 Koen Smets, "Organizational Leaders as Behavorial Economists?", medium.com.

out specific assignments, for example encouraging gender equality? Are they essentially financial in nature or do they include less material elements such as a team-building weekend? Have people been promoted for their spectacular financial performance in their area of responsibility, or do they have a more balanced profile that includes other types of broader successes such as elements related to the company's social responsibility? As soon as there is a drop in profitability, is the company's natural reaction (the 'default' option in Nudge terminology) to work out how to cut staff numbers or find other solutions to accelerate the growth of the company through innovation, or improve internal organization, or even find a way to rebalance the work that needs to be done? When allocating resources, do training investments go beyond what the law requires or are they driven down to the bare minimum? In the employee appraisal process, is the revered annual interview, which combines an evaluation of performance and remuneration, always the pivotal point or is feedback from managers more regular and genuinely focused on making improvements through training opportunities? What are the evaluation criteria for employees and to what extent do they combine financial performance with behavioral performance?

The list is very long. But I think you've got the idea: the key point is that the corporate culture needs to be a beacon of reliability at times when tensions are high. Because judgment calls are not easy for business leaders. They express the reality of a corporate culture much more strongly than words, speeches, or memos. When the choices are difficult, what should be prioritized, what decisions should be made and what do they reveal about the real concerns of the company and its leaders? And that's where the depth of a business culture shows its true colors.

Employees are fully aware of it, they can decode decisions and give them meaning, and that has the power to strengthen or destroy their belief in their company's culture.

In the end, the role of the leader in employee engagement is essential. As we have seen, effective leaders can create the physical and psychological conditions for success and well-being at work. From the strategic decisions they make to how they behave on a daily basis, from their ability to communicate about a transcendental mission and inspire their employees with motivational values to the art of developing the people around them, each word and each action can be a catalyst or an obstacle to gaining an employee's engagement. But even though they have power, they simply cannot do it alone.

From progress managers to "We're all leaders"!

The key role of direct supervisors

There are more cogs in the employee engagement machine. And plenty of them: direct supervisors.

Gallup found that they are the most important people in a company. From a meta-analysis of more than 2,500 business units including 105,000 employees, the results led to a surprising conclusion: engagement at work differs from one department to another, even within the same company. But that will come as no surprise to anyone who has worked at a big firm. Gallup writes: "The meta-analysis revealed that employees rated the items differently depending on which business unit they worked for rather than which company. This meant that, for the most part, these 12 opinions were being formed by the employee's immediate manager rather than by the policies or procedures of the overall company. We had discovered that the manager – not pay, benefits, perks or a charismatic corporate leader – was the critical player in building a strong workplace."[25] Yes, you can be an employee at an extraordinary company while remaining completely disengaged due to the behavior of your manager, and the opposite is also true: you can be very engaged and enjoy a high level of well-being in a run-of-the-mill company if you have an excellent direct supervisor. But what does excellent mean? Gallup states that it's the ability of a manager to generate satisfaction in his or her employees on the following six items:

- I know what is expected of me at work.

25   Don Clifton, *First, Break all the Rules, op. cit.*

- I have the materials and equipment I need to do my job well.
- At work, I have the opportunity to do what I do best every day.
- Over the past seven days, someone has recognized my work or I have felt proud that I have done my job well.
- My manager, or someone at work, seems to take care of me as a person.
- There is someone at work who encourages me to develop my skills.

In the conclusion of this study, Gallup underlines[26]: "Employees don't put their faith in the myths of 'great companies' or 'great leaders'. For employees, there are only managers: great ones, poor ones and many in between."

So if the role of the direct manager is so important, how can we make sure that those managers behave in a way that generates engagement?

First, recruit well! That means being able to define the profiles of candidates who, beyond their technical know-how, have a personality that is likely to adopt the behavior the company wants to encourage.

Then train well. If one of the company's genuine top-priority objectives is to create engagement among its employees, then managers in that company need to be fully trained on the specific behavioral practices that can bring about this engagement. Because in far too many companies, direct managers have been promoted mainly for their technical expertise or commercial success, while their managerial skills have often been overlooked. And yet, people management is without a doubt the most complex element in a leader's day-to-day mission. Especially if it's not just about having employees apply processes and checking them, but about creating an engaging workplace environment through recognition, support through challenges, and instilling confidence, autonomy and friendship.

It's about "technical" training in how to manage each of these elements, but also changing the vision of the manager's role. Old ideas are being replaced by a vision of a manager who is there for his or her employees, to help them succeed in their mission on a daily basis and to develop as individuals in the workplace. Managers are

....
26 *Id.*

no longer team bosses, but inspiring and demanding human coaches. Remember the wonderful research carried out by Teresa Amabile on the importance of a sense of purpose in engagement. Direct supervisors are the best placed to facilitate this progress by acting as a resource for expertise and advice to help their employees grow. But being human doesn't mean being lax or letting things slide: managers need to help an employee step out of his or her comfort zone by assigning new projects or setting ambitious objectives if they are to create the conditions for progress. In her book *Radical Candor*[27] – Kim Scott presents a very basic diagram made up of two axes that express this two-fold intention perfectly: she uses a vertical axis entitled "Care personally" and a horizontal axis labeled "Challenge directly." It's a very good way of expressing the two-edged ambition of a good manager and Scott uses the term "radical candor", which means the ability to show an employee that you're looking out for their interests and taking steps to help them succeed, while simultaneously making demands of them and setting out clear objectives, being honest and direct in your criticism and expectations. Fair behavior from a manager is about striking the right balance: if managers are only concerned about "caring personally" and make no demands, they bring about what Scott calls "destructive empathy." If the manager's behavior involves setting a constant set of challenges and shows no care for the employee's personal well-being, it comes across as aggression. Finally, behavior that involves no benevolence and no demands is quite simply no management at all.

Even though the business as a whole may be focused on getting this two-fold approach to management right, direct managers have the power to strengthen or reduce potential engagement and effectiveness in both individuals and teams simply by how they behave on a daily basis. People management can be learned, and it's even more crucial when a company bases its strategy on employee engagement.

While training is an essential prerequisite, it isn't enough to generate the desired behavior, because words are empty when they're not

....
27   Kim Scott, *Radical Candor: Be a Kick-Ass Boss Without Losing Your Humanity*, MacMillan, 2017.

backed up by actions. The company's entire ecosystem needs to work as an incentive for direct managers to implement good engagement practices if it really wants to achieve that. Everything about the company must be coherent with the engagement message, and show a clear path including two key elements:

- How managers are evaluated;
- How promotions work.

The way managers are evaluated sends a message to every employee in the company about what is really expected of them. For managers, how their performance is evaluated with regards to their ability to engage with their teams is directly proportional to the importance the company places on employee engagement. It's one of the clearest ways to set the course. In fact, evaluation criteria are less about motivating managers to take action towards employee engagement and more about ensuring coherence with the company's overall message. If engagement is proclaimed throughout the company as being vital but the evaluation system is based on technical or commercial performance, the company creates confusion or worse, shows that the quest for engagement is just a theme for a jazzy presentation rather than a goal with genuine importance. Evaluation systems for managers must therefore very clearly take into account their ability to engage, which can be assessed directly with their employees.

But for a company that really wants to incite direct supervisors to generate engagement, another major signal is who gets promoted. As Edgar Schein points out, this relates to one of the ways a company can spread the culture it wishes to promote, and sends out a very clear message. How do the people who receive a promotion convey the culture? And how are they recognized for their specific managerial qualities and not only for their technical or commercial successes? Those are the key questions whose answers can determine how other managers behave. People who are promoted are held up as an example, to incite everyone to act in similar ways.

Ultimately, encouraging leadership and direction shouldn't only be the business of the top echelons of a company, but should shine through in the behavior of all direct supervisors. And as a result, every employee must feel to a certain extent that they are the leader of their own life at work.

All employees should be in control of their own tasks

A feeling of autonomy at work is an important condition for engagement. When employees are given autonomy – within the confines of their specific responsibilities – they can tailor their work to their own aspirations and find greater motivation, more satisfaction, and enhanced pride in their accomplishments. Studies show that autonomy does indeed generate better individual and collective performance.

Giving employees more autonomy means giving them the chance to assume a degree of control over their own work.

The company has two roles to play in the perception of autonomy:
- Generally, when defining tasks for each employee;
- Individually, in how direct supervisors manage.

Within the scope of a specific framework, employees become their own leaders, and feel increased motivation. Motivation can be created by the entire company ecosystem, but granting autonomy to employees directly helps to bring about individual motivation. As we've seen, motivation isn't just an outcome, but a skill that can be developed and learned on an individual level as long as the person believes that they have control over part of the decision-making process, and over their actions and tasks, and that they are not robots performing duties decided upon by an external force.

We've now looked at the structural foundations for creating engagement and performance, and the physical and psychological work environment that encourages and facilitates productivity by using the teachings of behavioral science.

But in addition to these pillars for success, two other specific challenges are vital for long-lasting prosperity: how can a company attract the talent that will enact these teachings? How can it create an environment that promotes continuous learning and innovation? Because here again it doesn't come naturally, and now we're going to find out how it can be achieved.

Part 3

Encouraging groups to adopt winning behavior

Regardless of industry, size or positioning, from small businesses to corporations, everyone faces the same general context: a rapidly changing world. The famous VUCA (volatility, uncertainty, complexity and ambiguity) applies to all organizations and requires the same basic responses for success: employees need to work together productively on a daily basis, and companies need to know how to learn and transform effectively. Yves Morieux and Peter Tollman from BCG write: "Cooperation isn't just some taken-for-granted value or goal (the desire that people *work together as a team*). It is a complex social process, hard to create and easy to destroy. Organizations have to create the right context for cooperation."[1]

When striving to get employees to adopt winning behaviors, creating the right psychological environment for motivation to thrive is yet another challenge.

---

1   Yves Morieux and Peter Tollman, *Six Simple Rules: How to Manage Complexity without Getting Complicated*, Harvard Business Review Press, 2014.

Chapter 7

A basic requirement: talents that can work together

I'm a huge fan of soccer, and of Paris Saint-Germain in particular. As with any team sport, it isn't the sum of the talent in eleven outstanding individuals that makes a great soccer team, but a jigsaw puzzle of different talents who can play together to achieve the same objective: to win the match. The key to success is often the ability to work together, rather than individual talent: getting the members of the team to function as a group to achieve a common purpose.

In this respect, a business is no different to a team sport. Of course talent is fundamental, and attracting and retaining it is no mean feat. However, it's only the first stage of another, more complicated challenge, which is getting a variety of talents to pull together and achieve a shared goal: business performance. In today's increasingly complex world, where no individual has enough knowledge or information to move forward alone, cooperation is more crucial than ever. However, as is often the case, knowledge alone won't cut it, no matter how confidently anyone in the organization might claim otherwise. Employees won't work together and genuinely cooperate simply because their manager asks them to, but because the foundations have been laid to trigger factors that influence their behavior and make each person want to cooperate.

Yes, you need to hire talent... but they need grit and team spirit!

Almost twenty years ago, Jim Collins wrote in his worldwide best-seller *From Good to Great*[1] "The executives who ignited the transformations

1 Jim Collins, *Good to Great: Why Some Companies Make the Leap... and Others Don't*, William Collins, 2001.

from good to great did not first figure out where to drive the bus and then get people to take it there. No, they *first* got the right people on the bus (and the wrong people off the bus) and *then* figured out where to drive it... If we get the right people on the bus, the right people in the right seats, and the wrong people off the bus, then we'll figure out how to take it someplace great."

So, before you can get talented people to cooperate, you need to know how to recruit them. Talent that lacks team spirit will perform poorly due to internal rivalry, and a team that lacks talent will never be able to accomplish its goal. Behavioral science has no shortage of methods for avoiding the multitude of biases that can impede cooperation, which is crucial in a business context.

A structured process

The interview and hiring process that most companies use is highly simplistic: rather than following a clear structure, interviewers take an ad hoc approach to form an idea of the candidate's background and personality. Yet studies show that this is the worst possible way to go about recruiting. In a meta-analysis to evaluate the comparative relevance of nineteen different recruitment techniques based on the results of eighty-five years of research and publications on the matter, researchers Frank Schmidt and John Hunter demonstrated that unstructured interviews were unreliable for predicting the future performance of the candidate who was hired.[2] In fact those approaches were barely more effective than analyzing a candidate's handwriting or how many years of experience they had. Iris Bohnet, a behavioral scientist and Harvard Business School Professor says: "But while unstructured interviews consistently receive the highest ratings for perceived effectiveness from hiring managers, dozens of studies have found them to be among the *worst* predictors of actual

---

2 Frank L. Schmidt and John E. Hunter, "The Validity and Utility of Selection Methods in Personnel Psychology: Practical and Theoretical Implications of 85 Years of Research Findings", *Psychological Bulletin*, vol. 124, No.2, 1998.

on-the-job performance — far less reliable than general mental ability tests, aptitude tests, or personality tests."[3]

Bias rears its head once again. Most people who conduct interviews use this method, which has been proven to be ineffective, because they themselves are negatively influenced by various biases:

- Overconfidence – about their expertise and judgment skills (remember, the more of an expert a person is, the more susceptible they are to this type of bias) – which causes them to prefer their own way of doing things and reject any other methods that could jeopardize their autonomy.
- Hidden costs: potential failure that may arise as a result of hiring the wrong person can either be explained – again, don't forget that System 1 will automatically find causes that reinforce our self-confidence – or go unnoticed: we didn't know we had a better candidate because we weren't able to identify them, so we don't even know that a mistake has been made.
- The conformity bias, which stems from recruiters tending to veer towards candidates who are similar to themselves, especially in terms of their leisure interests, appearance, or experience.
- The confirmation bias also comes into play during the course of the interview: recruiters are likely to form an opinion in the first few minutes. Depending on whether that first impression is positive or negative, they will spend the rest of the time looking for ways to confirm their opinion.

A study carried out by the University of Texas Medical School demonstrated that conventional hiring processes fail to identify the best candidates. An initial selection of 150 medical students was made using a standard unstructured interview process. Once this had been done, the State of Texas asked the university to increase the class size to 200 rather than the initial 150. By this point, the pool of students available included only those considered to be less well-performing, who had not got into any of the universities to which they had applied.

....
3   Iris Bohnet, "How to Take the Bias Out of Interviews", *Harvard Business Review*, 18 April 2016, hbr.org.

Of the 50 extra students recruited, only seven of them had received an offer from another university. Researchers at the University of Texas decided to conduct a comparative analysis of the students selected during the first round and the 50 students from the second round, by studying them during their time at university and beyond. The result was unequivocal: there was no difference in performance between the students who had been selected the first time round, and those who had been rejected by most universities and given a second chance. What's more, the researchers demonstrated that almost 75% of the difference when assessing candidates during the hiring process was not due to objective factors such as grades or ranking, but the assessor's perception of them after the interview. Seeing the results of this study, Iris Bohnet wrote: "Faced with this finding, the researchers ask whether, after an initial assessment of academic and other performance measures, traditional interviews should be replaced by a lottery among the viable applicants."

Highly-qualified recruitment practitioner Laszlo Bock drives the point home further, saying[4]: "We all think we are great at it [hiring], but we never go back to check if we are, and so we never get better." There is a wealth of data showing that most assessment occurs within the first three to five minutes of an interview (or less), with the rest of the time spent confirming that bias; that subconsciously, interviewers are drawn to people who are like them; and that most interview techniques are worthless."[5] Basing an interview process on open, unstructured discussion can therefore be risky, because ultimately it does nothing to maximize the chances of recruiting people who will perform well on the job. Studies show that the solution hinges not on training, nor the interviewers – who can only make marginal progress given the power of the biases at work – nor is the solution to conduct interviews as a panel.

Unstructured interviews should actually be replaced by a structured process that limits recruitment biases and identifies the candidates who will succeed in the job and possess the qualities

....
4   Laszlo Bock, *Work Rules!*, *op. quote.*
5   *Ibid.*

required to ensure they will thrive. There is no miracle tool for this, although studies have proven the following practices to be effective:

- A detailed definition of the profile required, with the best companies clearly setting the bar high, and being willing to withstand pressing recruitment deadlines if it takes a while to find the right candidate.
- Conducting an initial cognitive ability test to assess the candidate's emotional intelligence and situational awareness, and their capacity for learning and development.
- Individual structured interviews whereby the same set of questions covering all the attributes to be assessed are put to each candidate in the same order so that comparisons are less subjective.
- Routinely including a role-play test, which is the single best predictor of future on-the-job performance.
- Rating each candidate immediately after assessing each attribute, to reduce the memorization and confirmation biases. Recent events are remembered more easily, so the candidate's later answers may be weighted disproportionately if an overall assessment is performed at the end of the interview.
- Getting a variety of people to assess the candidate; not just their future direct supervisor but also potential coworkers and direct reports, not only to assess the candidate's ability to fulfill the role, but also to gauge whether they are compatible with the company's culture.
- Comparing short-listed candidates horizontally (topic by topic for all candidates) rather than vertically (all topics for one candidate before moving on to the next), to limit the bias that arises from the halo effect and the order in which the questions are answered.
- Having all assessments aggregated and reviewed by a recruitment committee made up of people who are not directly concerned by the hire, who will make the final decision rather than it being entirely in the hands of the direct supervisor.
- Regularly assessing the efficiency of the hiring process and how it is perceived by candidates, including those who were unsuccessful, so that it can be constantly optimized.

Introducing a hiring process based on behavioral scientific findings isn't an easy thing to do. Aside from the process itself, it's absolutely essential to look at how talent recruitment is viewed within the company. If it is implemented as a strategic action, then it must be recognized as such in terms of the resources that are allocated to it: all too often, despite an admirable narrative, many companies neglect this process and prefer to take the easy option (carrying out non-directive interviews, for example) or try to identify a candidate as quickly as possible due to pressure from internal clients, which has a negative impact on the quality of the recruitment process. Google openly admits to spending more than twice as much as the average company on its hiring process (as a percentage of the HR budget). And to prove just how important it is to the company, Larry Page is personally involved in the whole process and gives his own views on all new potential hires. The way Laszlo Bock sees it, "More important than the feedback itself is the message from Larry to the company that hiring is taken seriously at the highest levels, and that we have a duty to continue doing a great job."[6] He adds: "And new Googlers ('Nooglers') are always delighted to learn that Larry personally reviewed their applications." Which goes to show that a company can start acknowledging and recognizing its employees from the moment it begins the hiring process.

Naturally, it's up to each company to determine which personal qualities should be sought in addition to technical expertise. And remember, over and above a candidate's intelligence, a superboss will intentionally seek to develop their creative ability and versatility. However, new research shows that qualities other than talent are the keys to professional success.

Grit and team spirit!

Angela Duckworth, Professor of Psychology at the University of Pennsylvania, has carried out substantial research in her quest to understand exceptional achievement, and recently published her

---

6   *Ibid.*

main findings in a book entitled *Grit*[7]. This illustrious researcher (watch her TedTalk if you need any more proof of her brilliance – it's been viewed by almost 12 million people) examined the specific characteristics of people who have achieved exceptional results in a wide range of fields, including sport, art, business and education. Her conclusions are clear and comprehensive: talent alone does not explain outstanding results. Those who become the best in their field combine two particular qualities at a very high level: they are passionate about what they do and show unwavering perseverance.

Expertise is generated almost naturally given this winning combination. When you "work" on something you are passionate about, you're not really working at all; you're simply doing what you love. Putting in long hours or suffering setbacks in a bid to improve isn't the same when you're doing what you love compared to when you're just doing a job. So, if your passion is also your living, you're far more likely to work more, and more efficiently, than anybody else. In doing so, you significantly increase your chances of becoming an expert in your field.

However, passion is only the first variable in the equation for outstanding success. The second is perseverance, or the ability to keep at it and stay focused on the same passion for years at a time, because someone who flits from one passion to another will never rack up the expertise that a rival may develop over a much longer period. As Angela Duckworth stresses, "Enthusiasm is common. Endurance is rare."[8] Success is underpinned by the combination of passion and perseverance, which she calls grit.

Indeed, that's why this research is both remarkable and very useful: it reframes the idea of hankering after pure talent. It turns out that the quest to secure the best talent may not be quite as good an idea for companies as we might think. Because what Duckworth shows through her research is that people with qualities that are less glitzy and less obvious than pure talent can be a valuable asset for the company that hires them. Their passion and perseverance mean they

---

7   Angela Duckworth, *Grit: The Power of Passion and Perseverance*, Scribner, 2016.
8   *Ibid.*

are "structurally" engaged in their work if the company's ecosystem allows them to flourish. They are the ones who will do their best every day – and their best is really, really excellent – to achieve the targets set and contribute to the company's overall performance. Looking for candidates who possess this combination of passion and perseverance in their work or in a certain industry is, therefore, the linchpin of good recruitment. Danger comes when recruiters focus solely on talent[9]: "By shining our spotlight on talent, we risk leaving everything else in the shadows. We inadvertently send the message that these other factors – including grit – don't matter as much as they really do." Now, let's be clear – talent matters and it matters a lot. However, people with pure talent aren't the ones who succeed the most, but those who are talented, passionate *and* determined.

And grit can be measured! Angela Duckworth designed the Grit Scale, a specially designed questionnaire to evaluate a candidate's grit. So, rather than just scouting for pure talent, try to track down people with a high grit factor for your sector by making this test part of the hiring process. Then, remember to carry out the final recommendation: test the process and find ways to optimize it.

Of course, in order to lay the foundations for genuine team spirit where cooperation is the norm, you need to make sure the candidates selected in the first place have a personality that fits. Which, in practical terms, means that although the talent you hire may be aware of their qualities, they need to have enough humility to be pleasant to work with, and enough empathy to prevent them from spending their time navel-gazing. The importance of emotional intelligence in great leaders that I referred to earlier also holds true for every individual in the company; therefore, the hiring process should include a thorough assessment which, at the very least, ensures that people with suitable personalities will be selected. That doesn't mean that everyone at the company has to have the same type of personality and conform to an ideal model, because in actual fact diversity – be it in terms of background, technical expertise, origin or personal traits – deepens and enhances a company's culture. This has also been demonstrated by a

....
9   *Ibid.*

number of studies on the subject that are cited in the excellent book *The Diversity Bonus*[10], by Professor Scott Page from the University of Michigan. Diversity unquestionably improves performance, especially when it comes to the most intricate and wide-ranging elements of the knowledge economy. For tasks like drafting a marketing plan, executing R&D and innovation programs, or designing sophisticated sales or logistics strategies, getting people on board who think differently benefits bottom-line performance.

However, while it's important to garner diversity, candidates whose personality wouldn't suit a cooperative environment should be rejected.

Once you've got the right people, you need to create the structural conditions for cooperation to become the default modus operandi.

Psychological safety generates cooperation

A business is inherently non-cooperative

A business is a somewhat singular environment where people don't tend to cooperate naturally. Risk aversion is built into all humans, and we have seen that it can hold people back in many ways, such as not asking questions for fear of sounding stupid or basic, not speaking up if their opinion goes against the tide, not suggesting innovative solutions in case they seem absurd, and, most certainly, not admitting to their mistakes. Basically, people shy away from cooperation for fear of damaging their image or career prospects. In fact, fear is one of the main things that a company's employees have in common; the most extreme fear is that of losing their job, but there is also the fear that their career won't turn out as planned. This can be explained by the existence of a hierarchy of people who wield substantial power over their subordinates. Amy Edmondson, Professor of Leadership and Management at Harvard Business School and a global leader

10 Scott E. Page, *The Diversity Bonus: How Great Teams Pay Off in the Knowledge Economy*, Princeton University Press, 2017.

in cooperation, wrote that: "Research shows that hierarchy, by its very nature, dramatically reduces speaking up by those lower in the pecking order. We are hard-wired, and then socialized, to be acutely sensitive to power, and to work to avoid being seen as deficient in any way by those in power. Most of this behavior is unconscious. As a result, in most organizations, even if leaders at the top of the hierarchy say they welcome employee feedback, and even if people have the knowledge and training to say something of importance, they still may remain silent out of fear of negative consequences."[11]

And yet, this is exactly the type of behavior the company needs. Asking questions to gain insight and enhance processes, offering constructive criticism to make better decisions, coming up with new and potentially more effective solutions, or allowing the rest of the company to benefit from one person's mistakes so that they are not repeated are all valuable tools for a company. Studies show that businesses in which this type of internal collaboration has been developed achieve better overall performance, but also higher levels of well-being and satisfaction among employees. When people work efficiently together, teams make the best decisions by drawing on the knowledge of all individuals, the company's pool of knowledge expands, and internal organization is transformed in a more controlled way.

However, on top of the individual biases mentioned above, there are a number of implicit and explicit factors that can curb cooperation and make it even harder to achieve. Studies by Amy Edmondson identified three main obstacles to cooperation in addition to individual biases:

- Physical distance
- Differences in status
- Diversity of knowledge

Physical distance may seem trivial, but it matters a great deal. It doesn't necessarily mean having colleagues at branches thousands of miles apart, it could simply be working with someone on a different floor, or even a coworker with an office just down the hall. Behavioral

....
11   Amy C. Edmondson, *Teaming, op. cit.*

science has proven that we are naturally inclined to save our energy, even when making the most trivial decisions, and we usually go for the easy option. In Dan Ariel's words, the "path of least resistance" is the most appealing, which explains much of our behavior. When it comes to our relationships in the workplace, this tendency means we're more likely to cooperate and engage with the colleagues nearest to us. However, once a company reaches a certain size, the notion of physical distance between individuals invariably crops up and throws a spanner in the works of communication, cooperation and interpersonal engagement outside of our immediate environment.

Differences in hierarchical status are another major obstacle and stir up the fear of authority that I mentioned earlier. However, it doesn't stop there; from a wider perspective, all types of differences come into play: age, gender, religion, social class, etc. Such diversity is a reality for many organizations and a challenge in itself, given the myriad stereotypes that can influence people's behavior towards each other. The bottom line is that it's just not that easy to chat freely, openly and on a level with people from other ranks. A person with a "lower" status in the organization, say a nurse compared with a doctor at a hospital, will tend to avoid discussions, adjust their judgment if they disagree, and, to a greater extent, avoid conflict. The outcome is a superficial working relationship whereby the organization misses out on what each party has to contribute.

Diversity of knowledge is the third structural limitation that Amy Edmondson identifies. This refers to the different skills that each person in the company can offer. The growing complexity that has characterized corporate growth in recent decades has translated into a multiplicity and diversity of internal expertise. The traditional major disciplines of human resources, finance, IT, marketing and sales have all splintered into an array of new subspecialties. For example, many marketing departments have evolved to include digital communication or social media specialists, and sales departments now include experts in e-commerce, customer relationship management or customer experience. Getting people to work together when they all have different backgrounds, baseline knowledge, standards and group bearings – not to mention different ways of communicating and inherent beliefs – is a considerable challenge, with the first step being simply to communicate without creating misunderstandings. Humans are creatures of habit: we'll open up to what we know and what we understand straight away, yet when dealing with the unknown – in this case, other people – our natural reaction and default setting is to be suspicious, watch and wait.

What's more, all these individual biases and obstacles are thrown into the mix in an environment where people are dealing with lots of tasks and responsibilities in a time-sensitive setting, making them even less receptive and less willing to cooperate with others, despite teamwork being the key factor for success in companies today.

So, unless measures are taken to purposefully turn it around, people's natural behavior in the workplace will be to collaborate as little as possible in order to avoid risk. Making internal cooperation standard practice means proactively dismantling the unhelpful default mode, to benefit individuals who all seek social interaction, and enhance the company's business performance.

Psychological safety, the key factor to cooperation

Psychological safety is the baseline requirement to encourage and facilitate cooperation. The concept arises from Professor Edgar Schein's work in 1965, and can be defined as "a climate in which people feel free to express their thoughts and feelings."[12] There are many advantages to this type of psychological environment for a company. First of all, individuals will say what they're really thinking without fearing other people's reactions. That is the crux of cooperation: benefitting from other people's insights and expertise in order to optimize progress or make the best decisions, but also for each person to adopt a more constructive mindset. Neuroscience studies have shown that a fear-induced defensive state of mind impedes communication and creative skills, whereas a feeling of safety does the opposite. More specifically, psychological safety encourages individuals to tell others about their mistakes, which is

----
12 Amy Edmondson, *Teaming, op. cit.*

one of the foundations for continuous improvement. It also sharpens a company's creative and innovative edge because everybody – even radicals and revolutionaries – feels entitled to express their ideas without the fear of ridicule. Finally, a climate of psychological safety allows people to focus on the shared goal that the group or the company is working towards; rather than spending time worrying about personal risk, focus can be shifted to the shared goal. For the same reason, employees are more willing to take responsibility and aim for more ambitious goals, because risk-taking and even failure are built into the culture of psychological safety.

So, the root of cooperation is a company's ability to create, disseminate and maintain this climate of psychological safety across the board.

However, while this is all very well in principle, actually creating and maintaining this type of climate is an uphill struggle. Studies show that psychological safety cannot be decreed and cannot be introduced from the top down. Amy Edmondson's work proves that success hinges more on the ability to encourage tangible changes in the way employees interact on a daily basis in the workplace.

Obviously, leaders also play a vital role in spreading and supporting a climate of psychological safety: the management team has to set the tone for the organization. But once again, it's essentially the day-to-day behavior of direct supervisors that has the most influence. Direct supervisors are best placed to spread this culture, to encourage everybody to express themselves openly for the benefit of the greater good. In practical terms, the first thing they need to do is make themselves available; managers create the foundations for cooperation by being as approachable as possible and genuinely engaged in the conversations they have with their staff. Being available may mean being physically accessible – not being in a separate office, or always leaving the door open – but it might also mean being mentally available, being prepared to engage with workers who initiate conversation. Likewise, as we saw when we looked at high quality connections, the quality of the conversation is equally as important. Not only is the manager approachable, but he or she is also available, attentive and genuinely engaged in the conversation, whatever the issue. Indeed, one of the prerequisites for psychological safety is that managers take on board any criticism that employees may put forward. That doesn't mean they have to agree with the criticism, simply that employees should feel safe to voice their views. Approachable and personally engaged managers lay the foundations for psychological safety.

Managers who are humble and willing to acknowledge the limits of their knowledge or their ability to answer their subordinates also help to create a culture of dialogue. Often, it's not easy for a manager to admit that they don't have the answer to everything, which equates to showing weakness or laying yourself bare. However, employees can see it as a show of confidence, which they appreciate. Not providing an answer is also an invitation to hear what employees have to say. When a manager doesn't have the answer, it is actually more likely to encourage dialogue than be seen as a weakness.

Humility aside, using psychological safety as a means to ensure cooperation and knowledge-sharing needs managers to be proactive and encourage employees to participate and contribute to the debate on matters that concern them. To ensure that words are backed up with actions, rather than caving in to the power of the biases and obstacles outlined above, specific meetings should be held to discuss specific matters. These meetings may be regular interactions among members of a permanent team, but can just as easily be held when needed for a team working on a one-off project. The two most important things are that first, they really do happen, and second, they are organized in way that allows each person to speak up based on the pre-established framework described earlier for executive meetings.

Clearly, one of the essential prerequisites for psychological safety is the management's willingness to accept mistakes and failures. Mistakes are inevitable whenever humans are involved in doing anything and the higher the risk, the more likely failure is to occur, yet risk-taking is essential for the survival of any company looking to grow and innovate. Talking about mistakes and failures is a great tool for improvement, but also incredibly difficult to achieve in the workplace, as the risk perceived by employees – ranging from getting a stern telling-off and tarnishing their image, through to losing their job – can be considerable. So, to counteract our natural tendency to sweep negative things under the carpet, managers should encourage their subordinates to be honest. They can do this in two ways: admit to their own mistakes, and, even more importantly, reframe them in a positive light by introducing a learning process whenever they happen. Naturally, measures should be taken to prevent mistakes from happening and minimize the risk of failure, but at the same time they should be accepted when they do occur, and people should be encouraged to talk about them in the interest of continuous improvement. When an idea fails, the company should learn from it by taking steps to reduce the likelihood of the same thing happening again. Even the best workers make mistakes; good managers know this and use it to benefit the organization.

Psychological safety is not created by lawlessness or sugarcoated compassion, which, contrary to the aim, would result in subpar performance for the company and a lack of individual accountability. Quite the opposite – psychological safety requires a clearly defined framework and boundaries within which people can express themselves freely. If everyone is fully aware what the boundaries are, then they can feel comfortable enough to say what they think. Conflict management is a good example of a situation in which these rules serve an excellent purpose. If a company encourages everybody to speak up and express their views, then the chances of conflict arising between people with different opinions are high. So the nature of such conflicts and the way they are handled are key concerns in these companies. Studies have shown that conflict is productive as long as interaction remains focused on ideas and does not become personal or emotional. The boundary that every person needs to clearly understand is that personal criticism is not allowed. It's okay, and even preferable, to challenge an idea, but respect must be shown to the person who brought it to the table. This rule should be reiterated before any discussion during which people are invited to give their opinions and anyone who violates the rule should be sanctioned. Free speech must be combined with respect for everybody to feel safe, in order to contribute to the common good without risking a personal attack. Therefore, psychological safety can only be formed and spread if there are clear and firm boundaries, and that those boundaries are understood by everyone involved.

Whenever sanctions are applied within the company and dismissals occur as a result of what is deemed to be inappropriate behavior, insufficient results, or inadequate job performance, the action taken must be explained. Such transparency preserves a climate of psychological safety. If people don't understand the reasons behind unpleasant decisions, then the rules may seem unclear and a feeling of "it could happen to me" can take hold. In cases like this, any suspicion that a decision has been made unfairly must be eliminated, to preserve the climate of psychological safety. Just like trust, psychological safety takes a long time to build but very little time to destroy. According to Amy Edmondson, "Setting boundaries and holding people accountable are critical for a leader hoping to cultivate an environment of psychological safety."[13]

Processes, routines and rewards to lock in best practices

While it is important to overcome the biases and mental blocks that prevent collaborative practices from becoming habits, specific action also needs to be taken for psychological safety to become a day-to-day reality throughout the workplace and to lock in best practices.

The right profile, with a "people-centric" induction process

This can start with the hiring process, by assigning extra weighting to candidates with strong empathy and relationship-building skills as discussed earlier, and involving colleagues and subordinates in the assessment process to maximize the chances of good relationships further down the line. This approach can then be pursued during the induction period. Rather than overwhelming new recruits with a torrent of information, more emphasis could be placed on getting to

----

13 *Ibid.*

know people. Research on best induction practices conducted by a team at MIT[14] highlights the need to switch from a traditional information-based process to a more people-centric approach. The authors write: "Managers tend to take an informational approach, providing exhaustive amounts of documentation and training. The assumption is that newcomers will somehow make sense of this information and augment it by seeking advice from coworkers. But the reality is that much of the organization's knowledge and expertise resides in people, and newcomers need to overcome their initial reluctance and develop a network of information relationships before they can truly become productive, creative employees who feel connected and satisfied."

Therefore, inductions need to be based on a combination of training and relationship building, with far more importance on the latter than is usually seen in companies. We need to stop introducing newcomers briefly to lots of people and instead adopt a process that gives these introductions the time and importance they deserve. In his book *The Best Place To Work*, Ron Friedman suggests going about it the way a person would if they were holding a party in their home and invited someone who didn't know any of the other guests. How would you make sure the person didn't feel left out, was quickly put at ease, and fitted into the group so they could enjoy the evening? You'd probably introduce the new person in a friendly and positive way and perhaps mention something they have in common with the other guests. "This is Rodney, and he has recently joined our marketing department. He's a black-belt in judo, a keen scuba diver, and has just returned from Indonesia." You may also have asked the other guests beforehand to make the new person feel welcome. And there might be other things throughout the evening that you've put some thought into, such as a table plan or entertainment, all with the aim of helping the newcomer feel at ease. Inductions for new employees will be more effective if they are designed with their feelings in mind – their expectations, hopes and fears – rather than the company's objectives. Friedman cites the case of Snagajob, which asks every new

---

14   Keith Rollag, Salvatore Parise and Rob Cross, "Getting New Hires Up to Speed Quickly", *MIT Sloan Management Review*, vol. 46, No.2, December 2005.

hire to fill out a short questionnaire in which they can describe themselves in terms of their hobbies and interests. It helps the manager to introduce them to their coworkers in a far more engaging manner by emphasizing personal information, just like a non-work related icebreaker. The first day at a new company is an important event for anybody: it should be used to lock in the company's values, starting with the importance of cooperation and team spirit.

The new employee's first tasks can also be carefully chosen to promote interaction and teamwork. Simple team projects will help the newcomer grow their network and understand how much importance the company places on this type of approach. It will also ensure a better chance of accomplishing their first tasks successfully, which in turn will help them fit into the team. The first steps are crucial, because System 1 is on high alert in this type of situation, grasping at any clues or signs that will form the person's long-term perception. The company therefore needs to pay particular attention to the induction process and focus on immersing the newcomer in its key cultural values, including cooperation, which will guide the employee on a daily basis, rather than force-feeding them information. However, while a successful induction is an important stage, it is still only the starting point on a long journey towards disseminating cooperation throughout the company.

Fostering familiarity and similarity

To encourage cooperation on a permanent basis, a company has to make it easier for people to interact with one another. It may seem trivial, but it is of vital importance. Building interpersonal relationships starts by simply getting to know each other. Earlier, we saw how workspaces with lots of smaller breakout areas facilitate meetings and discussions on a daily basis. However, it takes more than that to spark cooperation in a wider environment. To close the gap between geographical locations, regular meetings are a must, whether they are entirely work-based or combine work and leisure. Regular afterwork gatherings are a great way to initiate relaxed conversations in an informal setting where people can easily form bonds.

Getting to know other people generates the types of feelings that form relationships: familiarity and similarity. Behavioral science studies, in particular those mentioned earlier conducted by psychologist Robert Zajonc, have proven that familiarity and preference are closely linked; the more a person is in contact with something, be it a person or an object, the more they will develop an unconscious preference for it. Simply being exposed to a person is all it takes to reinforce the positive perception we have of them. This is one of things that was demonstrated in an amusing study carried out at a university. The school hired four different women who were simply instructed to attend a class with the other students for a semester, without ever talking to them or interacting with them. The only variable that was engineered by the researchers was the number of times each of the women attended the class: five times, ten times, fifteen times or never. At the end of the semester, the students were shown photos of the different women and were asked questions about them. Nobody remembered them. However, the more frequently the women had attended the class, the more the students said they liked their photo. In addition to this study, the links between exposure, familiarity and preference have been proven on many occasions. Companies can therefore facilitate good internal relations by prompting occasions for employees to interact with each other.[15]

Spending time with other people also increases familiarity. Having the opportunity to talk about things unrelated to work gives employees a chance to discover what they have in common, such as coming from or going on vacation to the same place, doing the same college degree, liking the same types of books, music or food, or having the same hobbies. The more similarities people find, the more they like each other. Similarity is a way of validating our choices and background, and that feeds our ego. We like people who think the same way or have done the same things as us. So in companies where people are encouraged to get to know each other and talk about topics

....
15   Richard L. Moreland and Scott R. Beach, "Exposure Effects in the Classroom: The Development of Affinity Among Students", *Journal of Experimental Social Psychology*, vol. 28, No.3, May 1992.

unrelated to work, it is likely that employees will find similarities and ultimately, build stronger personal relationships.

Rewarding cooperation

Managers can also send out a clear message to employees by explicitly rewarding collaborative behavior. This can be done through the assessment criteria for employee performance, the factors taken in account for variable remuneration, and the profile of employees who receive promotions. If collaborative behavior counts towards symbolic key factors such as remuneration and career development in alignment with the management's narrative about the importance of cooperation, then the entire corporate ecosystem will converge to encourage it. That immediately makes it clear and visible to everyone that financial and business results aside, the way people work – in this case, as a team – is important, and rewarded by the company.

Some businesses also give out special rewards to celebrate collaborative behavior and its ensuing success, handing out prizes to the teams that perform best in their interactions with colleagues. It's a way of emphasizing how much a company values cooperation and an opportunity to create an enjoyable event, which in turn encourages social interaction.

However, behind this genuine desire to encourage cooperation, it's important not to fall into the trap of excessive collaboration, which is a very real danger. Excessive collaboration, in particular endless meetings, can be detrimental to a company's performance. That was what Morten Hansen found in studies conducted for his book on the subject[16], which led him to recommend what he calls "disciplined collaboration", which means working together when it's required, and only calling on other people's time and skills if they genuinely contribute to the quality of the project. So it's not a case of simply encouraging collaboration, but working together more efficiently. It starts with a clearly-defined goal that will benefit all those involved

....
16   Morten T. Hansen, *Collaboration: How Leaders Avoid the Traps, Create Unity, and Reap Big Results*, Harvard Business Review Press, 2009.

and ends with the recognition of the success that has been achieved, rather than purely rewarding teamwork. Depending on the company's culture from the outset, the emphasis can either be placed on collaborative practices, if that's not how people usually work, or on "disciplined" practices if teamwork is already part of the business's basic culture.

While teamwork is absolutely essential for success, that success depends on striking exactly the right balance.

Breaking down silos

Over recent decades as organizations have become more complex, many departments have begun to develop their own individual cultures. This needs to be taken into account and silos need to be broken down in order to develop a cooperative environment. There are many ways of doing this, and they all stem from a simple idea: you need to create diversity and lateral working if you are to counter risk aversion, the fear of other people, or misunderstandings.

Diversity starts with recruitment in all departments, where complementarity should be prioritized, rather than similarity. To create an open environment, companies shouldn't consistently select candidates with similar backgrounds and experience.

Structured, *regular exchange programs* also heighten the potential for cooperation. For employees who are happy to do so, working in a different setting helps to enhance cultural diversity. This is the case for international companies where significant cultural differences among countries can be a major implicit barrier to cooperation that can only be overcome with technology. Social norms, and the behavioral practices they generate, are different: working with people from different countries helps everyone to understand and take on board the realities of other cultures.

Doing *taster programs* in other departments, even for a short period, also helps employees to gain a better understanding of different occupations and different people.

In their six rules for overcoming complexity, Yves Mureaux and Peter Tollman – both consultants at the Boston Consulting Group – put forward the idea of having "integrators". It's not a job creation, but an approach to working and how managers should go about their role. Rather than adding more duties in a bid to facilitate cooperation, the idea is to make sure that cooperation is non-negotiable in every managerial task: limiting the rules to give managers more scope to use their judgment; flattening the hierarchical pyramid in the organization; limiting the use of sophisticated KPIs to assess individual performance and assessing team performance instead.

Cooperation is also stimulated by *setting an inspiring overall team goal*. As a project grows, each person has to deal with lots of different sub-targets which can cause them to lose sight of the bigger picture and generate individualist behavior, with excessive focus on small tasks. Issuing a reminder of the overall objective, and putting it in inspiring terms can help to smooth out the creases and get the eyes of the whole team trained on the goal they are all working towards.

The company can also opt to *set up interest groups*, which may of course be work-related, but could also include personal interests: sports teams are a natural example, but there could be groups for other things that employees have in common, such as wine, music or gaming. Members of these groups could arrange to meet up in person or communicate virtually across corporate social media solutions such as Workplace. The more a company encourages and stimulates lateral initiatives between departments, the more it will lead to professional cooperation and motivate employees to want to work with other people.

Finally, the winning behavior of having people work together on a shared goal hinges on a company's ability to do two things: first, to create an environment that is conducive to psychological safety where individuals can contribute freely to collective decisions; and second, having processes in place that lock cooperation into daily practice by facilitating interaction, diversity and cross-departmental relationships, all while ensuring that the managerial narrative and incentive systems are in alignment with this goal.

Chapter 8

Encouraging innovation and lifelong learning

A company that has acquired talents and knows how to create the conditions that encourage cooperation among those talents has the internal structural conditions for lasting success.

Individual qualities and the collective intelligence generated by cooperation maximize the chances of designing and implementing winning strategies and being able to adapt quickly to changing conditions.

But these assets aren't enough. Because in today's ever-shifting world, the greatest challenge for a company's growth is its ability to innovate, as much in the products and services it offers its customers, or new targets, as its internal organization, processes, and more globally its business model. Given the dangers of risk aversion and the status quo bias, innovating, learning and transforming are not natural behaviors, especially in the specific context of a company with a community of employees. The company must therefore fight these biases and eliminate the default behaviors that lead to inertia.

Creating a culture of innovation

Cooperation can only thrive in a safe psychological environment, and the same goes for innovation. If your employees are confident enough to talk freely and express their views, new ideas will be generated naturally, and the conditions for learning and progress will be created by bringing together the points of view and expertise of a variety of people.

But while this culture of openness and debate is essential to ensure that innovation prospers, it's only a starting point. Employees also need to feel supported and encouraged as they innovate, whether that involves constantly seeking out ways to improve their daily productivity, or by proactively suggesting solutions to issues the company is facing.

A company's culture can nurture this global openness, but it all starts with a mission.

Top-down motivation: creating the desire to innovate

Innovating to benefit the mission

One of the world's leading innovation specialists Soren Kaplan – Associate Professor at the Center for Effective Organizations at the USC Marshall School of Business – believes that it's about being "intentional with your innovation intent"[1]: giving your intention meaning and making innovation the company's default approach.

It's not only about presenting innovation as a necessity, a way of surviving in an environment that renders it absolutely essential, but rather painting it as an inspiring and fun way to tackle the company's overall mission and make the world a better place while benefiting from personal progress. In a wonderful letter to its shareholders[2], Amazon's CEO Jeff Bezos emphasizes the "Day 1" concept, and its opposite number, the second day: "I've been reminding people that it's Day 1 for a couple of decades. I work in an Amazon building named Day 1, and when I moved buildings, I took the name with me. I spend time thinking about this topic. Day 2 is stasis. Followed by irrelevance. Followed by excruciating, painful decline. Followed by death. And *that* is why it is *always* Day 1."

He adds: "The outside world can push you into Day 2 if you won't or can't embrace powerful trends quickly. If you fight them, you're probably fighting the future. Embrace them and you have a tailwind."

It's possible to create intrinsic motivation and engagement in all employees by communicating in a way that appeals to their System 1.

---

1   Soren Kaplan, "6 Ways to Create a Culture of Innovation", Co.Design, 21 December 2013, fastcodesign.com.

2   "What is Jeff Bezos's 'Day 1' Philosophy?", Forbes, 21 April 2017, forbes.com.

Symbols, stories and rewards

A link with a real mission is a petri dish for innovation. But daily tasks and short-term troubleshooting are obstacles to making a company's intentions come to life. Employees' everyday experiences make innovation less and less of a priority. A culture of innovation must therefore counter a phenomenon known in behavioral science as mental availability. With our limited attention spans, the mental load of daily tasks relegates innovation to a lower position on our list of priorities. We still have good intentions, but they don't lead to actions. Innovation has to be part of an employee's daily life: it needs to shine through in symbols, stories and rewards.

Many different methods can be used to achieve that in both the physical and psychological environment. As we have seen, a company's offices can highlight the value of innovation. Its meeting rooms can be given the names of its biggest successes as is the case at Netflix. The walls of common areas can recall key moments in the company's history or the successes of new products and services. Quotes from great innovators may also be showcased, symbolic objects may be used, like at Intuit's innovation center, which houses the table where its founders Scott Cook and his wife Signe Ostby were sitting when they were inspired to create the company. Innovation in the premises themselves can also reflect this approach. The space may be designed to convey the culture of innovation and be a constant reminder for employees about the importance of this value.

The psychological environment must also be coherent with the culture, and a link with a mission is the starting point. The words and actions of leaders – like those of Larry Page – are vectors, but the entire company's ecosystem must adhere to the same message, and send it out to all employees. Formal prizegiving ceremonies such as "Innovation Awards" may be organized to acknowledge the internal efforts that are made. But even more importantly, to spread this culture of innovation on a daily basis, direct supervisors must encourage and recognize innovation as it happens. It might be a little message of encouragement, recognition for effort, or team celebrations that nurture the culture of innovation within the company. And as is often the case, while a firm's top directors are required to set the course, direct supervisors are those who start the engines, promoting or eroding the company culture on a daily basis, and driving the behavior of all its employees.

A culture of innovation must permeate a company's every nook and cranny.

Bottom-up motivation: counterbalancing the negative forces of the status quo

Countering risk aversion: failing smart

If a culture of innovation is to flourish, each person must be driven to contribute to it by innovating – in what I call top-down motivation – but they must also be able to fight the opposite forces that can erode or undermine that drive, counteracting the risk aversion effect by acknowledging and accepting the main obstacle to innovation: the fear of failure.

Unless the company clearly demonstrates otherwise, failure is naturally associated with incompetence. An individual who fails is also affected on a personal level, and may experience a loss of self-confidence. Employees can avoid this by simply not taking any sort of risk, and in doing so, dissociate themselves from any sort of failure.

Companies need to convey a very strong message that failure is acceptable, and part of the natural law of innovation. When she was Vice President at Google, Sheryl Sandberg made a mistake that cost the company millions of dollars, and her error became famous because of her superior's reaction. Larry Page held a meeting to tell her about the mistake, but said: "I'm so glad you made this mistake. Because I want to run a company where we are moving too quickly and doing too much, not being cautious and doing too little. If we don't have any of these mistakes, we're just not taking enough risks."[3]

---

3 Adam Lashinsky, "Chaos by Design: The Inside Story of Disorder, Disarray, and Uncertainty at Google. And Why It's All Part of the Plan. (They Hope.)" *Fortune*, 2 October 2006.

Obviously, when the head of a company takes this stance, it sends out a strong message to all employees: failure is allowed, because it's part of risk-taking. And in this case, the message is even more powerful because the failure was monumental. Even though claiming that failure is allowed and accepted might be a step in the right direction, employees need to see it in action to really take it on board. It's the only way of effectively counterbalancing the negative effect of risk aversion.

But Larry Page is smart, and goes further than just accepting failure when it happens. He put a positive spin on that failure by shining a light on the person responsible: failure isn't about incompetence, but it's actually a testament to her ability to take risks that might benefit the company. And that changes everything. It sends out a very positive sign to all the employees in a company.

Another way to put failure in a positive light is to present it as a way for the company to learn. In a very different context, it's also true in the famous quote by Nelson Mandela: "I never lose. I either win or learn." Upholding a vision like this is another way to make failure more acceptable, and reduce aversion to risk.

Countering the status quo bias: spotlighting long-term gains

The status quo bias also magnifies risk aversion to keep people in a rut, which is often so acceptable that it comforts us to believe that what made us successful yesterday will also work tomorrow. If we add a good dollop of the overconfidence bias to the mix, which drives people to overestimate the stability of a situation, and a dash of the present bias, which postpones any significant effort until tomorrow, it's easy to understand the strength of resistance that naturally prospers within a company. In addition, often very heavy daily workloads mean that setting aside time for reflection is extremely difficult. And innovating, improving, learning and replenishing take time away from essential daily tasks, which means that what's urgent takes precedence over what's important.

Again, these negative forces whose combined effects hold back constant transformation need to be destroyed. The present bias prevents us from estimating the genuine value of a long-term advantage. So the positive consequences for innovation need to be as visible, tangible, and concrete as possible, both for individuals and for the company as a whole. What will this innovative project change for you, the company, your customers and your environment? By looking to the future we make it easier to grasp, and in doing so we break through the negative dynamic of the present bias. Yves Morieux and Peter Tollman talk about "What game theory calls the shadow of the future which is the importance of what happens tomorrow to us as a result of what we do today. By extending the shadow of the future, we make the more-or-less distant horizon – that point at which our present behavior will eventually reveal its consequences – much more important and evident to us now."[4] Enabling people to see the advantages of their efforts today makes it easier to focus on the future. Innovation then becomes more desirable, because its benefits appear within reach.

Ultimately, a culture of innovation, rooted in a safe psychological environment, anchored in the company's overall mission, nurtured by the encouragement of risk-taking, the genuine and positive acceptance of failure and an ability to look to the future all help to break through the natural biases that draw people into ruts. But as fundamental as that may be, a culture of innovation can only truly thrive if it shines through a company's daily practices.

From a culture of innovation to winning practices

Allow time for free innovation

Soren Kaplan writes: "Innovation needs time to develop. No one ever feels like they have time to spare. People get so consumed with putting out fires and chasing short-term targets that most can't even think about the future."[5]

4   Yves Morieux and Peter Tollman, *Smart Simplicity*, *op. cit.*
5   Soren Kaplan, "6 Ways to Create a Culture of Innovation", *art. cit.*

In order to move from merely a culture of innovation to practicing innovation, a company must organize what Kaplan calls "a non-structured structure for time." He refers to the opportunity that Google and 3M give their employees to spend 10% of their working hours on projects of their choice, and to experiment with new ideas. This means that a proportion of those employees who wish to innovate can focus on that, and in doing so, maximize their chances of generating many different ideas. Now some of those ideas are bound to be brilliant! Allowing employees to take time out of their daily – and heavy – schedules to think about tomorrow is such a big challenge that it needs to be clearly stated in job descriptions. Setting aside time for innovation as a priority and assigning it as much importance as everyday tasks is the only way to prevent it from disappearing, regardless of individual intentions.

The innovation and R&D departments in companies are obviously supposed to innovate – in coordination with operational departments – while simultaneously tackling everyday necessities. And while that's a great way of bringing innovation into the company, the most innovative are the ones in which creating new ideas isn't only the domain of professional innovators, however brilliant they may be. My friend and colleague Richard Bordenave, head of innovation at BVA and an outstanding innovator, is always reminding his team how if all employees in the company share the same mindset, it can maximize an innovative project's chances of success. Project teams are combinations of individuals and experts with different experience, and that steps up their chances of success, with contributions and partnerships that go beyond the confines of the company. This vision of open innovation applies to academic researchers, collective intelligence from customers, and fresh start-ups. So innovation isn't only the domain of internal experts, but they do need to be the drivers and goads for open innovation that involves all the various players in the company, united around a shared vision that is presented from an inspiring angle. Here again, this open innovation can be organized structurally so that it permeates the company's practices, rather than leaving it up to individual motivation, which as we know, is soon exhausted by opposing forces.

Framing an innovative project, the psychological key to success

The way an innovative project is presented is crucial to its success. It's what behavioral economists call framing, and a study led by Amy Edmondson[6] shows what tremendous power it has.

Her research covers the implementation of a new approach to heart surgery known as MICS (minimally invasive cardiac surgery). This highly innovative technique is less invasive than traditional surgical procedures, and has many specific benefits for the patient. Furthermore, the ability to implement MICS is an important issue for hospital competitiveness. In her research, Amy Edmondson set out to understand the specific factors that made some hospitals succeed in integrating this new approach while others failed. What contributes to the success of a team with an innovative idea?

The study focused on sixteen hospitals and took into account all the variables that could have an impact on success: type of hospital, resources, support from management, status of the project leader, the hospital's track record on innovation, and the way the project was presented to participants.

And the results were striking. The only aspect that differentiated success from failure was how the project was framed: the way the leader presented the project, the leader's role and the roles of the various team members.

The leaders who managed to get MICS up and running presented the project to the members of their team in an aspirational way, while the leaders who failed presented it in a defensive way. Those who succeeded placed emphasis on a desire to do something important for the patients and the hospital, by going beyond the usual limits and moving forward with developments in cardiac surgery. Those who failed presented the project defensively, focusing on the need to move to this new approach because otherwise the hospital would be less competitive. Edmondson notes that in successful hospitals, "Members of the successful teams shared a sense of purpose that

6   Amy Edmondson, *Teaming, op. cit.*

can be described as aspirational – driven by a desire to accomplish compelling goals for patients or for the hospital."[7] In terms of the innovative project, the leaders inspired their teams by putting forward a clear and exciting project. Like a transcendental business mission, the innovative project generated commitment from those in charge of bringing it to fruition.

In successful hospitals, team leaders also presented their own role in a specific way, introducing themselves as interdependent facilitators rather than individual experts. By describing their own roles not as leaders on which other employees can depend, but as facilitators who need ideas and commitment from everyone else in order to succeed, each member of the team felt much more invested and important. In teams where the leader presented him or herself as an expert, the employees felt reduced to minion status, serving the expertise of their boss. The active listening and learning approach recommended by the leaders of winning teams was much more fruitful than the command and control approach used by the leaders of the teams who failed. Individual behaviors within each team were strongly affected by the role that the project leader put him or herself forward to fill.

Finally, the way the leader explicitly presented his or her expectations regarding the team members' work also played a major role. In successful teams, the mission was to enhance how the group learned together by communicating and sharing, and by considering all participants as valuable resources. In the teams that failed, the role of the participants was presented as that of performers who the group needed for their specific technical expertise: a "doer" in a specific field rather than a contributor to an overall project.

In the end, the way the project was presented, i.e. the language and words that were used by the project leader, made the difference between failure and success. And that's the power of framing for humans who are emotional, social and on the lookout for a mission that exceeds their own interest. Maximizing the chances of a project's success is not only the result of the material elements such as the resources, time

----

7   *Ibid.*

and people who are assigned to it, but also the standards of how the team functions, and how the project is presented as a whole.

Countering the overconfidence and possession biases

As the development process for an innovative project moves forward, the teams working on it may be victims of a bias which keeps their eyes trained on their project and may lead to failure: the overconfidence bias, which tends to anaesthetize and cause people to see a project in an excessively positive light. The possession bias also makes those working on a project feel very attached to it, and reluctant to let it go despite signs of failure or negativity. While we have seen that it is important to accept failure, it's also a good idea to do everything possible to avoid it, especially when it comes to countering the negative effects of these cognitive biases.

In performing regular and rigorous assessments of a situation we can try to objectivize progress, whether that applies to the overall innovation process or the development of a specific project. In terms of the overall process, the assessment must focus on quality and results: is the innovation process going as it was planned, and is it generating the expected results? Indicators may be connected to the project pipeline, taking into account the number of projects in terms of objectives, and the type of projects according to whether they are incremental or structural, short or long term, focused on internal processes or customers, or even the number of employees who have participated in innovative projects or have been trained to do so. The results of innovation processes can be measured using the number of innovative projects that have actually been launched, the success that each one has reported in relation to the objectives initially assigned to it, and the share of revenue (or margin) that has been generated by the new projects or services launched over a specific period in comparison with the existing portfolio, etc. The main point is to define a limited number of indicators – to make them easier to track and share – to gain clear insight into how the innovation process works, without being affected by negative biases. The shortfalls can be analyzed and corrective measures can be implemented. The aim is to be able to continually improve the innovation process with groups from different fields, to maximize the chances of success in the end, with a challenge that is specific to this analysis and improvement process: its flexibility. In the same way that putting a culture of innovation into practice means coping with everyday pressure, evaluation and improvement processes must also compete with the daily tasks that employees need to perform. Bringing a culture of innovation to life in daily practice must only require limited time and money resources if it is to be accepted by those responsible for implementing it. Otherwise it is doomed to vanish.

All innovation projects must benefit from evaluation and experimentation throughout their development. And the key point here is to evaluate – right from the very start – in order to retain an objective view of the project's purpose and chances of success without being a victim of the possession bias. Because the more team members invest in the project by devoting their time, resources, energy and engagement to it, the more they will feel connected to the projects and the more difficult it will be to present an objective analysis. The confirmation bias is also a threat: people involved in the project will tend to select elements and interpret them in a way that confirms their initial opinion, which often results in seeing the project they are working on through to the bitter end. When combined with loss aversion – in this case the pain of abandoning the project – those involved will probably want to see it right through to the bitter end. It's absolutely vital to conduct experiments and careful analysis of results, involving people who are not on the project team, in order to reduce that risk. Those onlookers can bring a "test/learn/correct" approach to the project, which must again be as flexible as possible. To avoid the pressure of tight deadlines, the initial plan must take into account frequent experimentation and optimization throughout the development process. Finally, the ability of these experiments to consider the reactions of users or end customers to finished prototypes will improve the quality of the data obtained and how predictable that data will be when applied to declarative and attitudinal studies. The Design Thinking approach, which is based on user experience and creates prototypes first and then goes ahead with a series of repetitions, is a good example of a quick, flexible and appropriate method to maximize a project's chances of success.

And if, despite efforts to readjust the new product or service according to what is discovered through experimentation, negative signs continue to grow, team members must have the courage to bring the project to a close. Because in innovation, failure is the norm – studies show that it varies between 70% and 90% for new products depending on the sector – and must be accepted not only as part of the process, but also as a source of progress. Here's where the culture of the company and its ability to accept failure play an important role in helping the members of the team admit this failure without feeling afraid or ashamed. Ultimately, as the innovation expert Ideo puts it "failing better to succees better!"[8]

Encouraging and promoting innovation means combining a culture that inspires all employees, motivates and creates the right state of mind based on a general feeling of psychological safety, with a process that nurtures and rewards innovative behavior. It also means being able to cope effectively with pressure and the biases that threaten success.

But while innovation is essential, learning and developing knowledge is just as important.

Learning by default

Learning: an absolute imperative in a knowledge economy

Learning isn't optional, it's absolutely crucial in what many call the knowledge economy, because intellectual skills are becoming the keys to success. In a constantly-changing world, obsolete knowledge is a threat to both individuals and companies. And in my view, that's why learning is one of the key winning behaviors that must be encouraged within a company. There is little debate on this matter,

8   Amy C. Edmondson and Laura R. Feldman, "Phase Zero: Introducing New Services at Ideo (A)", *Harvard Business Review Case* No.605-069, 2005.

and researchers and operational experts are in unanimous agreement. Along with other human resources specialists, Pat Wadors, former Senior Vice President Global Talent Organization at LinkedIn[9] says, "The only way for organizations to ensure their workforces are fully productive and able to achieve business goals is to make sure employees are continuously learning, so that they are driving the business forward."[10]

But even though there is no doubt about this absolute necessity, both in terms of individuals and the company as a whole...

... biases stop us from taking action

On an individual level, we know that merely being aware that we should act in a certain way to benefit our own interests and those of our community isn't enough for us to actually behave in that way. Most employees – from seasoned managers to new recruits – know full well that developing knowledge is a key driver for future performance. But here again, there are many biases at work to stop us from doing what we know we should. First, learning is about looking to the long-term future and putting in hard work now – setting aside time and attention – for a potential medium-term advantage. That probably reminds you of the present bias. And as you know, we find very little motivation in non-immediate rewards, and we are very reticent to work hard now on something we could put off until tomorrow. On top of that, there are the overconfidence and confirmation biases. Even though we are fully aware that it's a great idea to develop our knowledge, the overconfidence bias – and our egos – drive us to underestimate that necessity: after all, we're already pretty smart. In addition, the confirmation bias reassures: our career is proof of our ability, the latest project we finished was a success or we got good feedback from the boss. There are always things we can pick out to prove that the need for learning and developing our knowledge isn't all that important. And there is also

---

9 now Chief Talent Officer at ServiceNow.
10 Pat Wadors, "To Stay Relevant, Your Company and Employees Must Keep Learning", *Harvard Business Review*, 7 March 2016, hbr.org.

daily life and pressure: how is it possible to find the time for training when we can't even complete the tasks we need to work on every day? Work isn't always just stressful, it's exhausting too. Once we've done all our tasks, how can we possibly find the energy and motivation to learn?

The pressure that employees put on themselves is often magnified by their supervisors. Nick Gidwani who runs a talent development company says, "Managers are under tremendous pressure to generate results. You have annual quotas, quarterly goals, and increasing competition. Who has time to let employees go learn skills that may not be relevant for years, or may not serve your unit at all?"[11]

Once again, a business environment doesn't naturally encourage continuous learning for employees, and yet it's incredibly relevant to long-term performance. To counter the negative effect of these invisible biases and barriers to learning in the company, it can't only depend on its employees' individual motivation to learn, nor on that of its leaders. One of the most brilliant researchers into behavioral science – Francesca Gino from Harvard Business School – writes: "Virtually all leaders believe that to stay competitive, their enterprises must learn and improve every day. But even companies revered for their dedication to continuous learning find it difficult to always practice what they preach."[12]

As always, the combination of a favorable psychological environment with intelligent and flexible processes is what maximizes the chances that a continuous learning policy isn't just part of the spiel for most companies.

From leaders to new recruits: we're all teachers and we're all students

It all starts with a company's ability to create an environment that values and supports ongoing training and learning on a daily basis. The role

----

11   Nick Gidwani, "How to Support Employees' Learning Goals While Getting Day-to-Day Stuff Done", *Harvard Business Review*, August 1, 2017, hbr.org.

12   Francesca Gino and Bradley Staats, "Why Organizations Don't Learn", *Harvard Business Review*, November 2015, hbr.org.

of company leaders is key in disseminating this culture of learning. Their words and actions must show every employee that learning on a daily basis is of strategic importance. Their message must be clear: learning is a goal and a benefit, rather than a duty. The focus for the message should be on System 1, using emotion, rather than pure the logic and reason of System 2. The analysis carried out to identify the characteristics of the best leaders all point towards those who support and encourage continuous learning for themselves. But they are often wonderful mentors and teachers. Sydney Finkelstein, Professor at Dartmouth College and author of SuperBosses, writes: "I've spent more than 10 years studying world-class leaders like Kamath (CEO of the Indian bank Icici) to determine what sets them apart from typical leaders. One big surprise was the extent to which these star managers emphasize ongoing, intensive one-on-one tutoring of their direct reports, either in person or virtually, in the course of daily work."[13] As is often the case, leaders must set an example to build up a company of people who want to learn, they need to put across a strong message that learning is the key to business and individual success.

The recruitment process should also be a search for individuals who show strong interest and an ability for long-term learning and training, as they will tend to seize the opportunities that are offered to them, but also promote for their subordinates throughout their careers. Psychologist and Stanford Professor Carol Dweck has also shown that individuals who consider intelligence not as an innate genetic gift but a variable ability that can be enhanced with learning are much more inclined to educate themselves and educate others. If you believe that your level of intelligence is determined from birth, there's no point putting in the work to benefit others or develop their skills. If you believe the opposite is true, you are naturally drawn to learning and seek it out for yourself and for others.

The more a company attracts talent of this type and nurtures this mentality, the more of a hotbed it will be for learning. Recruiting employees with a thirst for constant learning and bringing in leaders

----

13 Sydney Finkelstein, "The Best Leaders Are Great Teachers", *Harvard Business Review*, January-February 2018, hbr.org

who also value and promote its benefits are the foundations for success.

Fail well to learn and improve: the default collective responsibility

We've already seen how a company that accepts failure generally and values it as the proof of an ability to take risks helps to bring about a culture of innovation and learning. When learning "on the job", it's not only big failures that are accepted and acknowledged, but also small mistakes and daily trials. All the hindrances that prevent you from being totally productive or throw up obstacles to what is being done are considered to be a source of progress. But beyond mere acceptance, studies show that there are different ways of failing and dealing with mistakes. And failing well is a privilege for companies that want to learn. So what does "failing well" actually mean?

First it means "un-learning" what we have been taught since child-hood: that failure is bad, and that you should do whatever you can to avoid it. That doesn't mean seeing failure as a good thing in itself, but recognizing that failure is part and parcel of all human activity, and inevitable. It is a source of progress and proof that you are willing to accept risk, as Larry Page so eloquently put it. This applies even more to innovation, where challenges are new and the environment uncer-tain. Failure is the rule, and success the exception. But this rule also applies to daily tasks that may turn out to be more and more complex given greater time constraints and diminishing resources. Failing well starts when you agree to share the failure and errors made by other people without being afraid of what they might mean for you personally. And that can only happen when a climate of psychological safety is instilled in a company, and where sanctions for mistakes are not a dead end, but rather the starting point for an improvement process. And that's the exact opposite of what actually happens in most companies. In a series of interviews that she carried out on the subject, Amy Edmondson found that 70% of mistakes are sanctioned by managers, and yet they admit that only 5% of those mistakes are genuinely due to one individual's own mistake.

Given the occurrence of mistakes, a company's go-to response should be to draw focus from the individual and place it on the group as a whole. How did the company allow that individual to make a mistake? Errors will only be revealed and used to improve how a company works when this approach is taken every time they occur. And only if employees trust in that system will they be able to get over the obstacles that make them want to cover up their mistakes. It's a long and winding path, because we have to be able to hate mistakes and try to avoid making them, while simultaneously accepting them when they do happen. You need to be able to call upon individual responsibility, make it important to the group as a whole, and find solutions to problems together.

The role of each employee's direct supervisor is to introduce a climate of trust, and to be able to strike a subtle yet essential balance. The managers' behavior and ability to create such an environment will establish the basic conditions for the company to go on improving. We saw previously how direct supervisors play a key role in employee engagement. This core responsibility is also important in supporting the progress of their subordinates. They need to create the psychological conditions for daily progress and constantly underline its importance.

And when a mistake is shared, failing well means having an internal process that helps the team to understand what caused the problem, and how corrective action can be put into place to prevent it from happening again. The goal is to set aside the resources to carry out an in-depth investigation – unless it's a basic individual mistake – to identify what underlying factors caused the error. It's very important to listen not only to the people who were directly involved, but also to bring in upstream players by going deeper into the issue, to reach a conclusion that gives enough information to design appropriate corrective measures. And it isn't easy, first because talking about mistakes is no fun for anyone, especially those who feel responsible – and second because a daily workload needs to take a back seat while the errors are analyzed and a conclusion is drawn. This process must be presented as being vitally important if it is to remain in place.

But in addition to simply underlining the importance of the process, which we now know may not be as effective as we'd like, it's important that it be made as flexible as possible, while always keeping the Nudge mantra in mind: "make it easy". If we want a behavior to be adopted and maintained over time, it needs to be easy. In this case, if the process used to understand failure is cumbersome and not seen as essential to constant improvement, then it will probably stop being applied. If it can be integrated into daily routines and doesn't sap resources, it is much more likely to succeed. The idea isn't to design a perfect quality system, but rather a system that is satisfactory and as invisible and transparent as possible for users; it mustn't be a heavy additional burden on those who will implement it.

The process is made up of five key phases: identifying errors, finding out what caused them, designing corrective actions, implementing them, and evaluating the results. It's an ongoing process that involves a learning loop and helps to generate constant improvement. And if it is to work properly, the process must be presented positively as a source of improvement and not a tool for control. Once again, framing – how the process is presented – determines how it is accepted and if it will succeed. And proof of this positivity – the absence of sanctions in most cases – must show each employee that the process is there to benefit everyone. The focus is on improving as a group rather than punishing individuals.

Learning by doing is the first step in this essential ongoing training approach to ensure that each employee can grow and that the company can thrive. But learning also involves another key element: the acquisition of new skills. And that's no mean feat.

Making it easier to acquire new skills

We all know that learning is an essential investment for the future. But sometimes just knowing something isn't enough to encourage the right behavior. A company must drive its employees to acquire new skills and make it easy for them to set the wheels of learning in motion.

A culture that values the acquisition of new skills is a rich breeding ground because it breaks through employees' own mental and psychological barriers. If a company recognizes the strategic importance of acquiring new skills, each employee can legitimately spend time on it, without feeling amateurish or individualistic. And training should be presented in an aspirational manner to create not only a need but also a desire on the part of employees to go on learning. Because studies show that when individuals want to learn something, their ability to learn is enhanced. Companies should therefore present training positively, especially by focusing on its benefits for the employee's future.

But that's still not enough. Training must be integrated into a daily routine and presented as a priority, with training programs that are tailored to employees' expectations and limitations.

It all begins with time. Training takes time. Highly motivated people will always find the time – even outside office hours – to acquire new skills through the opportunities available from MOOC (massive open online courses) or simply by reading books about the subjects that interest them. But for most people, the biases and obstacles we described earlier are too powerful to bring these behaviors into their everyday routine, and they become exceptional events. It's up to companies to set aside priority time for skills development. There are several ways of going about it, but first time must be allocated, and the training must be given the same importance as other tasks and operational duties. Some companies run "lunch and learn" sessions, others "inspiration days" with experts on issues of general interest. These allow employees to spend time learning autonomously, and use specific resources that have been made available for their benefit. Encouraging employees to take part in events and attend external conferences can stimulate their curiosity.

But in addition to training tools and knowledge acquisition, it's crucial to have high attendance for the sessions – because this is proof of the importance the company places on training – and strong discipline to keep up that attendance. The natural tension between daily emergencies and time spent on learning must be mitigated by making training one of the cornerstones of a day at work.

When each person has the time to benefit from the training, and to acquire new knowledge, the tools on offer must be personalized and easy to access.

The company's ability to offer personalized training is a way of showing recognition to each employee while optimizing the chances that the training will be successful. That doesn't necessarily involve developing individual programs – such as coaching – that may be costly and usually restricted to a small group of people. Many different training platforms are now available and can be personalized on various levels. Companies such as Lynda.com offer a wide range of training courses, and each employee can select the one that suits them best, while setting aside the required time and fitting it around their preferences and constraints. And others, such as Cerego.com, personalize their knowledge evaluation tests and responses to each participant, so offer a much more powerful learning tool than conventional solutions. Because it's not just about learning and knowing at a specific time, only to forget soon afterwards. The ability to retain information is important, so that the transfer of knowledge becomes a genuine asset for the person who benefited from the training. The combination of new possibilities that "machine learning" offers, with insight from cognitive science about understanding how the memory works, means that better performing programs can match each person's individual ability. The duration and number of sessions, the type of teaching, the techniques and number of assessments that are used to test the acquired knowledge can all be tailored to individual people so that it is more effective in the long term.

In addition, the lessons learned from video games can make training much more enjoyable and engaging. That's what's known as the "gamification" of training programs. Because while wanting to learn ahead of time is fundamental, the training must be enjoyable if it is to be pursued conscientiously. The best ambassador – the best messenger as we say in behavioral economics – is the training itself. It must be interesting in both form and content to make people want to stick to it. That's what Deloitte did when it created its Leadership Academy program, which is inspired by the principles of gamification. The results were spectacular: the site's return rate grew by 37% when these principles were applied.[14]

....
14 Jeanne C. Meister, "How Deloitte Made Learning a Game", *Harvard Business Review*, January 2, 2013, hbr.org.

So it's possible for companies to provide high-performance tools for their employees at very affordable prices if the acquisition of new skills is truly considered to be a strategic challenge.

Personalization promotes engagement and generates success

Knowledge acquisition must be personalized, because by adapting it to each person's own specific needs, it enhances motivation and is more likely to succeed. But one key element mustn't be ignored: training tools must be easy to access. Because behavioral science shows that the slightest micro-barrier, the slightest obstacle that would make the desired behavior more difficult, is a strong deterrent. Training platforms for employees must therefore be designed to eliminate all difficulties, even minor issues, by focusing clearly on the user experience. An access code that needs to be found or reinstalled with each session, a slow connection, an interface that isn't completely intuitive or clear are all it takes to significantly reduce participation or cause motivation to dwindle. Making people want to learn and designing tools that are appealing and fun to use, right down to the finest detail, are all essential to a successful internal training program.

And as always, direct supervisors have a core role to play because they are the ones who will support – or discourage – this approach to learning on a daily basis. Depending on whether priority is constantly given to daily tasks or to learning, both in how things are done as well as how they are learned, what subordinates do will be very different. If employees are genuinely encouraged to learn and if the above conditions are brought together, learning-oriented behavior can be developed. Basically, that means managers need to start by being proactive when they offer new training courses. It's simply not enough to ask each employee what type of training he or she wishes to do, but rather about thinking upstream about the person's strengths and weaknesses, as well as the direction the company wishes to take, and any possible technological developments that may be in the pipeline. Pat Wadors, who used to be responsible for talent at LinkedIn, also underlines the importance of being open when employees come with initiatives and aspirations. "Don't worry about what your employees are learning and if it directly relates to their work. We often see customers become concerned their employees are learning something not related to their job. Don't sweat it. Learning is a skill that requires practice, just like everything else. By learning something new, no matter what it is, your employees are practicing the skill of learning, which is invaluable."[15]

Managers can also promote learning by setting aside time for reflection in their subordinates' schedules. Studies have shown that having time every day to think about what has been learned – whether that's new skills or operational productivity – reinforces what has been learned. For example, in an experiment conducted by Francesca Gino in a call center owned by Wipro[16], having fifteen minutes thinking time from the sixth day of a 16-day training program allowed participants to increase their performance in their final assessment by 20% compared to those who had not had the thinking time.

15 Pat Wadors, "To Stay Relevant, Your Company and Employees Must Keep Learning", *art. cit.*

16 Giada Di Stefano, Gary P. Pisano, Francesca Gino *et al.*, "Making Experience Count: The Role of Reflection in Individual Learning", Harvard Business School, Working Paper 14-093, 2014.

Chapter 9

Applying Nudge management to any business challenge

Throughout this book, I've tried to present a new approach to business leadership – what I call Nudge management. It's based on behavioral science and seeks to design a physical and psychological environment with practices that generate engagement and effectiveness among employees to improve collective performance. Nudge management substitutes an approach based on extrinsic motivation with a holistic and coherent system that incites, encourages, and facilitates winning behavior based on real human experiences, to create an environment that cultivates engagement and boosts performance.

The principles of Nudge management are grounded in a specific physical and psychological environment and rooted in the concrete processes I have described.

These principles are hugely generalized and don't depend on specific contexts or situations. They are based on a fundamental understanding of how various factors and biases influence human behavior on a daily basis.

But while the catalysts for engagement and effectiveness apply to all human beings, situations in different companies can vary enormously. Each company has its own cultural environment, history, values, competitive environment and specific objectives. Each company is made up of individuals with their own experiences, who have developed a range of shared practices and those practices differ from one company to another.

The specific features of each organization naturally generate a variety of challenges: for one it may be a struggle to innovate, for another a lack of collaboration among individuals or departments, for a third, resistance to a transformation plan and for a fourth employees may feel that there is a lack of recognition or consideration.

Beyond the general guidelines, transformation using Nudge management involves specific actions which must be tailored to the challenges faced by each company, and according to the findings of behavioral science, may take different forms:

- *Personalized coaching for company directors* in order to:

  Help them gain a deeper understanding of the teachings of behavioral science and how the knowledge can be applied to the business world;

  Provide support to implement action plans and processes to avoid influences from biases in their individual strategic decisions (they should make decisions based on System 2) and to communicate better and demonstrate daily behavior that channels the power of System 1;

  Design a global or specific strategy to instill a psychological and physical environment that will improve performance;

  Be able to cope with specific crisis situations.

- *Training and support for managers:*

  For key factors from behavioral science that encourage engagement within teams, and especially the exact conditions required for them to be implemented in the company's day-to-day life;

  Support for business transformation plans tailored to specific challenges.

- *Training for company employees*, especially to ensure that everyone understands what generates individual effectiveness, so that overall performance can be improved, and to instill specific behavior taking daily workloads into account.

- *Support and guidance for the key people managers* in the company: from recruitment processes to reward and incentive programs, including individual assessments and promotion criteria, overall employee experience or training and development program methods all play a crucial role in creating the sought-after encouraging and supportive environment that will trigger the behavior and performance that the company wants.

- *Specific internal behavior*, for example a more in-depth look at safety procedures to reduce accidents at work, or a campaign to boost eco-responsible behavior in people's daily working lives.

Nudge management means providing personalized guidance throughout the various branches of the company, but is also based on a specific method that I'd like to share with you now.

This approach is designed to create the exact behavior that a company wants to encourage.

Obviously I'm going to present my approach on a general level, because I'm not looking to provide a solution to a specific case. Consider it as a sort of guidebook that needs to be tailored to each individual situation.

My friends and colleagues at BVA, especially those in the BVA Nudge Unit, have spent many long hours thinking, experimenting and practicing to create this approach.

So how can you find a solution to a specific challenge using the principles of Nudge management?

Identifying the right challenges

Just like Nudge, Nudge management isn't a miracle solution! It simply isn't possible to successfully tackle every single problem that a company faces. And it's important to correctly identify an issue that can be improved using the strengths and limitations of Nudge management to boost your chances of success.

So what kind of projects could benefit from Nudge management?

We've identified *four key criteria* to find out if an issue is appropriate. The final objective is to bring about a behavioral change within the company: to move from current behavior A, which is considered to be harmful, to future behavior B, which is considered to be beneficial. For example: stepping up cooperation among employees, generating more open discussion and debate during team leader meetings, changing how managers recognize the achievements of their employees, reducing staff turnover, making recruitment processes less biased, cutting down workplace accidents, promoting new practices through internal reorganization, creating a worksplace environment that breaks through silos and encourages people to get to know their colleagues better, etc.

- *The issue must be a strategic challenge for the company.* A successful process depends on putting in place specific guidelines and backing them up with proper resources. The approach isn't to resolve minor issues, though findings from behavioral science can be put into practice to eliminate them in other ways.
- *The scope of the project must be clearly defined* to avoid taking on too much, or too little. For example, the issue of employee engagement is so huge that it needs to be subdivided into more specific areas.
- *Conventional solutions are very limited.* They haven't been able to solve the problem thus far, and other options aren't feasible in terms of ROI or likelihood for success. Otherwise, there would be no need to look for a Nudge management approach.
- *The individuals involved must be motivated to change their behavior,* even if they have not yet begun. Nudge management mustn't be attempted if the individuals involved are hostile to it. Nudge management is about encouragement, and can only be effective if people really want to bring about behavioral changes.
- Deciding on the right issue is essential if the project is to be successful, and must be discussed in detail to create a consensus of opinion.

The criteria for success must also be considered at this stage. As Nudge management comes under the umbrella of the Nudge scientific approach, and as the actions will have to be tested before they are deployed, it's important to agree on what indicators will be used to decide they have been successful, and how those indicators will be measured in relation to the current situation.

Once the subject has been properly defined, the process can begin. And the reality of the current situation must be clearly understood if you are to get off to the right start.

Know your context inside out

Whatever the subject, the powerful Nudge solutions require a clear understanding of the current situation, because if employees are currently behaving in the "wrong" way, there are reasons for that behavior. They might be "bad" reasons, or they could be unconscious decisions influenced by the biases we talked about earlier, but they all need to be identified and acknowledged. The goal is to work out what causes them – the frictions and micro-barriers to these behaviors. If we know what we are up against, we can create relevant solutions that work to counter the harmful influences.

There's one basic rule for everyone to achieve this in-depth understanding, but many different ways to approach it.

The most important thing is to move beyond what people say about why they behave in certain ways. You are now well aware that many of the influences we are exposed to are completely unconscious. And that's even one of the main traits of biases: they work on us even when we know about them and think we can control them. We know that the ways people behave stem from personal character traits – which may be possible to learn and share – but also from social interactions and the contexts in which we find ourselves, and whose influence is much more difficult to pinpoint. Asking questions does help to understand and identify the influences that might be at work, but it's only the first step and won't eliminate those influences.

The process must involve observation, but we also need to use a specific analysis chart provided to us by behavioral science. It can be used to go beyond observation and discussion, and draw our attention to social and environmental factors. What impact does what other people think, say and do have on my own behavior? What influence does location have on employees' behavior? What is the influence of culture and unwritten rules? This observation will help you improve your understanding of how each potential influential factor works when the desired behavior seems out of reach.

Beyond this basic rule, there are many different methods to approach the limitations of each subject and each company. The observation may be carried out by someone outside the company, but only if that person is unobtrusive and does not have an effect on the behavior of the individuals under observation. Video cameras may also be used, as long as the individuals being observed have agreed. The observation may also be performed by the individuals themselves, who then report back on their own lives at work, perhaps using video tools or specific applications. Each method has advantages and disadvantages that must be discussed in order to identify the most useful for understanding what influences are at work.

Professor Teresa Amabile has devised a particularly interesting method[1] to monitor people's daily experiences at work. She uses micro-questionnaires that are completed each day. They include details about the nature of the tasks performed, how others behave in relation to those tasks, the satisfaction gained from ongoing projects and the employees' sense of motivation using clear academic measurement scales. My friend Laurent Bernelas of BVA also uses detailed quantitative measurements for his employees: time spent on the telephone, in internal meetings, traveling outside the company, on individual work, answering various requests, etc. His aim is to work with the departments and teams to understand the precise nature of the tasks performed. He can then play a useful role in re-organizing the physical spaces within the company because he understands what his employees really do.

These types of approaches, combined with individual interviews conducted by behavioral scientists and on-site observation sessions to understand environmental factors, provide a very solid basis for finding out what everyday practices really involve, and how they are connected to the life of the company, employee engagement and performance, and can precisely identify what prevents the desired behaviors from happening and the objective from being achieved.

Of course, as with all studies, data collection is fundamental, but it's only the first step in the quest for excellence.

For the data to really mean something, it must then be analyzed, and then the subsequent phases can play a useful role. And what really matters here is of course the analyst's expert knowledge of behavioral science, because the aim is to understand the biases at work, to go beyond descriptions and find the underlying mechanism that can explain why people don't behave how we'd like them to, or why they don't experience engagement. Each tiny hindrance must be understood and put into context. For example, if the objective is to

....
1   Teresa Amabile and Steven Kramer, *The Progress Principle: Using Small Wins to Ignite Joy, Engagement, and Creativity at Work*, Harvard Business Review Press, 2011.

ensure that employees feel that their direct supervisor values their work, then all the tiny actions and behaviors of each person, and all their interactions must be defined and examined. From the beginning of the day to the close of business and over a specific period of time, all interactions need to be analyzed to give meaning to each, using a specific grid that outlines the main biases and factors that influence behaviors, as identified in behavioral science and based on the three major personal, situational and relational elements.

The ultimate goal of the analysis is to obtain a detailed map of all the actions, gestures and behaviors that contribute to this lack of recognition and how the underlying biases work. From this basis, the company will be able to look for solutions.

Co-creating solutions in the spirit of Nudge

From a clear objective and a deeper understanding of why people are not behaving how we'd like them to behave, it is then possible to look for solutions that will encourage those individuals to switch to the right behavior.

And again, the process must be rigorous, because while the Nudge approach can be a huge benefit for management, it is only possible with clear goals. Once again, Nudge management is like applied science.

Effective ideas that will encourage people to behave how we want them to behave can only work if there is a process in place that:

- Involves motivated participants with varied experience who understand the challenge;
- Creates a specific state of mind that encourages and stimulates creativity;
- Draws on what has been understood during the research phase, and uses the lessons taught by behavioral science.

Let's take another more detailed look at each of these three elements.

First of all, academic research as well as my (many) years of marketing experience working with leading companies in the field, has taught me that nothing is more effective than co-creation when trying to come up with varied and appropriate ideas. So I'm very much in favor of co-creation workshops, including in the field of management where the approach is used much less frequently than in the development of new products or concepts.

Collective intelligence is potentially much more effective than individual intelligence. But now you know better than most that just because someone is part of a group, it doesn't mean that the group automatically works well: there are conditions that must be put in place for the group to reach its full creative potential. And the first is that the group must be formed of people with a diverse range of experiences with regard to the subject they are working on. Whenever I take part in Nudge creativity groups (we call them NudgeLabs at BVA) I am struck by the extent to which people with varied profiles and experiences stimulate creativity. Bringing together operational staff from the relevant departments, people from human resources, internal and external communication, marketing, innovation, IT and even finance, means that the group creates a whole range of different ideas based on their specific focuses. The closer the participants are to what really happens in the field, the more useful the ideas. Of course, the individuals must agree to participate, and their role must be explained and presented in a positive and aspirational way. They must also have a connection with the subject – however tenuous – or at least an opinion on it. In addition to being more creative and more relevant, a varied range of backgrounds and psychological profiles helps to develop ideas that everyone can appropriate, ideas that don't just belong to a specific individual or a department. This is a considerable advantage in the future deployment of ideas, because if the ideas are created by people working together, there are fewer psychological obstacles to deploying those ideas in the minds of other individuals or departments. Often when ideas are put forward by individual departments, other departments tend to criticize them immediately because they are under the influence of the possession bias. An idea to which everyone has made a contribution is much more likely to be developed and applied than the same idea that has been developed by just one individual or entity.

The second key element in designing powerful ideas is the state of mind that needs to be created within the group. Its way of working must encourage creativity. And that means using techniques that have been developed for many years by marketing experts to create an appropriate state of mind: simple and clear rules about encouraging the absence of self-censorship and the possibility that any idea might work – including ones that may be stupid or inapplicable. One of those techniques is ruling out "no" and using the "yes, and" technique. Welcoming new ideas, accepting and being open to them. Fun ice breaker exercises can also be used to instill a relaxed atmosphere that is conducive to creativity, to ensure that listening and respect are the basis for all interactions. Because countless academic studies have shown that innovation happens when a multitude of ideas are brought together. The more ideas there are, the greater the chances of finding that rare gem. We must therefore create the right conditions to generate lots of ideas.

But within a set framework. Although it may seem paradoxical, a truly creative workshop needs clear and precise organization; a combination of strict rules and free expression:

- The workshop needs a clear objective, so in this case the aim is to transform how people work to trigger specific behavior;
- Strict operational regulations that are shared and followed;
- Good quality facilitators – for example, I recommend taking part in a workshop led by my friends Pauline Le Golvan, Anne Charon or Beltrande Bakoula. Their workshops create a positive state of mind and respect timings and rules;
- Comprehensive and clearly presented data that has been produced during the learning phase to understand why people were not behaving in the desired way;
- Specific tools used to stimulate and guide the generation of ideas, with a firm basis in behavioral science.

This last point is key because it distinguishes regular creativity workshops from those that are based on behavioral science. And that's why experts in Nudge and behavioral science are required to make these workshops successful. It's not only about finding ideas that will encourage people to adopt the right behavior, but to make those ideas truly powerful because they activate a behavioral influence whose impact has been proven during experiments carried out by behavioral science researchers. If you take another look at the main successes of the Nudge approach that we presented at the beginning of the book, you'll find that the idea activates one of these factors every time: emotion, social norms, prominence, reciprocity, etc. At the BVA Nudge Unit, we select twenty-one of these fundamental factors that are described in my book *Nudge Marketing*[2] and we use them throughout the creativity workshop to help participants develop ideas whose basic mechanisms are likely to be powerful because they are firmly rooted in the genuine human experience. For each micro-barrier that has been identified during the in-depth understanding phase, the company and its employees must work together to review all the points of contact, by creating ideas that activate one or more of the influencing factors that will encourage the desired behavior. For example, if the aim is to reduce workplace accidents by reviewing safety, the first phase of the study will identify what is not currently in place to prevent accidents, and to understand the mechanisms and underlying biases that explain why. There might be a variety of reasons why employees don't wear their protective equipment, it might be cumbersome, unattractive, too hot, or it might take too long to put it on. There are lots of biases at work here, including the ego and the loss aversion bias (in terms of time in this case). After looking into it in more depth, it might be that employees have high individual productivity goals that make them see the loss of time as going against the important objective that they have been assigned. Their fear of risk – for their career or chances of promotion – will then be stronger than their fear of having an accident. And you now also know that the power of the overconfidence bias makes us believe that accidents happen to other people, but not to us! The information and processes put into place by the company might be combined with a goal to reduce the number of accidents at work, and not demonstrate a specific interest in employee well-being, which in this case brings about less personal motivation. The message

....
2   Eric Singler, *Nudge Marketing, op. cit.*

put across by management on safety at work might also be perceived as very technical and tedious – in behavioral science we'd say System 2-focused – and have little impact on the actual behaviors that result from such communication.

From these few examples of potential obstacles, each one must be reexamined both in terms of the contact points where changes can be made, and the influence we can have. Let's take the case of safety equipment: if it is perceived as unattractive or impractical, what ideas can we develop to improve its appearance? Could we use the ego bias and personalize the equipment by making it more appealing to wear and giving those who are required to wear it a chance to express their own personality? Could we create a process whereby everyone votes for the equipment they prefer to use, and in doing so use a tool that creates engagement or even autonomy? Let's look at the excessively technical language used to talk about workplace safety. Could we try to present a message from a more emotional angle? It's a legitimate approach: the risk can sometimes be fatal, as I was recently told by the manager of a nuclear power plant. Having employees experience the possible outcome of not following safety precautions by reminding them of genuine accidents and having them feel the emotional impact of those accidents can be much more effective. Those reminders might be verbal messages, or they could be conveyed by signs in the workplace. I'm not going to include a list of examples, I think you've probably now got some ideas about how to look for Nudge management solutions. You need to start with a tangible problem and then freely express and develop a whole range of ideas that will activate the influencing factors, then apply them to all points of contact: staircase, desktop screen, elevator, a machine lever, clothes or equipment, etc. always keeping in mind the imperative of a good Nudge, which is to come into play just when the decision is being made!

Preselect the best ideas: Golden Nudges

Once the ideas have been generated by the group, you need to start narrowing them down. Because the key to creativity is to start off by seeing the world through rose-colored glasses: with no constraints in terms of cost, regulations, technical feasibility, ethical issues, etc. There is a single initial objective, which is to come up with as many ideas as possible that will discourage the negative behavior through the use of behavioral science in a directive and stimulating environment. Genuinely effective ideas can only be created if we eliminate constraints. But, of course, the ultimate goal is to finish up with effective and enforceable actions. That's the purpose of the fourth stage, which involves taking another look at all the ideas you have developed and analyzing them in terms of both their power to bring about behavioral changes and how practical they are to implement.

A project group, again from a variety of departments, should be in charge of evaluating the ideas using a table of key evaluation criteria. The ideas must include every aspect of the Nudge approach, and be developed around the following two criteria:

- Feasibility: financial cost, technical feasibility, timing of development and implementation, internal acceptance by those who will be affected by the ideas, and the ethical element of each idea;
- Supposed effectiveness brought about by the desired behavior: the perception of how effective the mechanism will be, what impact the idea will have on the target and its ability to draw attention when it really matters, as well as how sustainable the desired behavior will be in real conditions.

The ideas must be evaluated and categorized in order of preference so that the group can discuss the initial ideas and optimize them having heard the criticism, which at this stage is not only authorized but encouraged. Then a consensus must gradually be reached on the best ideas, before a final evaluation pre-test on the initial objective.

The evaluation process has completely different rules from those that are applied during the creativity workshop, and is designed, in the words of Morten Hansen, to "fight and unite". To optimize the ideas that have been developed, it is now time to shine the spotlight on each of them, by taking a detailed look at how they might be implemented. Because, as in the title of the excellent book by my friend Professor Dilip Soman[3], Nudge is the art of the "last mile". It can only bring about spectacular changes in behavior if it is perfectly executed. And that's what Professor Hansen meant by "fight". A good partnership means being completely honest about each idea that is being developed so it can be optimized to its full extent. Morten Hansen says, "When teams have a good fight in their meetings, team membrs debate the issues, consider alternatives, challenge one another, listen to minority views, scrutinize assumptions, and enable every participant to speak up without fear."[4] That's how we must act to optimize the ideas we want to generate and finish up with truly powerful solutions.

But a good fight must always end well: everyone in the group must be completely committed to the decisions they make, and determined to do their best to ensure they are implemented successfully. There are no winners and no losers in a debate like this, only a group whose members have tried to come up with the best ideas and tailor them to the common goal: changing behavior. The ideas should each be described in detail in a Nudge logbook. This is science, and in science you test how effective your ideas are before you implement them.

Real-life experimentation

You now have a clear list of actions to encourage the targeted employees to behave as you wish them to behave, and your actions have been prioritized. At the very beginning of the process you established the criteria required to evaluate if the initiative has been successful. You now need to design an experimental plan, to measure your idea's effectiveness under real conditions. At this point it's very important to think methodically, because only the impact of the Nudges must be evaluated, and nothing else. There are many possible techniques and they all have advantages and disadvantages that need to be analyzed

3   Dilip Soman, *The Last Mile: Creating Social and Economic Value from Behavioral Insights*, University of Toronto Press, 2015.
4   Morten T. Hansen, *Great at Work, op. cit.*

in order to select the most relevant for each action, or more gene-rally which best suits the action plan. One of the main challenges is to measure how people really behave, and compare that to a control group, rather than measuring intentions to behave.

In addition, the experiment must be carried out on a small scale – one department, one office, one part of the team – but on a large enough group to obtain statistically sound results, while retaining the flexibility of the Nudge approach. It's about finding the best balance between scientific rigor and quick decision-making.

The results must be analyzed and evaluated so that the situation can constantly be improved. And that's what the Behavioural Insights Team call the "Test, Learn, Adapt" process[5]. The initial action plan can always be improved when insight is obtained from the results, and part of an iterative process for maximum effectiveness. But we still haven't quite reached the end of the process. Before the initiative is implemented throughout the entire company it must be very care-fully prepared.

Prepare the ecosystem, deploy... and measure

The measures have been designed with the active support of multi-functional groups, tested under rigorous conditions and then opti-mized again in light of the results obtained. But before they are rolled out to the entire company or entity, you need to make sure that the ecosystem is able to integrate the measures so that they are sources of progress and not obstacles. Because even the very best ideas have no chance of success if they are not supported by the world around them. Here again, it's about coherence between a company's physical environment and its psychological environ-ment. If the ideas developed do not fit with their environment, there is no chance of success. Because the environment always outweighs occasional actions. The environment needs to transform alongside

5   Behavioural Insights Team, *Test, Learn, Adapt: Developing Public Policy with Randomized Controlled Trials*, June 2012, behaviouralinsights.co.uk.

the desired behaviors if they are to be effective. For example, if the aim is to create opportunities for relaxation and to boost interpersonal relationships within the company to enhance team spirit and the idea was to provide specific facilities such as a gym, foosball table or ping-pong table, but managers never go into them (a nod to a friend of mine who is a brilliant businessman and chairman of Ogic, Emmanuel Launiau), there is a high chance that they won't be used at all because people don't want to give the impression that they have too much free time, or are not fully engaged with their work. In this case, managers need to set a good example by regularly using the equipment themselves. The system must support the actions that have been developed, and their implementation plan must incorporate this requirement. It may go as far as training or communication programs for specific targets who will have to modify their own behavior to encourage others to do the same. And beyond training, with its importance and its limitations, incentive systems and individual evaluations also need to be reconsidered so that they are in line with the behavioral objectives. A project's success depends on the ability of the entire business incentive ecosystem to converge, and encourage behavioral change. The plan for launching and implementing the actions must take all these considerations into account if it is to maximize its chances of success.

And it doesn't stop at the launch. It's the beginning of a new chapter, the progress must be monitored, and its results measured. Nudge management is an ongoing quest for continuous improvement in a constantly shifting environment. No organization is perfect, let alone in a world that is changing perhaps more quickly than at any other time in history. But it is my firm belief that the wonderful insight contributed by behavioral science about the factors that influence human behavior, as well as what we have learned about what brings about employee engagement, is the fundamental basis for building and developing businesses and organizations towards the holy grail of improved well-being at work, and better individual and collective performance.

Conclusion

I have a dream...

I have a dream... I have a dream that any company, or any organization can become a place of individual and collective performance AND a place of well-being and engagement or, more precisely, a place of performance *because* it is a place of well-being and engagement.

I know that the words "I have a dream" have already been said... And that those words had such power to inspire, such pertinence, and such beauty that they began one of the most important revolutions humanity has ever known. The fight for civil rights that was proclaimed on August 28, 1963 by Martin Luther King in front of the Lincoln Memorial in Washington will be remembered forever. In the aftermath, the American administration submitted the Civil Rights Act to Congress and in 1963 Martin Luther King was named "Person of the Year" by *Time* magazine, going on to win the Nobel Peace Prize in 1964. While the fight is obviously not yet over, the resulting progress for people of color throughout the world was outstanding. Because his dream was fair.

Obviously I'm not for one minute saying that my dream and the one so eloquently expressed by Martin Luther King have anything in common! I'm simply trying to help you realize that companies really do want to align performance with employee well-being. If people are happier at work, the world will be a better place.

And the best part is that there's no need to choose between performance and well-being. For companies and entrepreneurs who are looking to grow their business, this is clearly the way to go. For those who, like me, also believe that profit is a must, a company's primary focus must be its social responsibility and ability to contribute to a better world, so it is also the right path.

Because through the fascinating and inspiring work that is constantly being produced in behavioral science by the best researchers and academics, as well as the specific practices adopted by some of the most successful companies in the world, new managerial principles – the ones I call Nudge management – can generate this magical trio of performance, well-being and engagement.

Because employees are people first and foremost, and all they are looking for is to be engaged and achieve more than they think they can, as long as they are encouraged, supported, and given the means and the motivation to make those achievements happen. All they want is to be considered for who they really are: flesh and blood beings who need to find meaning in what they do, to be treated with respect and fairness, and feel that their work and efforts are recognized. They want to be part of a community they can trust and in which they enjoy working, and one whose members will be able to support each other in times of need. All they are looking for is the opportunity to develop their skills as individuals while contributing – even in a very small way – to a cause that is bigger than themselves. And this commitment will generate sustainable performance for the company in a knowledge economy where each person's intelligence benefits the community and constitutes an outstanding competitive advantage.

But unfortunately at the moment, these human beings are mostly disengaged and disinterested, even when we think we're motivating them with various rewards such as (fairly pathetic) salary increases, alluring career opportunities or financial bonuses for top performers. Or we use threats, whether in the form of dismissal or everyday stress, to get people to do more with less, always firmly focused on the ultimate goal of the highest quality product or the most complete customer satisfaction.

The main ideas in Nudge management do require an in-depth knowledge of human motivation and need to be implemented with a good deal of tact and commitment. But it's not about being permissive, it's about creating a physical and psychological environment that makes it easy for people to become engaged, and for performance to improve. These ideas are everyday words and actions, the combination of an encouraging culture and supportive leadership behaviors, workspaces that facilitate and convey the company's values, and processes that give meaning to practices as employees go about their daily lives. It is about co-creation and experimentation deep within the company, the constant search for improvement, innovation, and transformation, presented in an inspiring way and designed to integrate smoothly into the constraints of our busy schedules.

It's a huge challenge, but it has enormous potential.

The goal of this book is to share my dream of a management style that brings about performance by human beings and for human beings. My ultimate objective for as many entrepreneurs as possible, both now and in the future, to share this conviction and take possession of this dream so that together we can make a small contribution – with a lot of humility and plenty of passion and perseverance as Angela Duckworth would say – to making our world a better place.

Bibliography

Ackerman Joshua M., Nocera Christopher C. and Bargh John A., "Incidental Haptic Sensations Influence Social Judgments and Decisions" *Science*, vol. 328, No.5986, June 2010, p. 1712-1715.

Altmann Erik M., Trafton Gregory J. and Hambrick David Z., "Momentary Interruptions Can Derail the Train of Thought", *Journal of Experimental Psychology: General*, vol. 143, No.1, February 2014, p. 215-226.

Amabile Teresa M. and Kramer Steven J., "What Really Motivates Workers", *Harvard Business Review*, vol. 88, No. 1-2, January-February 2010, p. 44-45.

Amabile Teresa M. and Kramer Steven J., *The Progress Principle: Using Small Wins to Ignite Joy, Engagement and Creativity at Work*, Harvard Business Review Press, 2011.

Ariely Dan, *Predictably Irrational: The Hidden Forces that Shape Our Decisions* HarperCollins, 2008.

Ariely Dan, *The Upside of Irrationality: The Unexpected Benefits of Defying Logic at Work and at Home*, Harper, 2010.

Ariely Dan, *Payoff: The Hidden Logic That Shapes Our Motivations*, TED Books-Simon & Schuster, 2016.

Ariely Dan, *The Honest Truth about Dishonesty: How We Lie to Everyone – Especially Ourselves,* HarperCollins, 2012.

Ariely Dan and George Loewenstein, "The Heat of the Moment: The Effect of Sexual Arousal on Sexual Decision Making", *Journal of Behavioral Decision Making*, vol. 19, No.2, April 2006, p. 87-98.

Ariely Dan, Kamenica Emir and Prelec Dražen, "Man's Search for Meaning: The case of Legos", *Journal of Economic Behavior & Organization*, No.67, 2008, p. 671-677.

Ariely Dan, Gneezy Uri, Loewenstein George *et al.*, "Large Stakes and Big Mistakes", *The Review of Economic Studies*, vol. 76, No.2, April 2009, p. 451-469.

Ariely Dan, Hreha Jason and Berman Kristen, *Hacking Human Nature for Good: A Practical Guide to Changing Human Behavior*, Irrational Labs, 2014.

Atchley Ruth Ann, Strayer David L. and Atchley Paul, "Creativity in the Wild: Improving Creative Reasoning through Immersion in Natural Settings", *PLoS One*, vol. 7, No.12, December 2012.

Baard Paul, Deci Edward and Ryan Richard, "Intrinsic Need Satisfaction: A Motivational Basis of Performance and Well-Being in Two Work Settings", *Journal of Applied Social Psychology*, vol. 34, No.10, 2004, p. 2045-2068.

Bailey Catherine and Madden Adrian, "What Makes Work Meaningful – Or Meaningless", *MITSloan Management Review*, summer 2016.

Baldoni John "Employee Engagement Does More than Boost Productivity", *Harvard Business Review*, July 4, 2013.

Bargh John A., Chen Mark and Burrows Lara, "Automaticity of Social Behavior: Direct Effects of Trait Construct and Stereotype Activation in Action", *Journal of Personality and Social Psychology*, vol. 71, No.2, p. 230-244.

Barsade Sigal G., "The Ripple Effect: Emotional Contagion and Its Influence on Group Behavior", *Administrative Science Quarterly*, vol. 47, No.4, December 2002, p. 644-675.

Barsade Sigal G., Ward Andrew J., Turner Jean D. F. *et al.*, "To Your Heart's Content: A Model of Affective Diversity in Top Management Teams", *Administrative Science Quarterly*, vol. 45, No.4, December 2000, p. 802-836.

Baumeister Roy F. and Tierney John M., *Willpower: Rediscovering the Greatest Human Strength*, Penguin Books; Reprint edition, 2012.

Baumeister Roy F., Bratslavsky Ellen, Muraven Mark *et al.*, "Ego Depletion: Is the Active Self a Limited Resource?", *Journal of Personality and Social Psychology*, vol. 74, No.5, May 1998, p. 1252-1265.

Bazerman Max H. and Tenbrunsel Ann E., *Blind Spots: Why We Fail to Do What's Right and What to Do about It*, Princeton University Press, 2010.

Benartzi Shlomo, *Save More Tomorrow: Practical Behavioural Finance Solutions to Improve 401(K) Plans*, Portfolio-Penguin, 2012.

Berger Jonah, *Contagious: Why Things Catch On*, Simon & Schuster, 2013.

Berman Mark G., Jonides John and Kaplan Stephen, "The Cognitive Benefits of Interacting With Nature", *Psychological Science*, vol. 19, No.12, December 2008, p. 1207-1212.

Bloom Nicholas, Sadun Raffaella and Van Reenen John, "Does Management Really Work?" *Harvard Business Review*, November 2012.

Bloom Nicholas, Liang James, Roberts John *et al.*, "Does Working from Home Work? Evidence from a Chinese Experiment", *The Quarterly Journal of Economics*, vol. 130, No.1, February 2015, p. 165-218.

Bock Laszlo, *Work Rules! Insights from Inside Google That Will Transform How You Live and Lead*, John Murray Publishers, 2015.

Bohnet Iris, *What Works: Gender Equality by Design*, The Belknap Press of Harvard University Press, 2016.

Bohnet Iris, "How to Take the Bias Out of Interviews", *Harvard Business Review*, April 18, 2016.

Brooks David, *The Social Animal: The Hidden Sources of Love, Character and Achievement*, Random House, 2011.

Carrington Michal J., Neville Benjamin A. and Whitwell Gregory J., "Why Ethical Consumers Don't Walk Their Talk: Towards a Framework for Understanding the Gap Between the Ethical Purchase Intentions and Actual Buying Behaviour of Ethically Minded Consumers", *Journal of Business Ethics*, vol. 97, No.1, November 2010, p. 139-158.

Chan Amanda L., "Windows in the Workplace Linked with Better Sleep", *The Huffington Post*, December 6, 2013.

Christensen Clayton M., Hall Taddy, Dillon Karen *et al*, *Competing Against Luck: The Story of Innovation and Customer Choice*, Harper Business, 2016.

Cialdini Robert, B., *Principles of Persuasion*, Harvard Business Review Press, 2017

Cialdini Robert B., *Pre-suasion: A Revolutionary Way to Influence and Persuade*, Simon & Schuster, 2016.

Clifton Don, *First, Break all the Rules: What the World's Greatest Managers Do Differently*, Gallup Press, 2016.

Clouse R. Wilburn and Spurgeon Karen L., "Corporate Analysis of Humor", *Psychology: A Journal of Human Behavior*, vol. 32, No.3-4, 1995, p. 1-24.

Coleman John, Gulati Daniel and Segovia W. Oliver, *Passion & Purpose: Stories from the Best and Brightest Young Business Leaders*, Harvard Business Review Press, 2011.

Collins Jim, *Good to Great: Why Some Companies Make the Leap... and Others Don't*, William Collins, 2001.

Coyle Daniel, *The Talent Code: Greatness isn't born, it's grown, here's how*, Bantam Books, 2009.

Coyle Daniel, *The Culture Code: The Secrets of Highly Successful Groups*, Bantam Books, 2018.

Crabtree Steve, "Can People Collaborate Effectively While Working Remotely?" *Business Journal*, March 13, 2014.

Csíkszentmihályi Mihály, *Flow: The Psychology of Optimal Experience,* Harper Perennial Modern Classics; 1 edition, 2008

D'Abate Caroline P. and Eddy Erik R., "Engaging in Personal Business on the Job: Extending the Presenteeism Construct", *Human Resource Development Quarterly*, vol. 18, No.3, autumn 2007, p. 361-383.

Dai Hengchen, Milkman Katherine L., Hofmann David A. *et al.*, "The Impact of Time at Work and Time Off From Work on Rule Compliance: The Case of Hand Hygiene in Health Care", *Journal of Applied Psychology*, vol. 100, No.3, 2015, p. 846-862.

Damasio Antonio, *Descartes' Error* Vintage, 1994.

Danziger Shai, Levav Jonathan and Avnaim-Pesso Liora, "Extraneous Factors in Judicial Decisions", *PNAS*, vol. 108, No.17, April 2011, p. 6889-6892.

Daskal Lolly, *The Leadership Gap: What Gets Between You and Your Greatness*, Portfolio Penguin, 2017.

Davis Matthew C., Leach Desmond J. and Clegg Chris W., "The Physical Environment of the Office: Contemporary and Emerging Issues", *International Review of Industrial and Organizational Psychology*, vol; 26, 2011, p. 193-235.

Dean Jeremy, *Making Habits, Breaking Habits: Why We Do Things, Why We Don't, and How To Make Any Change Stick*, Da Capo Press, 2013.

Demirbilek Oya and Sener Bahar, "Product Design, Semantics and Emotional Response", *Ergonomics*, vol. 46, No.13-14, October 2003, p. 1346-1360.

DeSchriver Mary M. and Cutler Riddick Carol, "Effects of Watching Aquariums on Elders' Stress", *Anthrozoös*, vol. 4, No.1, January 1990, p. 44-48.

Di Stefano Giada, Pisano Gary P., Gino Francesca *et al.*, "Making Experience Count: The Role of Reflection in Individual Learning", Harvard Business School, Working Paper 14-093, 2014.

Dolan Paul, *Happiness by Design: Finding Pleasure and Purpose in Everyday Life*, Hudson Street Press, 2014.

Dolan Paul and Metcalfe Robert, "The Relationship Between Innovation and Subjective Wellbeing", *Research Policy*, vol. 41, No.8, October 2012, p. 1489-1498.

Dolan Paul, Foy Chloé and Smith Sophie, "The Salient Checklist: Gathering Up the Ways in Which Built Environnments Affect What We Do and How We Feel", *Buildings*, vol. 6, No.9, May 2016.

Duckworth Angela, *Grit: The Power of Passion and Perseverance*, Scribner, 2016.

Duhigg, Charles, *The Power of Habit: Why We Do What We Do in Life and Business*, Random House Trade Paperbacks, 2014.

Duhigg Charles, *Smarter, Faster, Better: The Transformative Power of Real Productivity*, Random House, 2016.

Dunn Elisabeth and Norton Michael, *Happy Money: The Science of Happier Spending*, Simon & Schuster, 2013.

Dutton Jane E., *Energize Your Workplace: How To Create and Sustain High-Quality Connections at Work*, John Wiley & Sons, 2003.

Dutton Jane E. and Heaphy Emily D., "The Power of High-Quality Connections", in Kim S. Cameron, Jane E. Dutton and Robert E. Quinn (eds), *Handbook of Positive Organizational Scholarship*, Berrett-Koehler Publishers, 2003, p. 263-278.

Dutton Jane E. and Spreitzer Gretchen M., *How To Be a Positive Leader: Small Actions, Big Impact*, Berrett-Koehler Publishers, 2014.

Dutton Jane E., Debebe Gelaye and Wrzesniewski Amy, "Being Valued and Devalued at Work: A Social Valuing Perspective", in Beth A. Bechky and Kimberly D. Elsbach (eds), *Qualitative Organizational Research: Best Papers from the Davis Conference on Qualitative Research*, vol. 3, Age Publishing, 2016, p. 9-51.

Dux Paul E., Ivanoff Jason, Asplund Christopher L. *et al.*, "Isolation of a Central Bottleneck of Information Processing With Time-Resolved FMRI", *Neuron*, vol. 52, No.6, December 2006, p. 1109-1120.

Dweck Carol S., *Mindset: The New Psychology of Success*, Ballantine Books, 2007.

Edmondson Amy C., *Teaming: How Organizations Learn, Innovate and Compete in the Knowledge Economy*, John Wiley & Sons, 2012.

Edmondson Amy C., *Teaming to innovate*, Jossey-Bass, 2013.

Edmondson Amy C. and Feldman Laura R., "Phase Zero: Introducing New Services at Ideo (A)", *Harvard Business Review Case* No.605-069, 2005.

Ellis Albert and Knaus William J., *Overcoming Procrastination: Or How to Think and Act Rationally in Spite of Life's Inevitable Hassles*, New Amercian Library, 1977.

Ericsson Anders and Pool Robert, *Peak: Secrets from the New Science of Expertise*, HMH, 2016.

Eyal Nir, *Hooked: How to Build Habit-Forming Products*, Portfolio-Penguin, 2014.

Fehr Ernst and Schmidt Klaus M., "The Economics of Fairness, Reciprocity and Altruism: Experimental Evidence and New Theories", in Serge-Christophe Kolm and Jean Mercier Ythier (dir.), *Handbook of the Economics of Giving: Altruism and Reciprocity*, vol. 1, Elsevier, 2006, p. 615-691.

Feldman Barrett Lisa, *How Emotions are Made: The Secret Life of The Brain*, MacMillan, 2017.

Ferrari Joseph R., Díaz-Morales Juan Francisco, O'Callaghan Jean *et al.*, "Frequent Behavioral Delay Tendencies by Adults: International Prevalence Rates of Chronic Procrastination", *Journal of Cross-Cultural Psychology*, vol. 38, No.4, July 2007, p. 458-464.

Finkelstein Sydney, *Superbosses: How Exceptional Leaders Master the Flow of Talent*, Portfolio-Penguin, 2016.

Finkelstein Sydney, "Secrets of the Superbosses", *Harvard Business Review*, January-February 2016.

Finkelstein Sydney, "The Best Leaders Are Great Teachers", *Harvard Business Review*, January-February 2018.

Fredrickson Barbara L., *Positivity*, Harmony, 2010.

Fredrickson Barbara L. and Branigan Christine, "Positive Emotions Broaden the Scope of Attention and Thought-Action Repertories", *Cognition and Emotion*, vol. 19, No.3, May 2005, p. 313-332.

Fredrickson Barbara L., "The broaden-and-build theory of positive emotions", *The Royal Society Publishing*, vol. 359, No 1449, September 2004, p. 1367-1378.

Friedman Ron, *The Best Place To Work: The Art and Science to Create an Extraordinary Workplace*, TarcherPerigee, 2014.

Friedman Stewart D., *Total Leadership: Be a Better Leader, Have a Richer Life*, Harvard Business Review Press, 2014.

Frijda Nico H., *The Laws of Emotion*, Lawrence Erlbaum, 2007.

Galinski Adam and Schweitzer Maurice, *Friend & Foe: When to Cooperate, When to Compete, and How to Succeed at Both*, Crown Business, 2015.

Gallup $Q^{12®}$, *The Relationship Between Engagement at Work and Organizational Outcomes*, April 2016.

Gidwani Nick, "How to Support Employees' Learning Goals While Getting Day-to-Day Stuff Done", *Harvard Business Review*, August 1, 2017.

Gigerenzer Gerd, *Gut Feelings: Short Cuts to Better Decision Making*, Penguin, 2008.

Gigerenzer Gerd, *Risk Savvy: How to Make Good Decisions*, Viking, 2014.

Gigerenzer Gerd and Selten Reinhard, *Bounded Rationality: The Adaptative Toolbox*, The MIT Press, 2001.

Gino Francesca and Staats Bradley, "Why Organizations Don't Learn", *Harvard Business Review*, November 2015.

Glimcher Paul W. and Fehr Ernst (dir.), *Neuroeconomics: Decision Making and the Brain*, Academic Press-Elsevier, 2014 (2nd ed.).

Gneezy Uri and List John A., *The Why Axis: Hidden Motives and the Undiscovered Economics of Everyday Life*, PublicAffairs, 2013.

Goldstein Noah J., Martin Steeve J. and Cialdini Robert B., *Yes!: 50 Scientifically Proven Ways to Be Persuasive*, 2015.

Goleman Daniel, *Emotional Intelligence: Why it can matter more than IQ*, Bloomsbury, 1995.

Goleman Daniel, "What makes a leader?", *Harvard Business Review*, November-December 1998.

Goleman Daniel, Boyatzis Richard and McKee Annie, *Working with Emotional Intelligence,* Bloomsbury, 1998.

Grant Adam, *Give and Take: Why Helping Others Drives Our Success,* Penguin, 2014.

Grant Adam, *Originals: How Non-Conformists Move the World,* Penguin Books, 2017.

Grant Adam, Campbell Elizabeth M., Chen Grace *et al.,* "Impact and the Art of Motivation Maintenance: The Effects of Contact With Beneficiaries on Persistence Behavior", *Organizational Behavior and Human Decision Processes,* vol. 103, No.1, May 2007, p. 53-67.

Haans Antal, "The Natural Preference in People's Appraisal of Light", *Journal of Environmental Psychology,* vol. 39, September 2014, p. 54-61.

Hansen Morten T., *Collaboration: How Leaders Avoid the Traps, Create Unity, and Reap Big Results,* Harvard Business Review Press, 2009.

Hansen Morten T., *Great at Work: How Top Performers Do Less, Work Better, and Achieve More,* Simon & Schuster, 2018.

Hartman Raymond S., Doane Michael J. and Woo Chi-Keung, "Consumer Rationality and the Status Quo", *The Quarterly Journal of Economics,* vol. 106, No.1, February 1991, p. 141-162.

Heath Chip and Heath Dan, *Made to Stick: Why Some Ideas Survive and Others Die,* Random House, 2007.

Heath Chip and Heath Dan, *Switch: How to Change Things When Change is Hard,* Broadway Books, 2010.

Heath Chip and Heath Dan, *The Power of Moments: Why Certain Experiences Have Extraordinary Impact,* Simon and Schuster, 2017.

Hedges Kristi, *The Inspiration Code: How the Best Leaders Energize People Everyday,* Amacom, 2017.

Heyman James E., Orhun Yesim and Ariely Dan, "Auction Fever: The Effect of Opponents and Quasi-Endowment on Product Valuations", *Journal of Interactive Marketing,* vol. 18, No.4, autumn 2004, p. 7-21.

Hirst Alison, "Settlers, Vagrants and Mutual Indifference: Unintended Consequences of Hot-Desking", *Journal of Organizational Change Management,* vol. 24, No.6, October 2011, p. 767-788.

Hobson J. Allan, "Sleep Is of the Brain, by the Brain and for the Brain", *Nature,* vol. 437, No.7063, October 2005, p. 1254-1256.

Horvitz Eric and Iqbal Shamsi T., "Disruption and Recovery of Computing Tasks: Field Study, Analysis, and Directions", *Proceedings of the 2007 Conference on Human Factors in Computing Systems*, San José, California, April 28-May 3 2007.

Hsieh Tony, *Delivering Happiness*, Grand Central Publishing, 2013.

Huffington Ariana, *The Sleep Revolution: Transforming Your Life, One Night at A Time*, Harmony, 2016.

Huselid Mark A., "The Impact of Human Resource Management Practices on Turnover, Productivity, and Corporate Financial Performance", *Academy of Management Journal*, vol. 38, No.3, 1995, p. 635-872.

Ibarra Herminia, *Act Like a Leader, Think Like a Leader*, Harvard Business School Press, 2015.

Ignatius Adi, "How Indra Nooyi Turned Design Thinking Into Strategy: An Interview with PepsiCo's CEO", *Harvard Business Review*, September 2015.

Isen Alice M., Rosenzweig Andrew S. and Young Mark J. , "The Influence of Positive Affect on Clinical Problem Solving", *Medical Decision Making*, vol. 11, No.3, July-September 1991, p. 221-227.

Jones Jeffrey M., "In U.S., 40% Get Less Than Recommended Amount of Sleep", December 19, 2013, news.gallup.com.

Judge Timothy A., Piccolo Ronald F., Podsakoff Nathan P. *et al.*, "The Relationship Between Pay and Job Satisfaction: A Meta-Analysis of the Literature", *Journal of Vocational Behavior*, vol. 77, No.2, October 2010, p. 157-167.

Kahneman Daniel, *Thinking, Fast and Slow*, Penguin, 2012 (revised edition).

Kahneman Daniel and Tversky Amos, "Choices, Values, and Frames", *American Psychologist*, vol. 39, No.4, January 1984, p. 341-350.

Kahneman Daniel, Knetsch Jack L. and Thaler Richard H., "Anomalies: The Endowment Effect, Loss Aversion, and Status Quo Bias", *The Journal of Economic Perspectives*, vol. 5, No.1, winter 1991, p. 193-206.

Kahneman Daniel, Diener Ed and Schwartz Norbert (dir.), *Well-Being: The Foundations of Hedonic Psychology*, Russell Sage Foundation, 1999.

Kahneman Daniel and Tversky Amos, *Choices, Values and Frames*, Cambridge University Press, 2000.

Kalev Alexandra, Kelly Erin and Dobbin Frank, "Best Practices or Best Guesses? Assessing the Efficacy of Corporate Affirmative Action and Diversity Policies", *American Sociological Review*, vol. 71, August 2006, p. 598-617.

Kaplan Soren, "6 Ways to Create a Culture of Innovation", Co. Design, December 21, 2013, fastcodesign.com.

Keltner Dacher, *Born to Be Good: The Science of a Meaningful Life*, W. W. Norton, 2009.

Kenrick Douglas T. and Griskevicius Vladas, *The Rational Animal: How Evolution Made Us Smarter than We Think*, Basic Books, 2013.

Knight Craig and Haslam S. Alexander, "Your Place or Mine? Organizational Identification and Comfort as Mediators of Relationships Between the Managerial Control of Workplace and Employees' Satisfaction and Well-Being", *British Journal of Management*, vol. 21, No.3, September 2010, p. 717-735.

Koelsch Stefan, "Towards a Neural Basis of Music-Evoked Emotions", *Trends in Cognitive Sciences*, vol. 14, No.3, March 2010, p. 131-137.

Kotter John, *The Heart of Change: Real Life Stories of How People Change their Organizations*, Harvard Business Review Press, 2002.

Kotter John, *Leading Change*, Harvard Business Review Press, 2012.

Kotter John and Rathgebber Holder, *Our Iceberg is Melting: Changing and Succeeding Under Any Conditions*, Penguin Random House, 2016.

Kramer Adam D. I., Guillory Jamie E. and Hancock Jeffrey T., "Experimental Evidence of Massive-Scale Emotional Contagion Through Social Networks", *Proceedings of the National Academy of Sciences*, vol. 111, No.24, June 2014, p. 8788-8790.

Lan Li, Lian Zhiwei and Pan Li, "The Effects of Air Temperature on Office Workers' Well-Being, Workload and Productivity-Evaluated with Subjective Ratings", *Applied Ergonomics*, vol. 42, No.1, December 2010, p. 29-36.

Lashinsky Adam, "Chaos by Design: The Inside Story of Disorder, Disarray, and Uncertainty at Google. And Why It's All Part of the Plan. (They Hope.)", *Fortune*, October 2, 2006.

Lazar Sara W., Kerr Catherine E., Wasserman Rachel H. *et al.*, "Meditation Experience Is Associated With Increased Cortical Thickness", *Neuroreport*, vol. 16, No.17, November 2005, p. 1893-1897.

Leakey Richard E. and Lewin Roger, *The Sixth Extinction: Biodiversity and its Survival* Phoenix, 1996.

LeDoux Joseph, *The Emotional Brain: The Mysterious Underpinnings of Emotional Life,* Simon & Schuster, 1998.

Lee Jooa Julie, Gino Francesca, Shuo Jin Ellie *et al.*, "Hormones and Ethics: Understanding the Biological Basis of Unethical Conduct", *Journal of Experimental Psychology: General*, vol. 144, No.5, October 2015, p. 891-897.

Lerner Jennifer, Small Deborah and Loewenstein George, "Heart Strings and Purse Strings: Carroyer Effects of Emotions on Economic Decisions", *Psychological Science*, vol. 15, No.5, May 2004, p. 337-341.

Lewis Michael, *The Undoing Project: A Friendship that Changed Our Minds*, W. W. Norton, 2016.

Lieberman Matthew, *Social: Why Our Brains Are Wired to Connect*, Crown, 2013.

Lo June C., Loh Kep Kee, Zheng Hui *et al.*, "Sleep Duration and Age-Related Changes in Brain Structure and Cognitive Performance", *Sleep*, vol. 37, No.7, July 2014, p. 1171-1178.

Loewenstein George, "Out of Control: Visceral Influences on Behavior", *Organizational Behavior and Human Decision Processes*, vol. 65, No.3, March 1996, p. 272-292.

Loewenstein George, *Exotic Preferences: Behavioral Economics and Human Motivation*, Oxford University Press, 2007.

Loewenstein George, Read Daniel and Baufmeister Roy F., *Time and Decision: Economic and Psychologic Perspectives on Intemporal Choice*, Russell Sage Foundation, 2003.

Lord Charles G., Ross Lee and Lepper Mark R., "Biased Assimilation and Attitude Polarization: The Effects of Prior Theories on Subsequently Considered Evidence", *Journal of Personality and Social Psychology*, vol. 37, No.11, 1979, p. 2098-2109.

Lovallo Dan and Sibony Olivier, "The Case for Behavioral Strategy", *McKinsey Quaterly*, March 2010.

Lyengar Sheena, *The Art of Choosing*, Twelve, 2010.

Lyubomirsky Sonja, *The How of Happiness: A Scientific Approach to Getting the Life You Want*, Penguin Books, 2008.

Martin Steve, Goldstein Noah and Cialdini Robert, *The Small BIG: small changes that spark big influence*, Grand Central Publishing, 2014.

Mather Mara and Lighthall Nichole R., "Both Risk and Reward are Processed Differently in Decisions Made Under Stress", *Current Directions in Psychological Science*, vol. 21, No.2, February 2012, p. 36-41.

McCord Patty, *Powerful: Building a Culture of Freedom and Responsibility*, Silicon Guilde, 2017.

McKee Annie, *How to Be Happy at Work: The Power of Purpose, Hope, and Friendship*, Harvard Business Review Press, 2017.

Medina John, *Brain Rules: 12 Principles for Surviving and Thriving at Work, Home and School*, Pear Press, 2014.

Mehta Ravi, Zhu Rui (Juliet) and Cheema Amar, "Is Noise Always Bad? Exploring the Effects of Ambient Noise on Creative Cognition", *Journal of Consumer Research*, vol. 39, No.4, December 2012, p. 784-799.

Mehta Ravi and Zhu Rui (Juliet), "Blue or Red? Exploring the Effect of Color on Cognitive Task Performances", *Science*, vol. 323, No.5918, February 2009, p. 1226-1229.

Meister Jeanne C., "How Deloitte Made Learning a Game", *Harvard Business Review*, January 2, 2013.

Milgram Stanley, "Behavioral Study of Obedience", *Journal of Abnormal and Social Psychology*, vol. 67, No.4, 1963, p. 371-378.

Miller George, "The Magical Number 7, Plus or Minus 2: Some Limits on Our Capacity for Processing Information", *Psychological Review*, vol. 63, No.2, March 1956, p. 81-97.

Mischel, Walter, *The Marshmallow Test: Understanding self-control and how to master it*, Corgi, September 2015.

Moll Jorge, Krueger Frank, Zahn Roland *et al.*, "Human Fronto-Mesolimbic Networks Guide Decisions About Charitable Donation", *Proceedings of the National Academy of Sciences USA*, vol. 103, No.42, October 2006, p. 15623-15628.

Montier James, *Global Equity Strategy: Behaving Badly*, Dresdner Kleinwort Wasserstein, February 2, 2006.

Moreland Richard L. and Beach Scott R., "Exposure Effects in the Classroom: The Development of Affinity Among Students", *Journal of Experimental Social Psychology*, vol. 28, No.3, May 1992, p. 255-276.

Yves Morieux and Peter Tollman, *Six Simple Rules: How to Manage Complexity without Getting Complicated*, Harvard Business Review Press, 2014.

Morrison Rachel L. and Macky Keith A., "The Demands and Resources Arising from Shared Office Spaces", *Applied Ergonomics*, vol. 60, April 2017, p. 103-115.

Nayar Vineet, *Employees First, Customers Second: Turning Conventional Management Upside Down*, Harvard Business Review Press, 2010.

Neal David T., Wood Wendy and Quinn Jeffrey M., "Habits: A Repeat Performance", *Association for Psychological Science*, vol. 15, No.4, August 2006, p. 198-202.

Newport Cal, *Deep Work: Rules for Focused Success in a Distracted World*, Grand Central Publishing, 2016.

Norton Michael I., Mochon Daniel and Ariely Dan, "The Ikea Effect: When Labor Leads to Love", *Journal of Consumer Psychology*, vol. 22, No.3, July 2012, p. 453-460.

OCDE, *Behavioural Insights and Public Policy: Lessons from Around the World*, OECD Publishing, 2017.

Oppezzo Marily and Schwartz Daniel L., "Give Your Ideas Some Legs: The Positive Effect of Walking on Creative Thinking", *Journal of Experimental Psychology: Learning, Memory and Cognition*, vol. 40, No.4, April 2014, p. 1142-1152.

Page Scott E., *The Diversity Bonus: How Great Teams Pay Off in the Knowledge Economy*, Princeton University Press, 2017.

Pfeffer Jeffrey, *The Human Equation: Building Profits by Putting People First*, Harvard Business School Press, 1998.

Pfeffer Jeffrey, *Leadership BS: Fixing Workplaces and Careers One Truth at a Time*, Harper Business, 2015.

Pfeffer Jeffrey and Sutton Robert, *Hard Facts, Dangerous Truths and Total Nonsense: Profiting From Evidence-Based Management*, Harvard Business Review Press, 2006.

Pink Daniel, *Drive: The Surprising Truth About What Motivates Us*, Riverhead Books, 2011.

Pink Daniel H., *When: The Scientific Secrets of Perfect Timing*, Random House Large Prints, 2018.

Pontefract Dan, *The Purpose Effect: Building Meaning in Yourself, Your Role and Your Organization*, Elevate, 2016.

Robinson Adam, *The Best Teams Wins: Build Your Business through Predictive Hiring*, GreenLeaf Book, 2017.

Rollag Keith, Parise Salvatore and Cross Rob, "Getting New Hires Up to Speed Quickly", *MIT Sloan Management Review*, vol. 46, No.2, December 2005, p. 35-41.

Rose Mike, *The Mind at Work: Valuing the Intelligence of the American Worker*, Penguin Books, 2014.

Ross Lee and Nisbett Richard E., *The Person and the Situation: Perspectives of Social Psychology*, McGraw-Hill, 1991.

Sami Saber, Robertson Edwin M. and Miall Chris, "The Time Course of Task-Specific Memory Consolidation Effects in Resting State Networks", *The Journal of Neuroscience*, vol. 34, No.11, March 2014, p. 3982-3992.

Sander Libby, "The Research on Hot-Desking and Activity-Based Work Isn't So Positive", *The Conversation*, April 11, 2017.

Schein Edgar H., *Organizational Culture and Leadership*, Wiley, 2017 (5th ed.).

Schmälzle Ralf, Häcker Frank E., Honey Christopher J. *et al.*, "Engage Listeners: Shared Neural Processing of Powerful Political Speeches", *Social Cognition and Affective Neuroscience*, vol. 10, No.8, p. 1137-1143.

Schmidt Frank L. and Hunter John E., "The Validity and Utility of Selection Methods in Personnel Psychology: Practical and Theoretical Implications of 85 Years of Research Findings", *Psychological Bulletin*, vol. 124, No.2, 1998, p. 262-274.

Schwabe Lars, Tegenthoff Martin, Höffken Oliver *et al.*, "Simultaneous Glucocorticoid and Noradrenergic Activity Disrupts the Neural Basis of Goal-Directed Action in the Human Brain", *Journal of Neuroscience*, vol. 32, No.30, July 2012, p. 10146-10155.

Schwartz, Barry, *Why We Work*, Simon & Schuster/TED, 2015.

Scott Kim, *Radical Candor: Be a Kick-Ass Boss Without Losing Your Humanity*, MacMillan, 2017.

Seligman, Martin, *Flourish: A Visionary New Understanding of Happiness and Well-being*, Atria, 2012.

Seppälä Emma, *The Happiness Track: How To Apply the Science of Happiness To Accelerate Your Success*, Harper One, 2016.

Shariatmadari David, "Daniel Kahneman: 'What Would I Eliminate If I Had A Magic Wand? Overconfidence'", *The Guardian*, July 18, 2005.

Sharot Tali, *The Influential Mind: What the Brain Reveals About Our Power to Change Others*, Little Brown, 2017.

Sinek, Simon, *Start With Why: How Great Leaders Inspire Everyone to Take Action*, Portfolio, Reprint edition, 2011.

Sinek, Simon, *Leaders Eat Last: Why Some Teams Pull Together and Others Don't*, Portfolio, 2017.

Sinek Simon, Mead David and Docker Peter, *Find Your Why: A Practical Guide for Discovering Purpose for You and Your Team*, Portfolio-Penguin, 2017.

Singler, Eric, *Nudge marketing: Winning at Behavioral Change*, Pearson, 2015.

(in French) Singler, Eric, *Green Nudge : réussir à changer les comportements pour sauver la planète*, Pearson, 2015.

Smith Emily Esfahani, *The Power of Meaning: Crafting a Life That Matters*, Crown, 2017.

Smith Emily Esfahani, "How to Find Meaning in a Job That Isn't Your 'True Calling'", *Harvard Business Review*, August 3, 2017.

Smolders Karine C. H. J. and Yvonne Kort A. W. de, "Bright Light and Mental Fatigue: Effects on Alertness, Vitality, Performance and Psychological Arousal", *Journal of Environmental Psychology*, vol. 39, September 2014, p. 77-91.

Soman Dilip, *The Last Mile: Creating Social and Economic Value from Behavioral Insights*, University of Toronto Press, 2015.

Sommers Sam, *Situations Matter: Understanding How Context Transforms Your World*, Riverhead Books, 2011.

Steel Piers, "The Nature of Procrastination: A Meta-Analytic and Theoretical Review of Quintessential Self-Regulatory Failure", *Psychological Bulletin*, vol. 133, No.1, 2007, p. 65-94.

Stephens Greg J., Silbert Lauren J. and Hasson Uri, "Speaker-Listener Neural Coupling Underlies Successful Communication", *Proceedings of the National Academy of Sciences*, vol. 107, No.32, August 2010, p. 14425-14430.

Strauss Iliana, "A Behavioral Scientist's Guide to Working from Home", From the grapevine, July 13, 2017, fromthegrapevine.com

Stulberg Brad and Magness Steve, *Peak Performance: Elevate Your Game, Avoid Burnout, and Thrive with the New Sciences of Success*, Rodale Books, 2017.

Sunstein Cass R., *Simpler: The Future of Government*, Simon & Schuster, 2013.

Sunstein Cass R., *Choosing Not To Choose: Understanding the Value of Choice*, Oxford University Press, 2015.

Sunstein Cass R. and Reid Hastie, *Wiser: Getting Beyond Groupthink to Make Groups Smarter*, Harvard Business Review Press, 2015.

Svenson Ola, "Are we all less risky and more skillful than our fellow drivers?", *Acta Psychologica*, vol. 47, No.2, February 1981, p. 143-148.

Tarran Jane, Torpy Fraser and Burchett Margaret, "Use of Living Pot-Plants to Cleanse Indoor Air: Research Review", *Proceedings of Sixth International Conference on Indoor Air Quality, Ventilation and Energy Conservation in Buildings – Sustainable Built Environment*, October 28-31, 2007, Sendai, Japan, vol. III, p. 249-256.

Thaler Richard H., *Misbehaving: The Making of Behavioral Economics*, W.W. Norton, 2016.

Thaler Richard H. & Sunstein Cass R., *Nudge: Improving Decisions about Health, Wealth and Happiness*, Yale University Press, 2008.

Ulrich Dave and Ulrich Wendy, *The Why of Work: How Great Leaders Built Abondant Organizations that Win*, Mc Graw Hill, 2010.

Virtanen Marianna, Singh-Manoux Archana, Ferrie Jane E. *et al.*, "Long Working Hours and Cognitive Function: The Whitehall II Study", *American Journal of Epidemiology*, vol. 169, No.5, March 2009, p. 596-605.

Vischer Jacqueline C., "Towards an Environmental Psychology of Workspace: How People are Affected by Environments for Work", *Architectural Science Review*, vol. 51, No.2, June 2008, p. 97-108.

Wadors Pat, "To Stay Relevant, Your Company and Employees Must Keep Learning", *Harvard Business Review*, March 7, 2016.

Waldinger Heather A. and Isaacowitz Derek M., "Positive Mood Broadens Visual Attention to Positive Stimuli", *Motivation and Emotion*, vol. 30, No.1, March 2006, p. 87-99.

Wargocki Pawel, Wyon David P., Sundell Jan *et al.*, "The Effects of Outdoor Air Supply in an Office on Perceived Air Quality, Sick Building Syndrome (SBS) Symptoms and Productivity", *Indoor Air*, vol. 10, No.4, December 2000, p. 222-236.

Webb, Caroline, *How to Have a Good Day*, Currency, 2016.

Wiseman Liz, *Multipliers: How the Best Leaders Make Everyone Smarter*, HarperBusiness, 2010.

Wiseman Liz, *Rookie Smarts: Why Learning Beats Knowing in the New Game of Work*, Harper Collins, 2014.

Wrzesniewski Amy, McCauley Clark, Rozin Paul *et al.*, "Jobs, Careers, and Callings: People's Relations to Their Work", *Journal of Research in Personality*, vol. 31, No.1, March 1997, p. 21-33.

Zhu Rui (Juliet) and Argo Jennifer J., "Exploring the Impact of Various Shaped Seating Arrangements on Persuasion", *Journal of Consumer Research*, vol. 40, No.2, August 2013, p. 336-349.

Zweig Jason, "Lesson from Buffett: Doubt Yourself", *The Wall Street Journal*, May 5, 2013.

IMPRIMÉ EN ESPAGNE

Imprimé par **GraphyCems**
31132 Villatuerta (Espagne)

Suivant sa politique de développement,
amélioration continue, qualité et gestion de l'environnement,
GraphyCems possède les certifications **ISO 9001**,
ISO 14001 et **FSC** (Forecast Stewardship Council).